W9-DDE-367

THIRD EDITION

"THEY SAY / I SAY"

*The Moves That Matter
in Academic Writing*

GERALD GRAFF
CATHY BIRKENSTEIN

both of the University of Illinois at Chicago

JOHN CARROLL UNIVERSITY

W· W· NORTON & COMPANY

NEW YORK | LONDON

DEPARTMENT OF ENGLISH

Directory

—🞜—

Department of English, Main Office
228 O'Malley Center
John Carroll University
University Heights, OH 44118
(216) 397-4221
http://sites.jcu.edu/english/

Chairperson, Department of English
Debra Rosenthal, Ph.D.
223 O'Malley Center
(216) 397-1721

Director of First-Year Writing
Tom Pace, Ph.D.
233 O'Malley Center
(216) 397-1736

Director of the Writing Center
Maria Soriano, M.A.
206 O'Malley Center
(216) 396-1911

FURTHER INFORMATION

If you need further information, or if you have questions about
First-Year Writing at John Carroll University, contact the English Department at (216) 397-4221, or log on to our website at
http://sites.jcu.edu/fycomp/

TABLE OF CONTENTS

Table of Contents

ONE

ABOUT *FIRST-YEAR WRITING AT JOHN CARROLL UNIVERSITY*

—▢—

The purpose of this handbook is to serve as a guide for all First-Year Writing students. This manual provides essential information on the general structure of the First-Year Writing program at John Carroll University. It also invites you to think carefully about the teaching of writing, about your status as a member of the university, and about your role in shaping the outcome of important issues through writing, both on campus and in the larger context of the public sphere.

We hope that you find valuable information in this edition of *FYWJCU*. Our goal is to invite you to begin thinking and reflecting on the First-Year Writing program at JCU and to help you look at your own writing, and others' writing, in fresh, meaningful, and critical ways.

TWO

MESSAGE FROM THE DIRECTOR OF FIRST-YEAR WRITING

Welcome to First-Year Writing at John Carroll University. It is my hope that your experience in EN 125 or EN 120 and 121 will prepare you for the many different kinds of writing you will encounter in your academic life, in your chosen professional career, and in your service to the public. No matter what you choose to do with your education, you cannot participate fully in academic life, in your profession, or in the world at large without a grounding in rhetoric and writing.

Indeed, today's careers place a premium on being able to communicate effectively through writing. A recent report by the National Commission on Writing found that top business leaders around the country see strong writing abilities as directly correlated to success in today's workplace. While writing has always been important in the workplace, today's high-tech, globalized workplace makes writing all that more important.

But, writing's importance goes beyond landing a job. Writing is instrumental to the health of the republic. Active citizens need to be able to analyze and make arguments in the public sphere. Years ago, citizens gathered at town hall meetings to debate, argue, and discuss topics of importance. Now, we gather on the Internet, on social networking sites, and in the blogo-sphere. These emerging modes of communication represent a new mode of writing in a globalized, interconnected world. America and the global economy need citizens who can criti-cally navigate and engage in these public spaces.

At John Carroll University, we link these new modes of writ-ing to the older, Jesuit principle of *cura personalis*, educating "the whole person." Instruction in rhetoric and writing is a key com-ponent of this goal. Since the founding of the Society of Jesus by St. Ignatius of Loyola in 1540, the Jesuits have been at the forefront of education in rhetoric. The Jesuits understood early that in order to persuade an audience and to spread their ideas, rhetorical skills must be taught in their schools and universities.

A defining characteristic of the ideals of Jesuit education, since the earliest Jesuit universities, is captured in the Latin phrase *elo-quentia perfecta*, meaning "perfect eloquence." In First-Year Writ-ing at John Carroll, you will begin to develop your own ability to write with power and clarity by focusing on the following: argumentation, audience awareness, organization, and style.

In short, you are the beneficiary of a grand tradition of teach-ing, and in your hands you hold the first tool on your own road to eloquence. This edition of *First-Year Writing at John Carroll University* provides an introduction to the kinds of writing you will undertake in your foundational writing courses, to the pur-poses of the writing assignments, and to the expectations you will be asked to meet. We believe strongly that all students can learn to write with clarity and grace, and this handbook will help you in developing your own strengths as a writer and thinker as you encounter many different rhetorical challenges at John Carroll.

Tom Pace, Ph.D.
Associate Professor of English
Director of First-Year Writing

THREE

OPEN LETTER TO FIRST-YEAR WRITING STUDENTS

By *Kate McConnell*

To the Class of 2020,

I remember sitting in my first-year composition course at my undergraduate university and hearing the word "rhetoric" mentioned for the first time. "Rhetoric," the professor told my class, "is defined as the art of persuasion, but it is much more than that. Rhetoric is the key to decoding and creating meaning. Your understanding of this term and your ability to employ it is imperative to your success in college, regardless of your major."

Although I pursued an English degree in the years that followed this pronouncement, I still agree wholeheartedly with my composition professor's words. The classmates that had sat alongside me in first-year composition course went on to become lawyers, doctors, scientists, and entrepreneurs. When looking back, I think it is fair to attribute—at least in part— our individual successes to our first-year composition class, where we began our exploration of writing, rhetoric, and the fundamental principles that taught us (as our instructor promised they would) to decode and create meaning.

This fall marks the start of my fifth year of teaching writing. Over the last half-decade, I have found that there are three key pieces of advice that all writers, myself included, should keep in mind:

1. Find a space in which to write. Here, I mean a *physical* space. Whether you live on campus or commute from home, finding a place that suits your individual study style is key. While some can compose a ten-page research essay whilst *The Price is Right* blares in the background, others will prefer a quiet corner of the library. If you are not sure what this space might look like for you, try out some different ones. Finding a writing/study space will help you "turn on" that part of your brain that allows you to really focus on the task at hand.

2. Pace yourself. Sure, we have all "crammed" for exams, and if you haven not, we should talk again in December. I will put it simply: writing an adequately supported, eloquent academic paper cannot be done overnight. I have tried it. My students have tried it. Trust me when I tell you that you will spare yourself significant agony by starting early. For many writers (first-year students and professionals alike), starting the essay is the most challenging part of the writing process. Find your writing space, pour yourself a cup of coffee, and get your thoughts down on paper, preferably at least a week before the paper is due.

3. Ask questions. John Carroll University has built-in resources for first-year writers, so if you are unsure as to how to proceed with an assignment, a paper topic, or even a sentence, do not

hesitate to ask for help. Your instructors and the consultants JCU Writing Center (see page 54 of this handbook for more information on the Writing Center) will be more than happy to help.

Isaac Newton is credited as having said, "If I have seen further, it by standing on the shoulders of giants." First-Year Writing at JCU will encourage you to read what others before you have said or discovered and employ those words, messages, and ideas to form and support your own original arguments. Work hard, and the outcome of that work is bound to be something that you are proud of.

Welcome to First-Year Writing at JCU, and best of luck!

KATE MCCONNELL

Kate is a 2016 MA graduate in English from John Carroll University, where she also worked as the Assistant Director in the JCU Writing Center and as a graduate assistant teaching EN 125.

FOUR

FIRST-YEAR WRITING

Our program is committed to university-wide writing excellence, a commitment that is reflected in the makeup of the English department, in its programs, and in the implementation of writing-intensive courses in John Carroll's Core Curriculum. The First-Year Writing course sequence is one of the requirements of the university's Core Curriculum in the Liberal Arts.

Our program is informed by process-based pedagogies, by social constructionist principles, and by cross-curricular writing instruction. The program draws on the ideas that best serve students' learning and development as thinkers, readers and writers. "Speaking, listening, reading, and writing," says educator Ann Berthoff, "are acts of mind by which we make meaning."

First-Year Writing instructors value the act of writing as a method for thinking and exploring. As such, you will be expected to learn new methods of written problem-solving, which will likely play an important role in your university education.

FIVE

PHILOSOPHY OF TEACHING WRITING

—⊡—

Five assumptions about the teaching of writing and about how students learn best to write guide the curriculum in First-Year Writing at John Carroll University.

1. Because good writing does not take place outside of a context, we design writing assignments that ask students to focus on a purpose, to address the needs of different audiences and rhetorical situations, and to use the conventions and form appropriate to the rhetorical situation, whether it's academic, public, or private.

2. Because critical thinking is a necessary component of all university learning, we teach students to weigh conflicting points of view on different issues, to evaluate, analyze, and synthesize appropriate primary and secondary sources, and to understand relationships among language, knowledge, and power.

3. Because writing is a process, we teach students to write multiple drafts as a method of creating and completing a successful text, to value the act of writing itself, and to develop appropriate strategies for generating, revising, editing, and proofreading texts.

4. Because reading is integral to writing, we teach students that reading provides support for various writing processes and that many writing assignments are structured around different readings. We also stress that reading itself is a social process indicative of a student's personal history, experience, and social context.

5. Because learning is social, we teach students to understand the collaborative and social aspects of writing processes, to critique their own and others' work, and to balance the advantages of relying on others with the responsibility of doing their part.

SIX

THE UNIVERSITY CORE CURRICULUM
IN THE LIBERAL ARTS

John Carroll's new Integrated Core Curriculum provides the foundation and the structure upon which all students build the major focus of their university studies. The courses that make up the Core Curriculum are informed by nine academic learning goals, which are rooted in the fundamental Jesuit heritage of the University and the particular history of John Carroll. These learning goals are value statements about what the University deems essential for each student's educational experience. They highlight key aspirations the JCU faculty and administration have for our students: We expect graduates of John Carroll University will be able to:

1. Demonstrate an integrative knowledge of human and natural worlds;
2. Develop habits of critical analysis and aesthetic appreciation;
3. Apply creative and innovative thinking;
4. Communicate skillfully in multiple forms of expression;
5. Act competently in a global and diverse world;
6. Understand and promote social justice;
7. Apply a framework for examining ethical dilemmas;

8. Employ leadership and collaborative skills;
9. Understand the religious dimensions of human experience.

The Core Curriculum intentionally ensures that these nine academic learning goals are met—not superficially, but in multiple places and times throughout the student's undergraduate years so that the skills, knowledge, competencies, and values they seek to instill are re-iterated, deepened, and actualized.

WRITTEN EXPRESSION IN THE NEW CORE

In the foundational writing course, students will gain knowledge of the expectations of academic writing, including the discovery and revision components of the writing process, and other principles of coherent and persuasive writing. This course will focus on the development of fundamental writing skills not tied to any particular discipline. Writing placement at entry to John Carroll will determine whether a student takes one or two courses in composition.

Students who need developmental writing will take two 3-credit courses. Other students will take one 3-credit course.

Competence in written expression will be further developed through writing required in all integrated courses and in one writing-intensive course in the major.

STANDARD COURSE OFFERINGS EN 125, 120, 121

The English Department offers two first-year writing tracks. Most students will take English 125 during either their first or second semester.

English 125 instructors are encouraged to teach a standard syllabus, where students are asked to complete four major projects. One of the goals of English 125 is to teach writing as a means of critical inquiry, stressing the centrality of writing to intellectual life. In English 125, you will learn how academic arguments are made in response to pre-existing arguments. Because good writing cannot be disassociated from careful reading, you will grapple with a diverse body of interrelated and sometimes difficult readings. Students who earn a grade below C- will be required to re-take the course.

English 120 provides additional practice in the reading and writing of expository prose for students who have placed below EN 125. Once students complete EN 120, with a grade of "D" or higher, they then proceed to EN 121. Students who earn a grade below C- in EN 121 will be required to re-take the course.

While individual classes will differ, First-Year Writing courses have several common aims. They are designed to provide a context in which you can begin to think of writing as the means by which you can learn and examine ideas in relation to those of others. These courses are also designed to prepare you to write for all your classes at John Carroll, offering practice in the rhetorical and stylistic strategies useful in academic writing. These strategies should help you to engage with writing in a wide variety of academic, professional, public, and private contexts.

LEARNING OUTCOMES

Below are the learning outcomes for foundational competency in written expression. To achieve effective writing in an academic context, students must demonstrate competency in the following:

1) Articulation of an argument
- Select and develop an appropriately complex argument, given audience, purpose, and length requirements.
- Develop and support an argument appropriate to context, audience, and purpose.

2) Source Integration
- Locate, engage with, and integrate evidence into your own argument.

3) Ethical Documentation
- Avoid plagiarism and include all important citation information.

4) Control of Syntax and Mechanics
- Use language that conveys meaning to readers with clarity.

SEVEN

STUDENTS' RIGHTS AND RESPONSIBILITIES

—回—

CLASS ATTENDANCE

Do I have to attend class? The answer is "yes." The *John Carroll University Undergraduate Bulletin, 2015–2017* states, "Students are expected to attend each and every scheduled meeting of all courses in which they are enrolled and to be present for the full class period." It stipulates further that:

a. During the first week of a semester each instructor will provide, as part of the class syllabus, a written statement of the attendance policy for the particular class and an explanation of the consequences for absences.

b. If you are absent from a class, you are responsible, nevertheless, for all material covered during the class period. You are also subject to appropriate consequences, as described by the instructor in the syllabus.

c. If you must miss a scheduled class meeting, you may be granted an excused absence at the discretion of the instructor. An excused absence, if granted, entitles the student to make up any required activity that took place on the day of the absence. The student is still responsible, however, for any material covered during the class period that was missed.

The nature of composition classes requires students to attend every class. Learning to write depends on the kind of thinking, practice, and feedback one gets in class.

CAN I KEEP MY PAPERS?

The papers you write for class belong to you. If you are not in class the day papers or exams are returned, it is your responsibility to find out from your instructor when and where you can pick up papers.

It is always a good idea for you to keep dated copies of all papers you hand in. That way, you can speedily replace a paper in case the instructor has lost or misplaced it. Also, you should keep a backup copy of all your work. If you save files on a hard drive, you should also back them up on disk or a supplemental drive.

STUDENTS WITH DISABILITIES

John Carroll University recognizes its responsibility for creating an institutional climate in which students with disabilities can succeed. In accordance with University policy, if you have a documented disability, you may be eligible to request accommodations from the Office of Services for Students with Disabilities. Students with disabilities are entitled to reasonable accommodations and should have equal access to learning.

Please contact the Office of Services for Students with Disabilities at (216) 397-4967 if you have any questions or to set up an appointment to meet with the director, Allison West. After your eligibility for accommodations is determined, you will be given a letter which, when presented to instructors, will help us know best how to assist you. Please keep in mind that accommodations are not retroactive so it is best to register with the Office of Services for Students with Disabilities at your earliest convenience.

EIGHT

WHAT IS "RHETORIC"?

The study of rhetoric is one of the oldest of the liberal arts, dating back to ancient Greece and Rome. The Greek philosophers Plato and Aristotle both wrote about rhetoric, and their ideas still influence current rhetoric scholars. Indeed, rhetoric was one of the standard course offerings in European and American colleges until the mid-nineteenth century, when it all but disappeared from the curriculum. Since about the 1960s, however, rhetoric has enjoyed something of a revival in American higher education, particularly in the way university students are taught to write.

But what *is* "rhetoric"? There are many different definitions and different ways to understand this often-puzzling term. For the purposes of First-Year Writing at John Carroll, rhetoric is defined as "the systematic study and intentional practice of effective symbolic expression."[1] The chief symbolic means of expression that we use, of course, is language. Therefore, think of rhetoric as the way we use language to achieve various aims: persuasion, clarity, beauty, or mutual understanding, to name only a few. In First-Year Writing, you will learn different methods and tools to help you argue effectively and to write clearly for different audiences and purposes.

WHY DO WE NEED RHETORIC?

By Susan C. Jarrett, University of California, Irvine

Rhetorical theorists, scholars, writers, politicians, and philosophers have provided a number of answers to this question over the 2,500 years of rhetoric's history:

> To figure out what we mean: as a mode of inquiry, a means of discovering knowledge and giving shape to experience;
>
> To persuade others to take our point of view and to accept the results of our inquiries as valid and useful;
>
> To protect ourselves from those who use it to their advantage (and others' disadvantage);
>
> To enhance our pleasure in using and experiencing symbol systems of all kinds: language, visual arts, even music;
>
> To define and preserve our humanity; as an alternative to solving conflicts through violence.

Most of these definitions can be traced back to rhetoric's origins in the cultures of ancient Greece and Rome.

THE RHETORICAL APPROACH TO WRITING IN FIRST-YEAR WRITING CLASSES AND IN YOUR MAJOR

Instructors and students alike can benefit from taking a rhetorical approach to writing in specific fields. For instructors, thinking about rhetorical elements will enable them to make visible to students conventions of writing in their field that they have come to take for granted. For students, asking rhetorical questions of the writing tasks you're given in each class will help you notice the differences among them and respond more effectively to each writing situation.

Here is a set of "rhetorical" questions to think about when responding to writing assignments:

What is the situation that gives rise to this writing?

In academic writing, this can become an empty question. Often, teachers ask you to write only to demonstrate your knowledge (as in an essay exam). So there isn't any real situation or exigency (to use a rhetorical term) for the writing outside the instructional context. Most writing specialists believe that asking students to write as though you were responding to a genuine rhetorical situation helps you to become better writers. Sometimes it is possible to give students opportunities to respond to actual situations (writing to public officials, businesses, other students, or scholars). Whatever the case, specifying the situation is most important because it enables you to answer the next questions . . .

Who is the speaker or writer in this situation? What kind of *ethos* should she or he adopt?

All writing and speaking has a performative quality. In every case, the writer (perhaps without thinking about it) takes on a persona, casting him/herself as a certain kind of person— sincere, witty, ironic, bland, authoritative, humble, anxious, earnest, etc. That persona dictates particular kinds of language choices and has an effect on the reader. In academic writing, you are often faced with a dilemma when it comes to creating an ethos in your writing. You, as students, are often asked by your instructors to write as authorities on subjects you're just learning about and to write to an audience (the instructor) who, you believe, already knows what the writer has to say. It's a difficult task and sometimes leads to bad writing: indirection, posturing, hypercorrectness, and other (sometimes humorous but nonetheless unsuccessful) strategies. When the instructor can give more direction about the kind of ethos the writer should adopt, the writing is often more successful. Here are some examples:

> Write as an upper-division major to a new student who is trying to decide whether to major in X;
>
> Write as a computer software salesperson to a client who is trying to decide whether to buy your product;
>
> Write as yourself (a student) to me (an instructor) about a subject that I don't know much about yet.

Often, as instructors, we want our student writers to adopt a disciplinary persona: scientist, literary critic, social science researcher—whatever we're preparing them to be. But if we do that without giving you specific instructions about the conventions of that voice or persona, we may be disappointed. How would you describe the ethos of writers in your major? Detached (no first person; passive voice) or engaged? Is the presence of the writer virtually effaced in this writing task (e.g., as in some technical documentation), or not? Would this writer need a rich, colorful vocabulary, or should the writer stick to a limited technical terminology? Of course, the persona of a "scientist" is not always the same. That's why you need answers to the next questions . . .

Who is the audience?

Audiences might be other students, academics in the field, a public of some sort, or a client. Knowing to whom you write can help you make important decisions as you write:

> **Appropriateness of subject matter** (What do these particular readers want to know?)
>
> **Hierarchy** (Should I be deferential or perhaps instructive?)
>
> **Levels of knowledge** (How much to assume, how much to provide)
>
> **Disposition toward my point of view** (Hostile? Sympathetic? Skeptical? Interested?)
>
> **Similarity or difference** (Am I a young person writing for mostly older people? Am I a single person writing about issues involving marriage and children? Am I a U.S. citizen writing about third world issues?)
>
> **Appropriateness of language** (Academic language? Jargon? Technical? Difficult vocabulary?)

In some cases, the writing assignment may include a pre-writing activity involving audience analysis. If the task is to write for a particular professional journal, your instructor may ask you to find a copy and read the editorial information for information about who reads the journal. Or if the writer will be addressing a public constituency, what are its demographics?

What is the purpose?

To inform? Persuade? Please? Instruct? Often purposes are blended. The most common purpose of academic writing is informative with a persuasive undercurrent. Scientific articles must present their evidence in a persuasive form, even though the modes of persuasion in scientific genres are circumscribed and highly conventional. Lab reports, field notes and software documentation may be almost purely informative. With literary criticism, on the other hand, your English teacher will often remind you repeatedly that an opinion is not sufficiently persuasive; there must also be abundant and supportive textual evidence. Specifying the purpose for writing is probably the single most helpful instruction a teacher can provide you in a writing assignment, *so don't hesitate to ask your professor what the purpose is for a given writing assignment.* Finding models of successful writing can help you get a fix on the appropriate ways to address purpose.

What is the genre or form of writing?

What are you writing? Proposal, case study, lab report, documentation, field notes, review article, policy statement, annotated bibliography, response, reflective journal, dialogue, script, sales presentation, editorial? The types of writing we produce in our academic, professional, public, commercial, and personal lives are amazingly varied. Yet sometimes when faculty assign writing, they revert to a few forms: the essay, the essay exam, and the research paper. When faculty assign forms of writing used by professionals in their field, you, as students, gain not only writing experience but deeper familiarity with disciplinary habits.

Different genres require different rhetorics; the questions above will all be inflected by genre. One of the most noticeable differences between the types of writing most commonly done in different disciplines is their format, or visual appearance on the page. Professors in different disciplines often give good, specific instructions about length, page layout (e.g., use of headings), font, margins, etc. In fact, this is often the kind of information that occurs first to faculty as they make up writing assignments. It is definitely important. As students, you need to be encouraged to attend to formal details. Addressing such conventions can open up a discussion about why knowledge is disposed in particular ways for particular subject matters. But attention to formal conventions should always be balanced with a focus on the substance of the writing.

Specific layout features, including aspects of visual design, especially in electronic texts, have become increasingly significant in some fields. With advances in electronic media, rhetoric has achieved new significance and has garnered additional dimensions with the increased use of computer-mediated communication and the growing popularity of visual media. Visual rhetoric is an exciting new area of study, leading to productive collaborations among rhetoricians, media theorists and producers, visual artists, and computer design specialists.

NOTES

[1]Herrick, James A, *The History and Theory of Rhetoric: An Introduction*. New York: Allyn and Bacon. 2005. Page 7.

NINE

ACADEMIC WRITING

—▣—

THE WRITING PROCESS

Speaking, listening, reading, and writing are acts of mind by which we make meaning. Ann E. Berthoff

When you are writing, you're trying to find out something which you don't know. James Baldwin.

In your writing courses at John Carroll, you will often hear the phrase "writing is a process." You may have even already heard it in high school or in other writing contexts. In First-Year Writing, we work under the assumption that writing is a tool of learning, that it's a process by which human beings learn about the world around them. Writing is not merely the act of transcribing what is already in your head onto a piece of paper or a computer screen. When writers sit down to write, as evidenced by the above quote from novelist James Baldwin, they often do not know where the writing will take them. The process of writing, therefore, is a process of discovery, of learning something new that can then be crafted for a reader who is genuinely interested in what you have to say. In other words, while the final written product is often linear, the process of creating that product is not, nor should you expect it to be.

In your writing classes at John Carroll, you will be asked to make arguments about issues, to take a stance, to use writing to learn about ideas. Therefore, you will be asked to use writing to work through various ideas and issues, to write multiple drafts, and to polish your writing so that it is appropriate to the academic audience to whom you write.

Since most of the writing you will do is "academic writing," it may be useful to define what academic writing is. To paraphrase writing scholar Peter Elbow, academic writing is the kind of writing academics do for other academics. Throughout your career at John Carroll, you will be expected to write for a variety of academic purposes: summaries, analyses, lab reports, syntheses, persuasive essays, interpretive essays, responses to reading, reflections on your learning, research-based arguments, and many, many more. You will do this writing for an audience of other students and faculty interested in what you have to say and eager to respond.

Much of the writing you will be asked to do in First-Year Writing and in other courses will be in response to the ideas of others. Most academic writing—indeed, most good writing—is often done in response to others' ideas. Gerald Graff, an English professor from the University of Illinois at Chicago, says this about academic writing:

> In our view, then, the best academic writing has one underlying feature: it is engaged in some way with other people's views. Too often, however, academic writing is taught as a process of saying 'true' or 'smart' things in a vacuum, as if it were possible to argue effectively without being in conversation *with* someone else. If you have been taught to write a traditional five-paragraph essay, for

example, you have learned how to develop a thesis and support it with evidence. This is good advice as far as it goes, but it leaves out the important fact that in the real world we don't make arguments without being provoked. We make arguments because someone has said or done something (or perhaps *not* said or done something) and we need to respond.[2]

Learning how to respond well to others' ideas—those you agree with and those you don't—and to use those ideas to build your own is, in part, what a liberal arts education is all about and is a necessary foundation for your education here at John Carroll.

At John Carroll, you will be expected to complete a variety of academic writing tasks in your different courses: you will compose lab reports in biology and chemistry; draft executive summaries in the business school; synthesize resources in history; analyze arguments in philosophy; analyze a soliloquy in your Shakespeare course, and many, many more. In performing these tasks, you will need to show how your own ideas relate to the ideas you read and write about and, in the process, learn about those ideas as you write about them.

So, in First-Year Writing, you will begin the process of learning the numerous conventions of academic discourse, of how to connect your ideas to others' texts, and of how to use the drafting process to develop ideas, revise, edit, and proofread those ideas for a reader genuinely interested in what you have to say.

NOTES

[2]From *Graff, Gerald and Cathy Birkenstein. They Say/I Say: The Moves that Matter in Academic Writing. New York: W.W. Norton, 2006. 3.*

TEN

GUIDE TO WRITING ACROSS THE CURRICULUM[3]

—▢—

NOTES ON CONVENTIONS AND STANDARDS ACROSS THE ACADEMIC DISCIPLINES

During the summer of 2012, we contacted key professors in disciplines across the university and asked to meet with them in-person to talk about writing and the nuances of their particular interests. We asked them what they look for in student writing, the common conventions of their academic disciplines, and how they teach writing in their own courses.

We discovered, as a result of our conversations, that some disciplines call for very particular citation styles, verb tenses, and ways of writing. Others follow what we would deem "academic standards" or may require students to pay specific attention to their professors' assignment sheets or recommendations. Indeed, there are some characteristics of effective writing that are consistent across *all* disciplines! When in doubt, always refer back to your professor for clarifications.

As a student, you are not expected to master the intricacies and requirements of each academic discipline, but you should familiarize yourself with this guide and consider it a resource for your own development and knowledge.

BIOLOGY – CONVENTIONS AND STANDARDS OF WRITING

Citation Style	*Student should ask for professor's preference *Often based on the style of a specific academic journal
Verb Tense	*Sections fluctuate between past and present tenses -past tense for "Results" section *1st person acceptable in *introductions* *1st person not acceptable in *body of essay/report*
Style of Expression	*Figures must be discussed in order *Writing must be concise and display no redundancy
Structure/Sections/ Thesis	*Discussion Section: in-depth interpretation of results in the context of the current field *Methods Section: write to an audience who has expertise in the field; no step-by-step explanations *End of each section acts as a "launchpad" for the next *Give audience signposts to differentiate each section
Active v. Passive Voice	*Fluctuates between sections

Academic and Visual Sources	*Never use footnotes *Alpha or numerical works cited page
Professor's Expectations and Evaluation Criteria	*Information displayed clearly *Sharp, clean figures *Factually correct *Displays what is necessary to interpret data *Points audience in the right direction *Makes a conclusion *Sticks to process *Followed directions
Source	Dr. Mike Martin mmartin@jcu.edu

CHEMISTRY — CONVENTIONS AND STANDARDS OF WRITING

Citation Style	*ACS Style guide is preferred *Student should ask professor's preference
Verb Tense	*Past tense for experiments done by others and comparing results *1st person acceptable for *journal articles* *No 1st person in *lab reports*
Style of Expression	*Concise, straightforward, and clear *Use appropriate language of the discipline
Structure/Sections/Thesis	*Audience must be able to understand procedure being followed
Active v. Passive Voice	*Passive voice acceptable for lab reports

Academic and Visual Sources	*ACS Style Guide *Superscript numbers for references *Research endnotes (per journal specifications)
Professor's Expectations and Evaluation Criteria	*Clarity *Concise writing *Audience can follow procedure *Appropriate conventions and language used
Source	Dr. Mark Waner mwaner@jcu.edu

COMMUNICATIONS – CONVENTIONS AND STANDARDS OF WRITING

Citation Style	*APA or MLA style guide is preferred *Students should ask professor's preference
Verb Tense	*Present tense is preferred
Style of Expression	*Concise sentence structure *Provide only the information needed *Active voice *Check with professor for preferred style
Structure/Sections/Thesis	*Write to audience expectations *Thesis statement should be present early in the paper
Active v. Passive Voice	*Active voice is preferred
Academic and Visual Sources	*Consult APA or MLA style guide based on professor's personal preference

Professor's Expectations and Evaluation Criteria	*Students should consult syllabi and individual professors for their expectations
Source	Bourhis, John, Carey Adams, and Scott Titsworth. *Style Manual for Communication Studies*. 3rded. Boston: McGraw Hill, 2009. Print.

ECONOMICS/FINANCE – CONVENTIONS AND STANDARDS OF WRITING

Citation Style	*No standard style of acknowledging sources in economics papers, but a good model is the style used in *The American Economics Review* *Student should consult professor for preferred style
Verb Tense	*Active verb tense is preferred *Summaries should stick to one verb tense
Style of Expression	*Define important terms used in the paper *State hypothesis and proceed deductively to reach conclusions *Avoid excessive verbage *Edit and revise to narrow writing to a simple, efficient way of communicating

Structure/Sections/ Thesis	*Literature review followed by the presentation of a simplified model (supply and demand, cost/benefit analysis, comparative advantage, etc.) *Follow a line of deductive reasoning to its conclusion and apply the rules of inference correctly
Active v. Passive Voice	*Active voice preferred
Academic and Visual Sources	*Style used by *The American Economic Review* is standard *Consult professor for preferred style
Professor's Expectations and Evaluation Criteria	*Consult individual professors for their expectations and evaluation criteria
Source	Neugeboren, Robert and Mireille Jacobson. *Writing Economics.* Published by The President and Fellows of Harvard University, 2005. Web.

EDUCATION – CONVENTIONS AND STANDARDS
OF WRITING

Citation Style	*APA Style guide is preferred *Student should ask professor's preference
Verb Tense	*3rd person for informational or instructional writing *1st person for qualitative information
Style of Expression	*Straightforward, simple sentences *Limit jargon *Write for an open audience
Structure/Sections/Thesis	*Scientific method style preferred
Active v. Passive Voice	*Active voice is preferred
Academic and Visual Sources	*APA Style Guide
Professor's Expectations and Evaluation Criteria	*Back up information with experience *Descriptive example of student experiences *Connect experiences with professional standards of the field *Must substantiate through data *Field specific content *Explain how conclusions were reached and what measures will be taken to solve problems
Source	Dr. Lisa Shoaf lshoaf@jcu.edu

ENGLISH – CONVENTIONS AND STANDARDS OF WRITING

Citation Style	*MLA Style guide is standard *Citation style can also be journal-specific
Verb Tense	*Active voice *Literary present tense
Style of Expression	*Vary sentence styles – paper should have "texture" *1st person used as a signpost
Structure/Sections/ Thesis	*Produce an argument and develop throughout paper *Good thesis statement shows organization of the paper *Conclusions as restatement and "escape" that pushes the author's thoughts
Active v. Passive Voice	*Active voice is preferred
Academic and Visual Sources	*MLA Style Guide *In-text citations
Professor's Expectations and Evaluation Criteria	*Knowledge of terms and concepts in the field *Thoughtful connection of imagination and judgment *Clarity and cohesion *Articulate argument
Source	Dr. John McBratney jmcbratney@jcu.edu

MANAGEMENT/MARKETING/LOGISTICS –
CONVENTIONS AND STANDARDS OF WRITING

Citation Style	*No specific style preferred *AP (Associated Press) style is close *Student should consult professor for preferred style
Verb Tense	* Present tense
Style of Expression	*Concise sentence structure *Provide only the information needed *Active voice *Conversational language *Think like the client
Structure/Sections/Thesis	*Provide results and not process *Write for audience expectations *Audience determines content *Include data *Adhere to expectations of corporate business world
Active v. Passive Voice	*Active voice is preferred
Academic and Visual Sources	*Students should consult professor for preferred style—no single standard
Professor's Expectations and Evaluation Criteria	*Concise sentences *Clarity *Data analysis and interpretation *Data-driven *Positive tone *Appropriate page design
Source	Dr. Ann Lee alee@jcu.edu

THEOLOGY AND RELIGIOUS STUDIES –
CONVENTIONS AND STANDARDS OF WRITING

Citation Style	*Chicago style is most common *MLA occasionally for shorter papers
Verb Tense	*Avoid past tense—present tense preferable
Style of Expression	*1st person is acceptable *Use gender-inclusive language *Straightforward, simple sentences *Crisp, journalistic style *Outline argument early on *Give the reader a reason to read beyond first sentence
Structure/Sections/ Thesis	*Thesis should be presented early on
Active v. Passive Voice	*Active voice is preferred
Academic and Visual Sources	*Chicago Style Guide *MLA acceptable for shorter papers *Either footnotes or parenthetical citations
Professor's Expecta-tions and Evaluation Criteria	*Clarity and focus *Supporting evidence
Source	Dr. Edward Hahnenberg ehahnenberg@jcu.edu

PHILOSOPHY — CONVENTIONS AND STANDARDS OF WRITING

Citation Style	*Chicago Style guide is preferred *Student should ask professor's preference
Verb Tense	*Passive voice is discouraged *Use of 1st person is standard practice
Style of Expression	*Argumentative *Support thesis statement through reason and textual analysis *Philosophy papers are not overly descriptive *Gender neutral language is encouraged
Structure/Sections/Thesis	*Thesis statement should appear in introductory paragraph
Active v. Passive Voice	*Active voice preferred
Academic and Visual Sources	*Chicago Style Guide
Professor's Expectations and Evaluation Criteria	*Clear and concise thesis statement *Clear transitions between ideas *Adequate support of points *Reasons to support your points *Paper indicates an understanding of material *Properly cited sources *Gender neutral language utilized *Free of grammatical and spelling errors *Separate title page
Source	Dr. Dianna Taylor dtaylor@jcu.edu

POLITICAL SCIENCE – CONVENTIONS AND STANDARDS OF WRITING

Citation Style	*MLA or Chicago Style guide is preferred *Student should ask professor's preference
Verb Tense	*Active voice verb tense
Style of Expression	*Compare and contrast ideas *Intervene in a discourse and distinguish from previous sources *Textual evidence (direct citations) to support thesis
Structure/Sections/ Thesis	*Thesis in introduction *Introduction used as overview of paper
Active v. Passive Voice	*Active voice is preferred
Academic and Visual Sources	*MLA or Chicago Style Guide
Professor's Expectations and Evaluation Criteria	*Paper is on-topic *Sophistication of ideas *Originality *Clear transitions between ideas *Textual evidence
Source	Dr. Mindy Peden mpeden@jcu.edu

PSYCHOLOGY — CONVENTIONS AND STANDARDS OF WRITING

Citation Style	*APA style is preferred *Student should consult professor concerning preference
Verb Tense	*Active voice is preferred *Use the present tense as much as possible except when referring to past research
Style of Expression	*Use bias-free language *Avoid jargon or overly unusual words except when it is absolutely necessary
Structure/Sections/ Thesis	*Thesis statement should be present early on in the paper *Be succinct and avoid wordiness
Active v. Passive Voice	*Use active rather than passive voice
Academic and Visual Sources	*Psychologists seldom use direct quotes *Distill the essence of the statements of other researchers and cite those researchers' work
Professor's Expectations and Evaluation Criteria	*Consult assignment sheets for specific requirements *Clarify with professors for individual expectations
Source	"A Brief Guide to Writing the Psychology Paper." Psychology Department, Harvard University, 2008. Web.

SOCIOLOGY/CRIMINOLOGY — CONVENTIONS AND STANDARDS OF WRITING

Citation Style	*Students should consult professor for preferred citation style
Verb Tense	*Active voice verb tense is preferred
Style of Expression	*Straightforward and to the point *Keep commentary and personal opinion to a minimum *Use of quotes is sparse *Paraphrasing is more common
Structure/Sections/ Thesis	*Thesis should be present early on depending on length of paper *Consult professor or assignment sheet for information about specific requirements based on the type of assignment
Active v. Passive Voice	*Active voice is preferred
Academic and Visual Sources	*Citations are kept to a minimum *Paraphrasing is preferred
Professor's Expectations and Evaluation Criteria	*Clear and concise writing that addresses all the points of the assignment *Demonstration of understanding of key theories and proper application of those theories
Source	Dr. Gloria Vaquera gvaquera@jcu.edu

FURTHER RESOURCES FOR CONVENTIONS AND STANDARDS OF WRITING ACROSS THE CURRICULUM

American Psychological Association. *Publication Manual for The American Psychological*

Association. 6th ed. Washington, D.C.: American Psychological Association, 2009. Print.

Associated Press. *The Associated Press Style Book and Briefing on Media Law 2011*.46th ed. New York: Basic Books, 2011. Print.

Bourhis, John, Carey Adams, and Scott Titsworth. *Style Manual for Communication Studies*. 3rd ed. Boston: McGraw Hill, 2009. Print.

Coghill, Anne M. and Lorrin R. Garson, eds. *The ACS Style Guide: Effective Communication of Scientific Information*. 3rd ed. Oxford, UK: Oxford UP, 2006. Print.

Council of Science Editors. *Scientific Style and Format: The CSE Manual for Authors, Editors, and Publishers*. 7th ed. New York: Rockefeller UP, 2006. Print.

Kinsley, Karin. *A Student Handbook for Writing in Biology*. 3rd ed. Sunderland, MA: Sinauer Associates, 2009. Print.

Modern Language Association. *MLA Handbook for Writers of Research Papers*. 7th ed. New York: Modern Language Association of America, 2009. Print.

Rubens, Philip, ed. *Science and Technical Writing: A Manual of Style*. 2nd ed. New York: Routledge, 2001. Print.

Scott, Gregory M. and Stephen M. Garrison. *The Political Science Student Writer's Manual*. 6th ed. Upper Saddle River, NJ: Pearson, 2008. Print.

Turabian, Kate et al. *A Manual for Writers of Research Papers, Theses, and Dissertations*, 7th ed. Chicago: University of Chicago Press, 2007. Print.

University of Chicago Press Staff. *The Chicago Manual of Style*. 16th ed. Chicago: University of Chicago Press, 2010. Print.

NOTES

[3]This information was collected for a summer research project completed by Maria Soriano, JCU Writing Center Director, and David Young, former Graduate Assistant.

ELEVEN

KEY TERMS IN THE WRITING PROCESS

—▣—

Invention: The process of discovering ideas to write about. Invention can take many different forms and activities: free-writing, brainstorming, class discussion, reading, in-class writing, drafting, and more.

Arrangement: The method of organizing the different parts of your argument. It goes beyond merely placing paragraphs together, but rather it concerns the global order of how the parts of discourse are placed together. The different parts of an argument in classical rhetoric were: the introduction, the narration of the events at hand, the statement of the issue at stake, the evidence uses to support the argument, the refutation of counter-arguments, and finally the conclusion.

Style: The choice of sentences, words, and paragraph structure used to make a written argument. If invention concerns *what* is being said, style is concerned with *how* it is said.

Focusing: This stage of the process refers to when student writers write a draft about the ideas they discovered during the invention stage. This early draft should be done in sentences and paragraphs but without worrying about surface concerns, grammar, punctuation, etc. Think of this draft as a "working draft."

Thesis: Usually the most important part of a paper, a thesis includes the author's main argument. The thesis usually appears in the introductory paragraph and should have a sufficiently narrow topic, at least one arguable point, and indicate the organization of the paper. A thesis acts as the controlling idea for a paper and addresses the what, how, and why of a specific issue, problem, or question.

Preliminary Draft: An important stage in the writing process when the author begins to construct his or her paper. A preliminary draft usually emerges out of a working draft and allows the author room to experiment with ideas and organization and to generate an appropriate thesis statement. Additionally, a rough draft should be revised many times before it is submitted as a final draft. Usually, rough drafts are not graded but are shared with peers who provide feedback to the author to help make main points in the paper more clear.

Peer Review Draft: A peer review draft is an early draft of your work that you will use during a peer review session. A peer review draft that is close to your intended final draft will benefit the most from classmates' additional tips for revision. Note that several changes will likely be made to this draft after the review, based on the feedback you have received. You may want to consider posing specific questions to your classmates in this draft, indicating what type of feedback or help you are seeking.

Peer Review: Peer review is a process during which peers examine each others' drafts. Although sometimes conducted by specific guidelines, peer reviews provide writers of all levels with additional feedback on drafts. Peer review should examine at great length global issues (higher-order concerns) such as structure, depth of critical thinking, and appropriate support for claims, and to a smaller degree, surface level issues (lower-order concerns) such as grammatical concerns, spelling, and matters related to formatting. These suggestions from peers should then be incorporated into later revisions.

Revision: A continuing process of "re-vision," in which writers alter their work throughout the writing process in order to communicate their ideas more clearly to a particular audience. Revision is not limited to mere grammatical correction, although some editing may play an important part in producing concise writing. Usually, revision refers to the recursive process of rewriting some or all of a particular paper, adding needed information, taking out unnecessary information, rearranging parts of the paper, and more.

Editing: Editing refers to the step of the writing process when the writer addresses local issues such as sentence structure, word choice, transitions, punctuation, parts of speech, and mechanics.

Proofreading: Proofreading is an element of the writing process which tends to focus most on surface errors. Frequently, writers proofread their own work while writing, by correcting "lower-order concerns" such as misspellings, word order, or citations. Proofreading also plays a part in peer review; however, examining these types of errors is a marginal component of the process, which should focus largely on higher-order concerns.

Recursive: This word refers to the idea that any stage of the writing process can occur at any time. Writers may find themselves going back to revision during the editing step to help them clarify ideas, or they may find after the focusing and rough draft stages, writers may rearrange sections of their paper, rewrite the thesis, or shuffle around sentences or paragraphs to help flesh out more ideas.

Polished Draft: In place of the idea that your projects are "final," an often misleading term, a polished draft is one that is submitted to the instructor but may come back with additional suggestions and comments. While the feedback may mean that the writer should return to the invention or focusing stage of the writing process, it usually requires addressing specific portions of the text, not starting over.

Portfolio: Refers to a selection of polished pieces of writing submitted by the writer to the instructor at the end of the semester. The polished pieces included in the portfolio have been extensively revised, edited, and proofread, and typically represent the writer's strongest work of the semester. Writing portfolios may be worth anywhere from 25-75 percent of the student's final grade. Many instructors note that students in portfolio-based writing classes receive higher grades than those in writing classrooms that rely on more traditional grading methods. This is, in part, because in the portfolio system students have the whole semester to revise their drafts, making the writing as strong as it can be.

TWELVE

FIGURES OF SPEECH

—◻—

Many First-Year Writing instructors will spend some time in class on the study of style. Style is the relationship between thought and language. Working on style does not mean simply "dressing up" your ideas. Rather, style can be viewed as a counterpart to invention, the discovery of ideas to write about. Or, as the Roman educator Quintilian said, it can "lend credibility to our arguments, exciting the emotions, and winning approval for our characters as pleaders." Rhetoricians call stylistic devices "figures of speech"—a form of speech artfully varied from common usage. At John Carroll, you will learn some of the types of figures of speech, and in the process, practice them in your writing.

There are two main types of figures of speech: schemes and tropes. Schemes generally refer to the playing around with the word order in your sentences; tropes generally refer to the playing around with meaning in your writing. Here is a list of some of the most frequently used schemes and tropes that you should become familiar with in your reading and writing.

Schemes

BALANCE:

Antithesis – juxtaposition of contrasting ideas, often in parallel order: *That's one small step for man, one giant leap for mankind. It was the best of times; it was the worst of times.*

Parallelism – similarity of structure in a pair or series of related words, phrases, or clauses: *We mutually pledge to each other our Lives, our Fortunes, and our sacred Honor. The government of the people, by the people, for the people, shall not perish from the earth.*

OMISSION:

Asyndeton – omission of conjunctions between series of words, phrases, clauses. *I came, I saw, I conquered. We shall pay any price, bear any burden, meet any hardship, support any friend, oppose any foe, to assure the survival and the success of liberty.*

REPETITION:

Polysyndeton – deliberate use of many conjunctions: *This semester I am taking History and English and Math and Sociology and Theater.*

Assonance – repetition of similar vowel sounds. *Stamper scampers around the pasture. Simon signs while his life is on the line. Toasty eats the most corn and grows the thickest coat.*

Anaphora – repetition at beginning of clauses: *We shall fight on the beaches, we shall fight on the landing-grounds, we shall fight in the fields and in the streets, we shall fight in the hills.*

Epistrophe – repetition at the end of clauses: *The white man sent you to Korea, you bled. He sent you to Germany, you bled. He sent you to the South Pacific to fight the Japanese, you bled. In a cake, nothing moistens like real butter, nothing tastes like real butter, nothing satisfies like real butter.*

Anadiplosis – repetition of last word of one clause at beginning of next: *Having power makes totalitarian leadership isolated; isolation breeds insecurity; insecurity breeds suspicion and fear; suspicion and fear breed violence.*

Climax – arrangement in increasing importance: *The goats provide me with work to do, leisure to enjoy, a reason to get up in the morning, and meaning to my life.*

Antimetabole – repetition of words, in successive clauses, in reverse grammatical order: *One should eat to live, not live to eat. Ask not what your country can do for you, ask what you can do for your country.*

Tropes

Metaphor – implied comparison between unlike things.

Simile – a direct comparison between unlike things. A simile is a type of metaphor, and uses "like" or "as" to make its comparison.

Synecdoche – Substituting a part for the whole: *Give us this day our daily bread. Lend me a hand.*

Metonymy – substitution of some attribute for literal meaning. *If history's ever told straight, you'll know it's the sunbonnet and not the Stetson that settled this country.*

Personification (Prosopopoeia) – giving abstractions or objects human qualities. *The ground thirsts for rain.*

Hyperbole – exaggeration for the sake of effect: *We walked along a road in Cumberland and stopped because the sky hung so low. The graduate seminar lasted ten years.*

Litotes – deliberate understatement. *Last week I saw a woman flayed, and you will hardly believe how much it altered her appearance for the worse.*

Rhetorical Question – asking a question in order to assert or deny. *How can the poor feel they have a stake in the system which says the rich may have due process but the poor may not?*

Oxymoron – joining two contradictory terms: *cruel kindness; sweet pain; conspicuous absence; cheerful pessimist; obedient donkey.*

Paradox – apparently contradictory statement: *We know too much for one person to know much. Art is a form of lying in order to tell the truth.*

THIRTEEN

EVALUATION OF STUDENT WORK

WRITING EVALUATION

In each class, instructors base evaluation of student work on the way each student has met the writing and class criteria articulated in class and on policy statements and assignments, criteria that have evolved from an instructor's concept of good writing and a productive classroom, based on his or her teaching and writing experience and study of rhetoric. Most instructors are concerned with content, organization, style, and mechanics in student papers. They would like students to hand in thoughtful papers, with vivid supporting details. Instructors like to see that students did not simply produce one draft and clean it up (changing a word here, a sentence there) before submission, but that students wrote and rewrote before final editing and proofreading.

Note: Keep in mind that most English teachers see revision as "re-vision" – seeing the project in a different way, from a different perspective. A revision is not just changing small details, editing or moving paragraphs around. It is restructuring the writing to substantially further the idea or move in a new direction.

Many instructors believe that grades, which are just one form of evaluation, have to be viewed in a larger context. In courses that emphasize the writing process (such as English 120, 121, and 125), instructors want to enter into a dialogue – a discussion between two writers – with you about your own process. To facilitate such a conversation, instructors will provide you with feedback designed to engage you in rethinking your papers. However, writing teachers will not simply "tell" you how to "fix" drafts. In becoming a stronger writer, it is up to you to determine, with guidance from the instructor, the answers to your writing questions and to become a more self-reflective critic.

OVERVIEW OF GRADING PRACTICES

Most teachers would agree that the complexity of responding to and grading student texts nearly matches (and sometimes surpasses) the complexity of writing itself. As a student at John Carroll, you will encounter a variety of grading styles and teaching practices based on instructors' professional, theoretically-informed beliefs about good teaching and good writing. *We encourage you to talk to your instructors about their grading practices during the early part of the semester in order to prevent misunderstandings.*

DEFINITIONS OF LETTER GRADES

Letter grades for courses are determined by a variety of factors, and these factors may vary somewhat with individual instructors. Many instructors use different evaluation methods other than letter grades (point systems, portfolios, contract grading, check plus/minus systems). Some instructors do not put traditional letter grades on each draft, but students have the right to ask their instructor what his or her letter grade for a draft or for the overall course is during the semester, and instructors should respond in a timely manner. The following criteria provide a general outline for letter grades given to papers, though they are not the sole criteria used to determine course grades:

The **"A" paper** has numerous and significant strengths. It is substantial in intellectual and rhetorical development. There is evidence of critical analysis and critical thought based on convincing use of various types of evidence. "A" papers often successfully execute a graceful style and unique approach to the subject matter in a manner that treats the assignment carefully. They are free of errors in grammar, mechanics, and usage.

The **"B" paper** has strengths that outweigh its weaknesses, but it may be lacking in some significant areas. While the "B" paper engages the material and explores useful questions, it does not articulate ideas as clearly or convincingly as the "A" paper. It may have less detail or substantial supports for claims than an "A" paper, but there should be evidence of careful critical thinking. It is relatively free of errors in grammar, mechanics, and usage.

The **"C" paper** is a satisfactory response to the assignment; its strengths and weaknesses are about equally balanced. The "C" paper generally has a central idea which is executed and developed clearly enough to be understood by the reader. The "C" paper may express useful ideas or arguments but lacks substantial support or explanation of these ideas. "C" work can be mechanically clean, but lacking intellectual development.

The **"D" paper** indicates below-average achievement in expressing and developing ideas. It is vague and underdeveloped and does not exhibit strong critical thinking and the essay may not respond carefully to the aims of the assignment. Its central ideas may be unclear or are supported illogically or inconsistently. The "D" paper contains repeated, serious grammatical errors.

The "F" paper fails to respond appropriately to the assignment. Whereas the "D" paper may be weak in its support of its own focus, the "F" paper will simply fail to have a focus or support it adequately. The paper may contain serious errors in grammar, spelling, and sentence structure that interfere with the readers' understanding. The paper appears to have been put together with little time or thought.

FOURTEEN

GUIDELINES FOR USING NON-SEXIST LANGUAGE

—◻—

Language not only reflects the world around us, but it also shapes people's thoughts and attitudes. In other words, when we write or speak we are actually affecting our audience: pleasing them, amusing them, informing them, or perhaps offending them. The fact that words, as symbolic acts, can harm us every bit as much as physical acts demands that we be responsible for what we say and write and how we phrase things. Realizing this, most of us try to rid our vocabularies of words that label people on the basis of their race, religion, class, gender, ethnic origin, or sexual orientation – words we know are painful. But our language still contains conventions that in more subtle ways can often be just as hurtful as obviously offensive words.

One area where this is particularly true is in the area of gender, where we can do harm without even realizing it. For instance, if we use the pronouns "he," "his," or "him" to represent both men and women, if we use "man" or "mankind" to represent all human beings, or if we label people as "mailman" or "chairman" regardless of their gender, we are using biased language. By not being aware that even seemingly insignificant parts of our language (like the use of pronouns) can have a powerful impact on our readers and listeners, we can potentially trivialize and make irrelevant the existence and contributions of half of humanity.

Thus, we ask you to use gender-neutral language in papers written for First-Year Writing classes. In this policy, the English Department is following the guidelines used in all John Carroll University publications, as well as in professional journals in academic fields.

Organizations such as the National Council of Teachers of English and the Modern Language Association have required the use of non-sexist language in their publications for more than a decade. The examples that follow are some ways you can avoid accidentally transmitting gender-biased messages along with the messages you mean to send. Such careful attention directed toward all members of your reading audience makes you a more thoughtful and powerful writer.

1. **Avoid the pronoun problem by using plurals in sentences.**
   Example: Give each student his paper as soon as *he* asks for it.
   Alternative: Give students their papers as soon as *they* ask for them.

2. **Eliminate words that cause unnecessary sex/gender references.**
   Example: A nurse must take care of *her* patients.
   Alternative: A nurse must take care of *the* patient.

3. **Use inclusive nouns.**
   Example: freshman, mankind, chairman.
   Alternative: first-year student, humankind, chairperson

4. **Use alternatives to phrases that demean or stereotype women.**

Example: lady lawyer, woman doctor, career girl, poetess

Alternative: lawyer, doctor, professional, poet

5. **When necessary, consider compound constructions.**

Example: The student may turn in *his* paper.

Alternatives: Students may turn in *their* paper.

The student may turn in *their* paper.

FIFTEEN

PLAGIARISM DEFINED

Plagiarism is the unacknowledged use of another person's writing or of his or her words, ideas, facts, and arguments. Plagiarism is never acceptable in university writing.

1. You plagiarize when, in quoting phrases, sentences, or paragraphs, you fail to use quotation marks (or, for longer passages, blocked quotes) or when you fail to identify the source of each quotation.

2. You plagiarize when, in restating borrowed material in the original language *or rewritten in your own words*, you fail to identify the source of each borrowing. Proper source documentation requires that you provide at least the author, work, place and date of publication, and page number, or URL from the Internet.

3. You plagiarize when, in taking from another writer ideas or facts which cannot be considered common knowledge, you fail to identify the source of each borrowing, giving the author, work, place and date of publication, and page number, or URL from the Internet.

4. You plagiarize when, without acknowledgment, you submit as your own work a paper written wholly or in part by some

other person. It is wrong to claim as your own the words, ideas, or facts of another person, or an anonymous source such as the Internet.

5. You plagiarize when you use material you wrote in high school or for another class and turn it in as though it is new work written for a current course. Though it is your material, it was not produced as part of a course for which you submit it, and therefore can be considered a form of cheating. This is often referred to as self-plagiarism. The purpose of John Carroll University writing courses is to engage students in the act of writing and revision, not simply the production of finished papers. Recycling earlier works omits a major component of the course.

INTENTIONAL VERSUS UNINTENTIONAL PLAGIARISM

There is an important difference between intentionally seeking to deceive when plagiarizing and unintentionally plagiarizing. Because writing can be a collaborative or cooperative act, inexperienced writers can be confused about the difference between collaboration and plagiarism, and inexperienced writers can sometimes submit work that has plagiarized passages without the intent to deceive. Two important rules should be followed to avoid unintentional plagiarism:

1. Any help that you receive from another person, or an idea or a plan from someone else, must be acknowledged. In the case of working with a tutor or writing consultant, consult your course instructor about your responsibility for acknowledging that person's aid.

2. If you have any questions or doubts about that difference between what you are required to acknowledge and what you need not acknowledge, talk to your instructor.

PENALTIES FOR PLAGIARISM

1. The penalty for plagiarism is failure for the course.

2. When there is evidence of a high degree of premeditation, as when a student submits a paper as original that is purchased from a business engaged in selling papers, or a paper copied from the Internet, a student may be suspended from the university.

3. A student who in any way cooperates with another student in an act of plagiarism is equally guilty and is subject to comparable penalties.

4. In cases involving mitigating circumstances, such as unintentional plagiarism, penalties may be reduced.

5. For possible additional penalties, a case of academic dishonesty may be heard by the University Disciplinary Board.

The university's general policy on Academic Honesty is described in the *John Carroll University Undergraduate Bulletin, 2015–2017* and on the First-Year Writing website at http://sites.jcu.edu/fycomp/.

Students should be aware that John Carroll instructors and administrators have software and search engines at their disposal designed for finding the sources for plagiarized work.

PROCEDURE FOR PLAGIARISM VIOLATIONS

1. If an instructor finds evidence for plagiarism, that instructor may:

   A) Discuss the case with the student while also reporting the incident and submitting evidence to the English Department Chair.

   OR

   B) Report the incident and forward the evidence to the English Department Chair without discussing the case with the student. In this instance, the Department Chair contacts the student.

   In both cases materials submitted by the instructor to the Department Chair are made available to the student.

2. Even in cases with mitigating factors, instructors are required to report incidents of plagiarism to the English Department Chair. A letter is written that includes the student's name and student number, the evidence of plagiarized work, any other relevant details, the penalty imposed, and acknowledgement of a student's right to appeal. The letter is forwarded to the Dean of Arts and Sciences, who determines if further disciplinary action is warranted, and places the letter in the student's file.

3. Students have the right to appeal a penalty to the English Department Chair. If a student is unsatisfied with the Chair's decision after the appeal, he or she can appeal the decision to the Dean of Arts and Sciences.

PLAGIARISM'S EFFECTS

Who is hurt by plagiarism?

The student
Plagiarism is a self-destructive act that sabotages learning, which is the most important reason a student attends John Carroll University.

Other students
Those who work hard to complete assignments honestly can rightfully feel betrayed by those who do not make the same effort and who may gain an unfair advantage when it comes to course grades. A student who knowingly plagiarizes is no different than an athlete who cheats and takes banned drugs to gain an unfair advantage.

The instructor
Instructors spend much time and expend much effort preparing classes, carefully reading and commenting on student writing, and meeting with students. Because of this, an instructor may rightfully feel disrespected and betrayed when a student plagiarizes.

What is damaged by plagiarism?

The student-teacher relationship
If teachers cannot trust students they cannot teach them. Plagiarism turns the student-teacher relationship into a perpetrator-cop relationship, which signals the end of the learning process.

Critical, creative, and independent thinking
When a student plagiarizes, that person loses the chance to develop skills which make for a productive life.

An atmosphere conducive to learning
Plagiarism replaces curiosity, effort, and trust with cynicism and distrust.

John Carroll's reputation
Potential employers will hesitate to hire a student from a school that has a reputation for students who practice plagiarism.

The value of a degree from John Carroll
Students who plagiarize graduate lacking important knowledge and skills, diminishing the value of their John Carroll education.

The values of a Jesuit Education
Students who plagiarize do not prepare themselves to lead and serve others.

WRITING CENTER

The John Carroll University Writing Center is located in the O'Malley Center, Room 207. The service is free and available on a first-come, first-serve basis as well as by appointment. The Writing Center is staffed by writing consultants consisting of both undergraduate and graduate students. Sessions last approximately 20-30 minutes, depending upon consultant availability.

Writing Center consultants are trained to work with writers of all skill levels, to provide useful feedback on any kind of writing, and to assist at any stage in the writing process. In most situations, they employ *interactive* teaching methods aimed primarily at helping you develop more effective composing strategies. Writing consultants are not "editors"; they will not, without your active involvement, simply proofread your work. Instead, you are encouraged to take the initiative and ask writing-specific questions about the draft-in-progress. For example, "How can I make the introduction more focused and interesting?" "How can I include more specific details or extra source material in my text without making my essay sound like a summary?" "How might I reword this sentence so that the idea is clearer?"

For hours, please contact the Writing Center at (216) 397-4529 or visit the Center's website at http://sites.jcu.edu/writingcenter/.

SEVENTEEN

LIBRARY INFORMATION

Grasselli Library is located across from the O'Malley Center. A library directory is located in the lobby. The library uses the Library of Congress classification system. If the library does not carry a copy of the book you are looking for, you can request a copy from another university library in Ohio via OhioLINK. You can access the library catalog, and a wide variety of database services, online at http://lib.jcu.edu/page/10000. Be sure to get your student identification number validated at the Circulation/Reserve Desk. Once this is done, you are free to check out materials, initiate OhioLINK loans, and use databases from off-campus locations.

Instructors will often ask for journal articles for research assignments. Grasselli Library carries a variety of journal subscriptions in electronic and/or printed formats. Journal articles are usually more focused and current than books and can be copied for future reference. Books are good sources for general treatments of topics with which you may not be familiar. You should choose sources carefully; many students make the mistake that easy-to-read information from popular magazines (Time, Newsweek, People, etc.) is just as reliable or appropriate as information from professional journals. Rather than assuming all periodicals are the same, you should show your instructor a list of sources and ask for suggestions. Many academic journals can be accessed on-line through the library website. (See "Articles and Data").

If you have any questions, you should ask your instructor or a reference librarian for help. Or, contact Nevin Mayer, the Grasselli Library liaison to the English Department, at (216) 397-3055 for more in-depth help with research.

EIGHTEEN

MLA FORMAT

MLA (Modern Language Association) style is the standard format for citing outside sources for almost all humanities disciplines, including most of the papers you will write in First-Year Writing at JCU. The following examples offer a brief overview of how writers commonly use MLA format in their writing. For a more extensive listing of citation examples, please consult the following website: https://owl.english.purdue.edu/owl/resource/747/01/.

The following information was drawn from The Purdue Online Writing Lab (OWL). Purdue OWL is a helpful resource students can consult for questions regarding MLA format, in-text citations, and works cited documentation. The Purdue OWL contains similarly helpful information on other documentation styles as well, including APA and Chicago style.

The MLA divides sources into three categories: print, Web, and other common sources. What follows are sample works-cited entries drawn from the Purdue OWL:

Print Sources: Books

Gleick, James. *Chaos: Making a New Science*. New York: Penguin, 1987. Print.

Gillespie, Paula, and Neal Lerner. *The Allyn and Bacon Guide to Peer Tutoring*. Boston: Allyn, 2000. Print.

Print Sources: Periodicals

Poniewozik, James. "TV Makes a Too-Close Call." *Time* 20 Nov. 2000: 70-71. Print.

Duvall, John N. "The (Super)Marketplace of Images: Television as Unmediated Mediation in DeLillo's *White Noise*." *Arizona Quarterly* 50.3 (1994): 127-53. Print.

Web Sources:

Note: MLA style no longer requires the inclusion of webpage URLs in works cited entries. Be aware that some online sources and automatic bibliography builders do not reflect this change.

Entire online site

Felluga, Dino. *Guide to Literary and Critical Theory.* Purdue U, 28 Nov. 2003. Web. 10 May 2006.

Part of a site

"How to Make Vegetarian Chili." *eHow.* Demand Media, Inc., n.d. Web. 24 Feb. 2009.

Sources Found Through a Database

Langhamer, Claire. "Love and Courtship in Mid-Twentieth-Century England." *Historical Journal* 50.1 (2007): 173-96. *ProQuest.* Web. 27 May 2009.

Junge, Wolfgang, and Nathan Nelson. "Nature's Rotary Electromotors." *Science* 29 Apr. 2005: 642-44. *Science Online.* Web. 5 Mar. 2009.

Blog

Salmar1515 [Sal Hernandez]. "Re: Best Strategy: Fenced Pastures vs. Max Number of Rooms?" *BoardGameGeek.* BoardGameGeek, 29 Sept. 2008. Web. 5 Apr. 2009.

NINETEEN

WEBSITES FOR FURTHER RESEARCH AND STUDY

The following websites are intended to provide you with additional resources and study aids to help you in First-Year Writing, as well as in other classes, at John Carroll. For more resources, please consult the composition program website: http://sites.jcu.edu/fycomp/.

Online Dictionaries: http://www.yourdictionary.com/ http://www.oxforddictionaries.com/us

Purdue's Online Writing Lab: http://owl.english.purdue.edu/

APA Format: http://owl.english.purdue.edu/owl/resource/560/01/

Chicago Style Format: http://owl.english.purdue.edu/owl/ resource/717/01/

Proofreading Strategies: https://owl.english.purdue.edu/owl/ resource/561/01/

University of California-Irvine Resources for Writing and

Research: http://www.writingcenter.uci.edu/resources/resources-for-students/

Duke University Resources: Writing for Specific Disciplines: http://twp.duke.edu/writing-studio/resources/writing-for-specific-disciplines

TWENTY

ENGLISH 125: COURSE PHILOSOPHY AND DESCRIPTION

PHILOSOPHY

The standard English 125 syllabus at John Carroll University stresses writing that focuses on learning different approaches: rhetorical knowledge; critical thinking, research; the process of writing; and the knowledge of academic conventions. Primarily, you will learn that academic arguments emerge in response to other arguments. You will also learn various rhetorical strategies necessary for successful research-based writing in diverse academic and non-academic situations. You will use these approaches to acquire the writing skills necessary to succeed in college and beyond: summary; revision; analysis of textual evidence; arguing a position; analyzing different audiences; researching and documenting source materials; writing introductions and conclusions; writing with coherence, cohesion, and completeness; and, showing proficiency in grammar and punctuation. Although English 125 instructors use a standard syllabus, each instructor makes the course his or her own by focusing on a central theme, by assigning various readings, and by developing in-class activities and writing assignments.

DESCRIPTION

The standard syllabus is held together by a common philosophy and a common set of learning outcomes, not by a rigid schedule or specific readings. If a student and his or her roommate are taking English 125, they may have different readings, assignments, and discussion/writing topics. The following descriptions are not absolute, but may help students to understand the different units.

These are the assignments you may be asked to complete in EN 125:

- *Project #1: What Do You Have to Say?* The purpose of the semester's first major project essay is to introduce students to academic research and writing. To do so, students will choose one of the essays we read in this section, conduct some minor library research, and write a well-developed paper that makes an argument about an issue and supports it with evidence from your reading and your research (4-5 pages).

- *Project #2: Introduction to Text-Based Research.* As a class, we will either read a short novel, read a piece of non-fiction, watch a film, or read some other kind of academic writing that revolves around the course theme. Then, students will pick a research topic or question based on their reading and write an annotated bibliography and paper proposal: 1-2 page proposal with 5-7 –item bibliography.

- *Project #3: Formal Research-Based Project.* Students will write a research-based project based on their proposal and annotated bibliography from Project #2.

- *Project #4. Academic Literacy Narrative.* Students will compose an academic narrative on their learning about writing over the course of the semester, integrating the narrative with research on the kind of writing performed in their major. This assignment can stand alone as a separate project, or students can use this narrative as their final portfolio letter.

TWENTY-ONE

ENGLISH 120: COURSE PHILOSOPHY AND DESCRIPTION

English 120 is for students who require more explicit empha-sis on addressing problems in grammar, mechanics, and usage. Students in the course engage in the following: reading and writing expository prose; studying the principles of invention, arrangement, and style; working to develop a sense of audience and purpose in their writing; and, studying matters of grammar, mechanics, and usage to support their writing skills. English 120 also introduces students to the basics of research.

At the end of English 120, students should be able to draft, revise, edit, and proofread. Their writing should demonstrate: the formulation of a central idea; the organization of a convinc-ing argument; the development of unified, coherent paragraphs; the construction of correct and effective sentences; and, the command of an appropriate vocabulary. In writing the research-based papers, students should also demonstrate the ability to select, assimilate, and document source material in support of a thesis.

Students are placed in English 120 based on their prior aca-demic record.

These are the assignments you may be asked to write in English 120:

- *Project #1: Four-Paragraph Set (Summary, Analysis, and Argument).* Students begin writing a series of short, 4-paragraph long essays that focus on analysis, description, and argument. These short essays give students practice in fundamental academic skills such as summary, analysis, and argument.

- *Project #2: Exemplification and Description Essay.* Students write a short essay in which they use the skills of exemplification and description.

- *Project #3: Cause and Effect Essay.* Students write a short essay that introduces them to the argumentative idea of cause and effect.

- *Project #4: Visual Argument Analysis Essay.* Students study and analyze a piece of visual rhetoric and write a short essay analyzing the visual elements and how they are used to make either an implicit or explicit argument.

- *Project #5: Argument Essay with Visual Component and Annotated Bibliography.* Students write an academic, argument-based essay with annotated bibliography and include a visual representation of their argument.

TWENTY-TWO

ENGLISH 121: COURSE PHILOSOPHY AND DESCRIPTION

English 121 is the spring semester course taking by students who complete EN 120 in the fall semester. The EN 121 curriculum mirrors much of what is taught in the standard EN 125 curriculum, as it focuses on academic research, but the assignments and activities are constructed specifically for a developmental writing population. In the course, students: read and write expository prose; study the principles of invention, arrangement, and style; work to develop a sense of audience and purpose in their writing; and, study matters of grammar, mechanics, and usage to support their writing skills. English 121 also introduces students to the fundamentals of academic research.

At the end of English 121, students should be able to draft, revise, edit, and proofread. Their writing should demonstrate: the formulation of a central idea; the organization of a convincing argument; the development of unified, coherent paragraphs; the construction of correct and effective sentences; and, the command of an appropriate vocabulary. They should also be able to perform various academic research tasks, including the ability to select, assimilate, and document source material in support of a thesis.

These are the assignments you may be asked to write in English 121:

- *Project #1: Introduction to Course and Course Theme.* The purpose of the semester's first major project essay is to introduce students to the theme of the course, to pick up on skills from EN 120, and to lay the groundwork for the remaining projects. Students will write two short essays. The first essay asks students to read an assigned text, discuss their reactions in their small groups, and write a short page essay analyzing their group's experiences and understanding of the theme. The second essay asks students to read an assigned text and write an essay analyzing how the text fits into the course theme.

- *Project #2: Introduction to Text-Based Research.* The class will watch a relevant film in class, or read a short work of fiction or non-fiction, and then, with the additional use of assigned texts, students will analyze an aspect of the course theme presented in the film or the reading. To help them develop their arguments, students will conduct library-based research and integrated those sources into their essay.

- *Project #3: Annotated Bibliography.* Students will continue their research practices by selecting a topic relevant to the course theme, write a proposal, and a 5-7 item annotated bibliography.

- *Project #4. Formal Research-Based Project.* Students will write a research project based on their proposal and annotated bibliography (6-7 pages).

In their final portfolio, students will revise two of the three major essays and also write a reflection of their learning about writing over the course of the year (2-3 pages).

TWENTY-THREE

STUDENT WRITING

—▣—

The student texts that follow were produced in English 125 courses during the 2015–2016 academic year. This collection represents a variety of academic genres and purposes: summaries, close textual analyses, and academic research essays.

The following student essays were solicited by the English department's First-Year Writing Program and chosen by the Director of First-Year Writing, Tom Pace. These essays were selected because they represent the type of engaged intellectual effort that we encourage and applaud in first-year writing courses at John Carroll. We do not offer these essays only as models or exemplars for you to imitate. Rather, we believe they provide examples of different rhetorical strategies and approaches from which other students can benefit and, accordingly, they may work as texts for class discussion within the context of the standard syllabus.

The Editor's Note before each essay articulates why the Writing Committee selected the essay and offers questions to consider while you read. We ask that you read these essays critically and engage in thoughtful and stimulating conversations about them, both in and out of class.

ESSAY CONTEST

Awarding the finest in John Carroll University First-Year Writing

Open to all essays written for a first-year composition classes in the 2016–2017 academic year.
(EN 120, 121, or 125)

Send questions or submissions to:
compcontestJCU@gmail.com
Deadline: April 1, 2017

The Effects of Mass Media on Juror Impartiality

ABBY LENHART

—▣—

Recently, it has become commonplace to find information within seconds, using smart phones, social media apps, laptops, or even turning on the television. Not only has the media developed greatly and become more widespread in recent years, it has also had a remarkable amount of influence on people of many ages today. This influence is merely due to

———

Editor's Note: In this research essay, Abby examines the role that mass media play on the way jurors, in highly-publicized criminal trials, make impartial decisions. She argues that jury bias is prevalent in many of these cases, in large part, due to the abundance of mass media, including social media . Specifically, she draws from recent well-publicized cases, as well as from older cases, to show how media impacts juror impartiality.

When reading Abby's essay, consider the following: How does Abby introduce, cite, and explain each quote and each paraphrase that she includes from her research in her own essay? How does Abby connect the evidence in a way that supports her conclusion regarding the role of mass media? Do you agree with Abby's postion?

the ever-growing content the media covers and consists of, and to the simple accessibility of the information. As a result of widespread media coverage, information about almost any crime can be viewed on the news or found online. Sometimes, the degree to which the media covers certain crimes can offer a challenge to the courts when a case goes to trial because, often times, the reports on the court proceedings can affect the way a jury reaches its verdict. This is to say that jury bias is prevalent in today's court system due to the extensive media coverage of certain trials.

The most critical requirement of a jury in almost any case is for jurors to remain impartial. All defendants are supposed to receive a fair trial by an unbiased jury, according to the defendant's Sixth Amendment rights ("Media Influence in Capital Cases"). Nicole Waters and Paula Hannaford-Agor, researchers for the Center for Jury Studies at the National Center for State Courts (NCSC), have published their findings in an article regarding the impact of media on jurors. According to their examination, unbiased and impartial jurors are "those who are willing and able to consider the evidence presented at trial without preconceived opinions about the defendant's guilt or innocence." The article goes on to stress that such jurors should be able to "deliberate in good faith" and return an honest and reasonable verdict to the court (Waters and Hannaford-Agor 1). Here, Waters and Hannaford-Agor define what an impartial juror is and ought to be, and they emphasize the importance of a truthful verdict with no biases or hindrances.

The impartiality of jurors could be seriously threatened in cases where there has been extensive media coverage. One possible reason for this threat is that members of the jury could be exposed to pre-trial publicity, which might possibly lead to bias among some of them. Indeed, jurors can access published information about a case very easily from newspapers, magazines, online articles, news broadcasts, blogs, or social media sites such as Facebook or Twitter. With a vast variety of ways to access this material, jurors are likely to come across some biased information which could in turn affect their outlook on a trial or about a particular defendant (1-2). However, Jon Bruschke at Fullerton College in California ardently maintains that pre-trial publicity does not directly affect the outcome of a trial. In a recent news piece at California State-Fullerton, Valerie Orleans cites Bruschke, a published researcher who has conducted studies on numerous court cases in which some type of media coverage or reporting was involved, and emphasizes that Bruschke concurs that most pre-trial coverage displays defendants in a negative manner. Yet, according to Orleans, Bruschke still asserts that it does not have an impact on the verdict because it is usually presented months before the court proceedings even begin, and that potential jurors are unlikely to still be affected by it once they are selected. To corroborate this claim, Orleans cites Bruschke's statistics that out of 1,100 murder and robbery cases he studied, there was no difference in the court or jury proceedings for cases with harsh pre-trial publicity and cases that received no publicity (Orleans). While Bruschke's research is valid, it cannot completely rule out the possibility of pre-trial publicity affecting the juror's attitudes and behaviors.

A recent and popular example of where pre-trial coverage impacted juror impartiality stems from the trial of convicted criminal Steve Avery, whose case was the foundation for the popular Netflix show *Making a Murderer*. In 1985, Avery was convicted for the sexual assault of a young woman. He served 18 years before being released in 2003, after DNA testing revealed another person committed the crime. Before Avery's trial began, potential jurors admitted to having preconceived notions about Avery's guilt. During jury selection, Avery's lawyers discovered that 129 out of 130 potential jurors thought Avery was guilty before the trial even began. This was due, in part, to the extensive pre-trial coverage of Avery's case which depicted him as a brutal murderer. Although the dynamics of this case have proven to be widely controversial, it is undeniable that the media coverage before the trial played a large role in affecting the jury (Stuart).

Also, in a study conducted by the National Center of State Courts (NCSC) on the frequency of juror use of the media, researchers Waters and Hannaford-Agor found that the majority of jurors involved in the study used the internet to discover details about the cases with which they were involved. In this report, they cite Thomson Reuters, an informational source for businesses and professionals, who noted that ninety verdicts out of all state court verdicts in the United States were questioned due to wrongdoing of jurors involving the media between 1998 and 2010 (Waters and Hannaford-Agor). The report also claimed that in twenty-eight of these cases, the verdicts were overturned (3-4).

Aside from internet content and news stories affecting the jury directly, the jury could also be biased towards one verdict or another based on how the media portrays the jury if they do not return the verdict the public was expecting. A prime example comes from the trial of convicted murderer Dr. Sam Sheppard. Sheppard was convicted of murdering his pregnant wife in 1954 in Bay Village, Ohio. Even though his trial took place long before the era of cell phones, 24-hour news cycles, and social media, it still received enormous media attention through radio, television, and newspapers. The reports portrayed Sheppard as a vicious killer and basically convicted him in the public eye, although he maintained his innocence. According to Megan Thielking's reporting in *North by Northwestern Magazine*, the jury in this particular case was heavily exposed to this publicity during the trial and returned a verdict of guilty very quickly, despite lack of evidence from the prosecution (Thielking). After serving ten years in prison, Sheppard was acquitted of the murder because of a DNA test that proved his innocence. Additionally, some of the jurors involved eventually reported that they did not believe there was enough evidence to convict Sheppard and that they allowed the public's emotional appeal to get the best of them (Linder). The outcomes of this particular case support the idea that some juries show an unfair bias towards the defendant because of the pressure they feel from the media.

Another essential factor to consider when thinking about jury bias arises from the use of cameras in a courtroom. Almost twenty-five years ago, trials began to be televised for the American public to see. Now, all fifty states permit courtroom proceedings to be broadcasted. Only federal courts have banned cameras from the courtroom. On the one hand, as Supreme Court Justice Anthony Kennedy contends, cameras in the courtroom are a distraction from the course of the trial and can make witnesses, attorneys, judges, and juries uncomfortable. On the other hand, proponents of televised trials insist that the live feeds educate the public on the legal system and the operations of the courts. In an article that appears in *Pacific Standard Magazine*, Kate Wheeling presents both sides of this debate. She observes that those who support trials shown on television assert that the public should not develop any biases towards a case one way or another because these viewers are simply watching the trial and not following a certain media outlet such as Fox News or MSNBC. While this distinction is acceptable and logical, it overlooks the fact that displaying broadcasts of the proceedings does not guarantee that people will not tune into the news or check social media to see a brief but probably biased update on the trial (Wheeling).

To illustrate this point, the highly-publicized Casey Anthony trial offers a prime example. Anthony was accused of murdering her young daughter and pleaded not guilty, although considerable evidence was stacked against her. Details of this case could be found in almost any form of media and the public began to develop opinions on Anthony's guilt almost instantly. For instance, Nancy Grace and her followers pinned Anthony as guilty from the very beginning and were among the many people outraged when the jury returned a verdict of not guilty. This verdict and the jurors alike were extensively criticized in the media. As a result, the judge opted to conceal the names of the jurors from the public to protect them from any potential backlash. Although this verdict was controversial, this case epitomizes how a televised trial can lead to bias and disruption within a court system due to excessive media coverage and its influence on public opinion ("Media Influence in Capital Cases").

With the question of bias in the courtroom associated with cameras at hand, it should be recognized that the presence of cameras sometimes triggers witnesses to testify differently because they fear criticism from the public based on their testimony. For example, if the person called to testify has witnessed a gang-related crime, he or she may provide a false testimony due to fear of retribution from the gang ("Media Influence in Capital Cases"). When examining the impact of televised trials, one can conclude that jurors may be affected by being filmed in the same way witnesses are. This is to say that jurors could potentially develop biases against a case because they are aware that an audience is watching them and most likely scrutinizing their decision. Additionally, cameras in the courtroom offer added pressure on the jury since the jurors' identities will be known to those who view the case, which could possibly lead the jurors to fear for their safety based on the attitudes of their audience. This issue raises some serious concerns when exploring the origin of jury bias and whether or not the defendant is receiving a fair trial.

It is crucial to understand that there is no concrete way to avoid bias among juries. The media will always influence people, especially when it comes to the criminal justice system. It is actually a Supreme Court ruling that courts are not permitted to try to stop the media from covering their cases. However, according to Capital Punishment in Context, a judge may delay a case so that the publicity surrounding it can die down before a trial ("Media Influence in Capital Cases"). Though it is possible that certain measures can be taken to avoid jury bias, these measures cannot eliminate bias altogether. A jury may be biased for numerous reasons, but it seems that the most prominent reasons in today's society are issues dealing with the media through the forms of social media services, newspapers, magazines, websites, talk shows, and news broadcasts. There are several factors to consider when it comes to jury bias, but some of the most prominent are pre-trial publicity, pre-determined attitudes set forth by jurors, the expectations of the public for a certain verdict, and televised trials. Whether the jurors themselves allow media coverage to influence their opinions, or they feel pressure from the media to return a certain verdict, it can be seen that in some cases, the media does indeed affect the way jurors behave in the criminal justice system.

WORKS CITED

Linder, Douglas. "The Dr. Sam Sheppard Trials." *Umkc.edu*. University of
    Missouri – Kansas City School of Law, 2006. Web. 14 Feb. 2016.

"Media Influence in Capital Cases." *CapitalPunishmentinContext.org*. Capital
    Punishment in Context, 2012. Web. 29 Jan. 2016.

Orleans, Valerie. "Pretrial Publicity: Does it Impact Verdicts?" *Calstate.
    Fullerton.edu*. CSUF News, 28 Oct. 2004. Web. 14 Feb. 2016.

Stuart, Tessa. "Making a Murderer: Steven Avery's Lawyer on Suspicions
    About Jury." *Rolling Stone Magazine*, 14 Jan. 2016. Web. 29 Jan. 2016.

Thielking, Megan. "Five trials by media." *North By Northwestern Magazine*,
    13 Oct. 2011. Web. 14 Feb. 2016.

Waters, Nicole L., and Hannaford-Agor, Paula. "The Impact of New Media
    on Jurors, Public Perceptions of the Jury System, and the American
    Criminal Justice System." *National Center for State Courts: Center for Jury
    Studies* (2012) : n. pag. Web. 29 Jan. 2016.

Wheeling, Kate. "Should There Be Cameras in Courtrooms?" *Pacific Standard
    Magazine*, 6 March 2015. Web. 14 Feb. 2016.

Therapy that Does not Hurt

SARAH HAREN

In his book *Musicophilia*, neurologist Oliver Sacks writes, "Music can lift us out of depression or move us to tears- it is a remedy, a tonic, orange juice for the ear. But for many of my neurological patients, music is even more- it can provide access, even when no medication can, to movement, to speech, to life. For them, music is not a luxury, but a necessity" ("8 Beautiful Oliver Sacks Quotes"). As this quote implies, music can be a form of therapy for many. I often find myself, for instance, when I am having a rough day, turning to music to help me evaluate

---

Editor's Head Note here. In her research essay, Sarah explores the role of music therapy in treating both children and adults who have cancer. By bringing in research from scholarly sources, as well as from non-scholarly, yet substantive, source, Sarah argues that such therapy can be highly beneficial and , in some cases, just as beneficial as traditional medicines. Sarah weaves this research through her own personal experiences with her mother's aunt to create a provocative case for music therapy.

When reading Sarah's essay, consider the following: Are you persuaded by Haren's argument? If not, do you find her argument valid? Why or why not? Haren, near the end of the essay, brings in a naysayer. Is the naysayer fair to the opposing arguments? Why or why not?

my emotions. In addition to helping us when we feel down, though, Sacks's quote points toward a different take on music. Yes, he refers to music as a remedy and a tonic but, perhaps most importantly, he stresses it can help people through tough periods of their life that even medicine cannot.

When I think of people who are going through difficult times, I often think of my mom's aunt. She has battled and won against cancer before, but now they have found a large tumor in her brain. There is nothing that can be done, and she has lost hope. No amount of medicine or surgery is going to change her condition. Something that she can change, however is her outlook on life. Music therapy is a way for patients to relax, enjoy themselves, and to improve their overall wellbeing by either listening to or participating in music. So, when I started researching music therapy it hit me that there is something more for them; something that does not hurt like chemotherapy or surgery. Music therapy is a reputable source of treatment for all cancer patients during every stage of their illness to help them deal with the harshness of the disease.

Before we get too far, let us go over the basics of music therapy. In her article, "Music Therapy for Children and Adults with Cancer: Alternative and Complementary Therapies," Jane Hart addresses music therapy as an alternative rehabilitation for people. Here, she uses a definition from the American Music Therapy Association to define music therapy as, "an established healthcare profession that uses music to address physical, emotional, cognitive, and social needs of individuals of all ages. Music therapy improves the quality of life for persons who are well and meets the needs of children and adults with disabilities or illnesses" (221). The article explains that music therapy also has a variety of different set ups being classified as active and passive. On the one hand, active music therapy is where the patient is involved in the making of music with their therapist. On the other hand, passive music therapy is where the therapist finds already made music that fits the patient's mood or needs and the patient listens to the music. There are also two types of sessions where the patient can either participate in a group or have a session where it is just the patient themselves with the music therapist (Hart). What is beneficial about music therapy, then, is that a variety of set-ups exist for each patient to choose from and that no session is the same, since patients are not the same. Through this personalization, music therapy aids any patient, young or old, at any stage of their battle with cancer.

Music therapy can help children, for instance, to deal with cancer in many different ways. Children, of course, are not the only ones who are helped by music therapy, but children do face different obstacles when battling cancer than adults battling cancer. Therefore, it is important to look at them separately from adults. Children dealing with leukemia are put into isolation rooms, because sometimes if they get sick it can become fatal. In his article, "Music Therapy as an Intervention for Children with Cancer in Isolation Rooms," Warren Brodsky focuses on children in isolation for his research, where he points out that in the isolation rooms, these children experience less social interaction, very few physical activities, and decreased stimulation. They often become lonely, depressed, and angry because they do not understand (Brodsky). The fact that isolated children are having these feelings is not surprising. To be in a hospital with limited interaction away from how their life was before cancer, would be very hard on a young person due to the anger and frustration they can feel. Sometimes, because of this lack of interaction, they do not want to verbalize their feelings. For example, as Brodsky states, "Anxiety about death may not be verbalized immediately because children may be hesitant to voice these concerns to their favorite nurse or doctor. But the bond and relationship created through satisfying musical encounters with the music therapist has been found to be an outlet for children to verbalize freely" (20-21). This outlet is crucial for these children in this stage of their life. A child's music therapist connects with them first through something they can enjoy which is music. If the child is singing/ playing an instrument with their therapist it is building a friendship where they trust their therapist. Even if the music therapist is just picking music for their patient, the therapist is still showing that they understand what is going on or trying to understand which also creates trust. To have someone to talk to that they trust will help these children to express feeling that they had pent up inside and gives their therapist room to explain what is going on to the child if they have any misconceptions. No matter what point in their battle these children are at they are always going to need someone to talk to.

Not only can music therapy help children emotionally, but it can also help children physiologically. In a 2010 study on children who underwent lumbar punctures, Thanh Nhan Nguyen, et al. conducted a trial involving two groups: those receiving music therapy and those who were not (control group). The researchers show that all patients had decreased pain, heart rate, respiratory rates, and anxiety (Nguyen et. al). In the article, they observed that, "When the children had earphones with music, they felt less pain and were calmer and relaxed during and after the procedure. All these children definitely wanted to have earphones with music the next time they were treated. Almost all the children in the control group expressed pain, fear, and anxiety" (153). The fact that the children wanted to have music to help them the next time shows that music therapy does indeed have a positive effect on people. It is also important to note that without music therapy children go into surgeries with fear and come out with pain. However, with music therapy patients go into procedures and come out with less pain and fear. Quotes were gathered after the lumbar puncture from the children involved in the study and one in particular stuck out to me. In their research, Nguyen, et al. quote a child who received music therapy: "I didn't feel any pain," the child declared. "I felt less afraid than last time. The last time, I had to hold my mother's hand very tightly during the LP. I didn't need to do that this time . . . [smiles]" (151). While there are well-researched drugs that can certainly lower anxiety in people before a surgery, music therapy is a way to do help decrease anxiety naturally, and it assists after a surgery as well, without relying too much on drugs. So, not only does music therapy help to lower anxiety all though out the battle against cancer, but it also can help before a surgery or procedure.

Not only does music therapy help before surgeries/procedures it can also help during and after. In her *New Yorker* article, "How Music Makes Us Feel Better," Maria Konnikova explores the workings of our bodies in response to music. Specifically, she examines how music helps patients throughout their surgeries as well as after them. Konnikova writes that, "In 2006, researchers discovered that even something as complex as open-heart surgery could be improved with a musical intervention: patients who listened to music during and after heart surgery not only felt less anxious but required, on average, two hundred fewer minutes of intubation than those who had undergone standard procedure," (Konnikova). This procedure strongly suggests that just listening to music helps patients long after listening to it. Healing is another phase of the cancer process that people can experience and music can help during the recovery stage.

SARAH HAREN

Konnikova also addresses how music theraphy works on the brain. She explains that, "The human auditory cortex—the part of our brain devoted to hearing and listening—can differentiate between extremely specific frequencies of sound". This part of the brain is crucial to telling how effective a type of music is. Music that have tempos similar to that of a heart rate can help heart rate, breathing, and circulation. Music with lyrical melodies like classical music can help with relaxation (Konnikova). It is extremely important to know what type of music to listen to, to get the result wanted for a patient to help them throughout their battle.

Music therapy can also help patients in hospitals have a way to workout in addition to all the other aspects of life that I have discussed so far. In her article and accompanying PBS video, "When Music Is Medicine for Kids Coping with Cancer," Laila Kazmi interviews a music therapist and her young patient. In the article, Kazmi addresses music therapy in a manner I would have never thought of. Kazmi notes, "For patients who need exercise, but feel too exhausted because of the harsh medicines and treatments they are receiving, music provides a physical outlet" (Kazmi). The physical exercise is either in playing instruments or dancing. Exercise is an important aspect of life and is needed for everyone, including people who are ill. Playing instruments and dancing are forms of active music therapy. So, even if these patients cannot perform regular exercises, music therapy helps them, at this stage in their battle with cancer, to provide a substitution for this lack of something vital to life they might have enjoyed before becoming sick.

Now that we have explored adults and children with cancer, now let us look at a specific stage of cancer that some will go through and some will not. This stage of cancer that music therapy can help is with those with terminal cancer. Certainly, children can also have terminal cancer, but here I am going to focus on adults with terminal cancer. In his article, "The Effects of Music Therapy on the Quality and Length of Life of People Diagnosed with Terminal Cancer," Russell E. Hilliard studied patients in hospice care receiving music therapy. There were also two groups in this study containing a control group and those receiving music therapy. In this study quality of life was measured to see how music therapy was helping patients. Quality of life was measured with a self-test by the patients. (Hilliard). Hilliard States that the, "Quality of life was higher for those subjects receiving music therapy, and their quality of life increased over time as they received more music therapy sessions. Subjects in the control group, however, experienced a lower quality of life than those in the experimental group, and without music, their quality of life decreased over time" (113). Hilliard's research suggests that the quality of life for these patients increased with each music therapy session. Increased quality of life means that these patients looked at life in a more positive light than before. Music therapy is just not just something that will only help once, but it can help patients every time. The study also states that these hospice care patients, who were receiving music therapy, scored closer on the test to a healthy adult that took the same test than to other terminally ill patients (Hilliard). It is remarkable that these patients, who were once considered terminally ill and then received music therapy, had about the same quality of life as people who were not deemed terminally ill. Helping people at the end of their battle with cancer is still extremely important even if they have been deemed as people who cannot be saved.

At this point I would like to identify a topic many people bring up when talking about the effectiveness of music therapy. This topic is people who claim it works as a placebo or that the patients just think that music therapy is helping them when it is not. This is simply not true. Music therapy has shown to help, as I mentioned before, with respiratory rates, heart rate, and blood pressure. There is no way to fake these results as they are proven to be real with science. There is also talk that music therapy requires those participating in it to be musically inclined for it to be effective. Music therapy does not require any skill in playing an instrument or singing and is meant to be relaxing and a way to express emotions.

Music therapy, ultimately, is something that can help every person with cancer no matter where they are in their cancer battle. Music therapy can help children, adults and all people with terminal cancer in a variety of different ways. Emotionally, physically, and physiologically patients are able to improve with the help of music therapy. Music therapy can also be used before and after procedures to continually help patients. Music therapy is not just a placebo effect where patients think they are improving, they actually are. Patients that have a lot on their minds can be helped with music during this tough time for. I know now, and I hope you do too, that music therapy is something that can change with the patient and is always there for them.

Works Cited

"8 Beautiful Oliver Sacks Quotes That Illustrate his Inspiring Mission to Understand the Mind." *Bustle.com*, 15 August 2015. Web. 12 April 2016.

Brodsky, Warren. "Music Therapy as an Intervention for Children with Cancer in Isolation Rooms." *Music Therapy* 8.1 (1989): 17-34. Print.

Hart, Jane. "Music Therapy for Children and Adults with Cancer: Alternative and Complementary Therapies." *CINAHL* 15.5 (2009): 221-25. Print.

Hilliard, Russell E. "The Effects of Music Therapy on the Quality and Length of Life of People Diagnosed with Terminal Cancer." *Journal of Music Therapy* 40.2 (2003): 113-137. Print.

Kazmi, Laila. "When Music Is Medicine for Kids Coping with Cancer." PBS. 24 Mar. 2015. Web. 04 Oct. 2015.

Konnikova, Maria. "How Music Makes Us Feel Better." *The New Yorker.* 26 Sept. 2013. Web. 04 Oct. 2015.

Nguyen, Thanh Nhan, S. Nilsson, A. L. Hellstrom, and A. Bengtson. "Music Therapy to Reduce Pain and Anxiety in Children With Cancer Undergoing Lumbar Puncture: A Randomized Clinical Trial." *Journal of Pediatric Oncology Nursing* 27.3 (2010): 146-55. Web. 3 Nov. 2015.

When Words Won't Work

CAYLAN FAZIO

—❐—

I remember walking into my AP History class, slightly embarrassed but determined to be truthful. Right through the door and straight to his desk: "Mr. Heider, I don't have my paper."

Sudden severity, "you had a week, why don't you have it?"

"Mr. Heider, I have to be honest with you. I lost my words."

Growing up I never particularly enjoyed writing. My mom used writing as a punishment, because I despised it so much.

———

In this personal narrative, Caylan traces her frustrations and breakthroughs as a writer. She artfully recounts several pivotal experiences from her childhood and adolescence that have shaped her relationship to the written word. Although Caylan admits that she still struggles to find the "right" words, she leaves us with the final impression that this struggle is both necessary and productive.

When reading Caylan's essay, consider the following: What do you make of Caylan's decision to include an introductory scene before presenting her title? How does she maintain her unique voice throughout the essay? To what extent do Caylan's observations reflect your experiences as a writer? What insights into your own writing process can you take away from this narrative?

I remember having to write ten times, "I'm sorry for (insert crime committed here)." I've always had a tight writing grip and sometimes I think it's from my tense writing as an angry kid. If I wasn't forced to write, I wouldn't. I could tell you for a long time that I hated writing.

I remember during my awkward freshman year of high school, I was assigned a research paper for English class. I got it back recalling a particular sentence underlined. Scribbled in the margin was a note from my well-intentioned teacher: "awkward phrasing." How could phrasing be awkward? Recounting the memory still makes me uncomfortable. . . Yes, maybe the sentence did sound awkward, but to me, my freshman awkwardness was perpetrating much of my being, spilling out onto my homework like orange juice would do on the kitchen table after school. To say the least, being self-conscious of my writing was the norm every time I touched a pen.

English teachers frighten me. I must say the fear is a sort of awe-struck respect for their eloquence. Nonetheless, I can't recall a writing teacher that I did not try to avoid. That was until Mr. Hemmert. While most of his students couldn't tell you what they learned, we all knew we learned something. To sum it up: "don't be a pig in a jar." For illustration, Mr. Hemmert even had a pink stuffed-animal pig shoved into a glass jar sitting on his filing cabinet. Being a pig in a jar meant to write like everyone else. To not be a pig in the jar, you had to find your own voice.

In the two years of English and a semester of creative writing that I spent with Mr. Hemmert, I barely branched out in my writing. I still had neither the words nor the ways to accurately convey my ideas for assignments. But thank goodness Mr. Hemmert lived outside the box. One assignment at the end of each semester was the personal section of our binders. This section had no rules except for the necessary written explanation of each creative outbursts. My senior year, I included a drawing in that section: black ink, nothing but a series of lines in a curvy, egg-like shape. I found my Etch-A-Sketch-masterpiece therapeutic, and for some reason the picture reminded me of two important women: my sister and the Virgin Mary, although I'm not quite sure why. The written addition was overlaid on top with a green highlighter, nothing more than a brief reflection of how my day was. Although my ideas and words were not very coherent, I unbridled my pen for the first time. The comment I received back, "this is really you." I think that was when I began to find my voice.

Even though my pen was free to wind and wander, I still found difficulty in finding words when trying to communicate how I felt. I remember sitting in my '97 Odyssey with my boyfriend at the time. We weren't working out, but still I considered it polite to provide a short explanation of how I felt. This started out with a lot of fragmented sentences followed by a pause then a defeated "I don't know." After much frustration for both of us, it hit me. "Dante, I feel like a brick."

Unfortunately, Dante was an exquisitely eloquent individual. To put it simply, words never failed him. Named after the Italian poet Dante Alighieri, his dad an English teacher and writer, his mom an English major and head of a Montessori school, he grew up like a modern William Faulkner.

"You feel like a brick? What's that supposed to mean?" In the waiting silence between us, I thought: well, I had one thing going for me, now I have nothing. It was time to start from scratch.

Now that I've given it some thought for the purpose of writing this paper, I will provide a translation of what I meant by "I feel like a brick:"

I felt stuck, like how a brick endures a river's rapid current dispassionately while becoming eroded by it.

I felt stubborn, not of my own choosing, but by design, fixed into a hardened clay.

I felt sharp. The texture I remember as a kid picking up some of the deep burgundy bricks in the garage.

And easily breakable. Like when my dad hammered the bricks in half to build our mailbox.

Still I couldn't completely tell you how exactly I felt like a brick. But for the most part, I *was* a brick. That same brick that the six-year-old me picked up and brought to the tree lawn for my dad while he was building the mailbox. That brick was the singular thing in this world that I emotionally identified most with. How could someone not understand me? I finally had the words.

The place where I am free to use words as they choose is my journal. Some entries are lists, others letters, a few lengthy analyses of my days, every so often a poem, a short captions to capture a moment. I journal whatever I feel knowing that no one can judge what they can't see. I guess that's why I was so frightened of my childhood English teachers, because their painful but necessary judgement and critique. While I no longer could say I hate words, I would never say I like them either. I see words as little trolls clinging to my back both helping and hindering my expression. The bittersweet relationship I have with my vocabulary of trolls helps me communicate, yet impedes what I try to mean. With words as the creatures and I, the cooperating agent, we scream futilely into an apparent vacuum, and wait for our voice to be heard.

WHAT THEY'RE SAYING ABOUT *"THEY SAY / I SAY"*

"The best book that's happened to teaching composition— ever!"   —**Karen Gaffney,** *Raritan Valley Community College*

"A brilliant book. . . . It's like a membership card in the academic club."   —**Eileen Seifert,** *DePaul University*

"This book demystifies rhetorical moves, tricks of the trade that many students are unsure about. It's reasonable, helpful, nicely written . . . and hey, it's true. I would have found it immensely helpful myself in high school and college."

—**Mike Rose,** *University of California, Los Angeles*

"The argument of this book is important—that there are 'moves' to academic writing . . . and that knowledge of them can be generative. The template format is a good way to teach and demystify the moves that matter. I like this book a lot."

—**David Bartholomae,** *University of Pittsburgh*

"Students need to walk a fine line between their work and that of others, and this book helps them walk that line, providing specific methods and techniques for introducing, explaining, and integrating other voices with their own ideas."

—**Libby Miles,** *University of Rhode Island*

"A beautifully lucid way to approach argument—different from any rhetoric I've ever seen."

—**Anne-Marie Thomas,** *Austin Community College, Riverside*

"It offers students the formulas we, as academic writers, all carry in our heads."   —**Karen Gardiner,** *University of Alabama*

"Many students say that it is the first book they've found that actually helps them with writing in all disciplines."

—**Laura Sonderman,** *Marshall University*

"As a WPA, I'm constantly thinking about how I can help instructors teach their students to make specific rhetorical moves on the page. This book offers a powerful way of teaching students to do just that."   —Joseph Bizup, *Boston University*

"The best tribute to '*They Say / I Say*' I've heard is this, from a student: 'This is one book I'm not selling back to the bookstore.' Nods all around the room. The students love this book."
                               —Christine Ross, *Quinnipiac University*

"What effect has '*They Say*' had on my students' writing? They are finally entering the Burkian Parlor of the university. This book uncovers the rhetorical conventions that transcend disciplinary boundaries, so that even freshmen, newcomers to the academy, are immediately able to join in the conversation."
                               —Margaret Weaver, *Missouri State University*

"It's the anti-composition text: Fun, creative, humorous, brilliant, effective."
                               —Perry Cumbie, *Durham Technical Community College*

"Loved by students, reasonable priced, manageable size, readable."
                               —Roxanne Munch, *Joliet Junior College*

"This book explains in clear detail what skilled writers take for granted."   —John Hyman, *American University*

"The ability to engage with the thoughts of others is one of the most important skills taught in any college-level writing course, and this book does as good a job teaching that skill as any text I have ever encountered."   —William Smith, *Weatherford College*

"A fabulous resource for my students (and for me). I like that it's small, and not overwhelming. It's very practical, and really demystifies the new kind of writing students have to figure out as they transition to college."   —Sara Glennon, *Landmark College*

THIRD EDITION

"THEY SAY/I SAY"

*The Moves That Matter
in Academic Writing*

THIRD EDITION

"THEY SAY / I SAY"

The Moves That Matter
in Academic Writing

GERALD GRAFF
CATHY BIRKENSTEIN

both of the University of Illinois at Chicago

W· W· NORTON & COMPANY

NEW YORK | LONDON

For
Aaron David

W. W. Norton & Company has been independent since its founding in 1923, when William Warder Norton and Mary D. Herter Norton first published lectures delivered at the People's Institute, the adult education division of New York City's Cooper Union. The firm soon expanded its program beyond the Institute, publishing books by celebrated academics from America and abroad. By mid-century, the two major pillars of Norton's publishing program—trade books and college texts—were firmly established. In the 1950s, the Norton family transferred control of the company to its employees, and today—with a staff of four hundred and a comparable number of trade, college, and professional titles published each year—W. W. Norton & Company stands as the largest and oldest publishing house owned wholly by its employees.

Composition: Cenveo® Publisher Services
Book design: Jo Anne Metsch
Production manager: Andrew Ensor
Manufacturing: Quad/Graphics

Library of Congress Cataloging-in-Publication Data

Graff, Gerald.
 "They say / I say" : the Moves that Matter in Academic Writing / Gerald Graff,
Cathy Birkenstein, Both of the University of Illinois at Chicago.—Third Edition.
  pages cm
 Includes bibliographical references and index.
 ISBN 978-0-393-93584-4 (paperback)
1. English language—Rhetoric—Handbooks, manuals, etc. 2. Persuasion
(Rhetoric)—Handbooks, manuals, etc. 3. Report writing—Handbooks, manuals,
etc. I. Birkenstein, Cathy. II. Title.
 PE1431.G73 2013
 808'.042—dc23

                                                                    2013039137

W. W. Norton & Company, Inc., 500 Fifth Avenue, New York, N.Y. 10110
www.wwnorton.com

W. W. Norton & Company Ltd., Castle House, 75/76 Wells Street,
London W1T 3QT

1 2 3 4 5 6 7 8 9 0

BRIEF CONTENTS

CONTENTS

Contents

Contents

PREFACE
TO THE THIRD EDITION

WE CONTINUE TO BE THRILLED BY THE RECEPTION OF OUR BOOK, which has now sold over a million copies and is assigned in more than 1,500 (over half) of the colleges and universities in the United States. We are also delighted that while the audience for our book in composition courses continues to grow, the book is increasingly being adopted in disciplines across the curriculum, confirming our view that the moves taught in the book are central to every academic discipline.

At the same time, we continue to adapt our approach to the specific ways the "they say / I say" moves are deployed in different disciplines. To that end, this edition adds a **new chapter on writing about literature** to the chapters already in the Second Edition on writing in the sciences and social sciences. In this new chapter, "Entering Conversations about Literature," we suggest ways in which students and teachers can move beyond the type of essay that analyzes literary works in isolation from the conversations and debates about those works. One of our premises here is that writing about literature, as about any subject, gains in urgency, motivation, and engagement when the writer responds to the work not in a vacuum, but in conversation with other readers and critics. We believe that engaging with other readers, far from distracting attention from the literary text itself, should help bring that text into sharper focus. Another premise is that the class discussions that are a daily feature of literature courses can be a rich and provocative source of "they says" that student writers can respond to in generating their own interpretations. Throughout the chapter are numerous templates that provide writers with language for entering into conversations and debates with these "they says": published critics, classmates and teachers, their own previous interpretations, and the authors of literary works themselves.

This new edition also includes a **chapter on "Using the Templates to Revise,"** which grew out of our own teaching experience, where we found that the templates in this book had the unexpected benefit of helping students when they revise. We found that when students read over their drafts with an eye for the rhetorical moves represented by the templates they were able to spot gaps in their argument, concessions they needed to make, disconnections among ideas, inadequate summaries, poorly integrated quotations, and other questions they needed to address when revising. Have they incorporated the views of naysayers with their own? If not, our brief revision guidelines can help them do so. The new chapter includes a full essay written by a student, annotated to show how the student used all the rhetorical moves taught in this book.

Finally, this edition adds a **new chapter on writing online** exploring the debate about whether digital technologies improve or degrade the way we think and write, and whether they foster or impede the meeting of minds. And given the importance of online communication, we're pleased that our book now has its own blog, **theysayiblog**. Updated monthly with current articles from across media, this blog provides a space where students and teachers can literally join the conversation.

Even as we have revised and added to *"They Say / I Say,"* our basic goals remain unchanged: to demystify academic writing and reading by identifying the key moves of persuasive argument and representing those moves in forms that students can put into practice. We hope this Third Edition will get us even closer to these goals, equipping students with the writing skills they need to enter the academic world and beyond.

PREFACE

Demystifying Academic Conversation

EXPERIENCED WRITING INSTRUCTORS have long recognized that writing well means entering into conversation with others. Academic writing in particular calls upon writers not simply to express their own ideas, but to do so as a response to what others have said. The first-year writing program at our own university, according to its mission statement, asks "students to participate in ongoing conversations about vitally important academic and public issues." A similar statement by another program holds that "intellectual writing is almost always composed in response to others' texts." These statements echo the ideas of rhetorical theorists like Kenneth Burke, Mikhail Bakhtin, and Wayne Booth as well as recent composition scholars like David Bartholomae, John Bean, Patricia Bizzell, Irene Clark, Greg Colomb, Lisa Ede, Peter Elbow, Joseph Harris, Andrea Lunsford, Elaine Maimon, Gary Olson, Mike Rose, John Swales and Christine Feak, Tilly Warnock, and others who argue that writing well means engaging the voices of others and letting them in turn engage us.

Yet despite this growing consensus that writing is a social, conversational act, helping student writers actually participate in these conversations remains a formidable challenge. This book aims to meet that challenge. Its goal is to demystify academic writing by isolating its basic moves, explaining them clearly, and representing them in the form of templates.

In this way, we hope to help students become active participants in the important conversations of the academic world
and the wider public sphere.

HIGHLIGHTS

- *Shows that writing well means entering a conversation*, summarizing others ("they say") to set up one's own argument
  ("I say").
- *Demystifies academic writing*, showing students "the moves
  that matter" in language they can readily apply.
- *Provides user-friendly templates* to help writers make those
  moves in their own writing.
- *Shows that reading is a way of entering a conversation*—not just
  of passively absorbing information but of understanding and
  actively entering dialogues and debates.

HOW THIS BOOK CAME TO BE

The original idea for this book grew out of our shared interest in democratizing academic culture. First, it grew out of
arguments that Gerald Graff has been making throughout his
career that schools and colleges need to invite students into
the conversations and debates that surround them. More specifically, it is a practical, hands-on companion to his recent
book, *Clueless in Academe: How Schooling Obscures the Life of
the Mind*, in which he looks at academic conversations from the
perspective of those who find them mysterious and proposes
ways in which such mystification can be overcome. Second,

this book grew out of writing templates that Cathy Birkenstein developed in the 1990s, for use in writing and literature courses she was teaching. Many students, she found, could readily grasp what it meant to support a thesis with evidence, to entertain a counterargument, to identify a textual contradiction, and ultimately to summarize and respond to challenging arguments, but they often had trouble putting these concepts into practice in their own writing. When Cathy sketched out templates on the board, however, giving her students some of the language and patterns that these sophisticated moves require, their writing—and even their quality of thought—significantly improved.

This book began, then, when we put our ideas together and realized that these templates might have the potential to open up and clarify academic conversation. We proceeded from the premise that all writers rely on certain stock formulas that they themselves didn't invent—and that many of these formulas are so commonly used that they can be represented in model templates that students can use to structure and even generate what they want to say.

As we developed a working draft of this book, we began using it in first-year writing courses that we teach at UIC. In classroom exercises and writing assignments, we found that students who otherwise struggled to organize their thoughts, or even to think of something to say, did much better when we provided them with templates like the following.

▸ In discussions of _____, a controversial issue is whether _____. While some argue that _____, others contend that _____.

▸ This is not to say that _____.

One virtue of such templates, we found, is that they focus writers' attention not just on what is being said, but on the *forms* that structure what is being said. In other words, they make students more conscious of the rhetorical patterns that are key to academic success but often pass under the classroom radar.

THE CENTRALITY OF "THEY SAY / I SAY"

The central rhetorical move that we focus on in this book is the "they say/I say" template that gives our book its title. In our view, this template represents the deep, underlying structure, the internal DNA as it were, of all effective argument. Effective persuasive writers do more than make well-supported claims ("I say"); they also map those claims relative to the claims of others ("they say").

Here, for example, the "they say/I say" pattern structures a passage from an essay by the media and technology critic Steven Johnson.

> For decades, we've worked under the assumption that mass culture follows a path declining steadily toward lowest-common-denominator standards, presumably because the "masses" want dumb, simple pleasures and big media companies try to give the masses what they want. But . . . the exact opposite is happening: the culture is getting more cognitively demanding, not less.
>
> STEVEN JOHNSON, "Watching TV Makes You Smarter"

In generating his own argument from something "they say," Johnson suggests *why* he needs to say what he is saying: to correct a popular misconception.

Even when writers do not explicitly identify the views they are responding to, as Johnson does, an implicit "they say" can often be discerned, as in the following passage by Zora Neale Hurston.

> I remember the day I became colored.
>
> ZORA NEALE HURSTON, "How It Feels to Be Colored Me"

In order to grasp Hurston's point here, we need to be able to reconstruct the implicit view she is responding to and question- ing: that racial identity is an innate quality we are simply born with. On the contrary, Hurston suggests, our race is imposed on us by society—something we "become" by virtue of how we are treated.

As these examples suggest, the "they say/I say" model can improve not just student writing, but student reading compre- hension as well. Since reading and writing are deeply recipro- cal activities, students who learn to make the rhetorical moves represented by the templates in this book figure to become more adept at identifying these same moves in the texts they read. And if we are right that effective arguments are always in dialogue with other arguments, then it follows that in order to understand the types of challenging texts assigned in college, students need to identify the views to which those texts are responding.

Working with the "they say/I say" model can also help with invention, finding something to say. In our experience, students best discover what they want to say not by thinking about a subject in an isolation booth, but by reading texts, listening closely to what other writers say, and looking for an opening through which they can enter the conversation. In other words, listening closely to others and summarizing what they have to say can help writers generate their own ideas.

THE USEFULNESS OF TEMPLATES

Our templates also have a generative quality, prompting students to make moves in their writing that they might not otherwise make or even know they should make. The templates in this book can be particularly helpful for students who are unsure about what to say, or who have trouble finding enough to say, often because they consider their own beliefs so self-evident that they need not be argued for. Students like this are often helped, we've found, when we give them a simple template like the following one for entertaining a counterargument (or planting a naysayer, as we call it in Chapter 6).

▸ **Of course some might object that _____ . Although I concede that _____ , I still maintain that _____ .**

What this particular template helps students do is make the seemingly counterintuitive move of questioning their own beliefs, of looking at them from the perspective of those who disagree. In so doing, templates can bring out aspects of students' thoughts that, as they themselves sometimes remark, they didn't even realize were there.

Other templates in this book help students make a host of sophisticated moves that they might not otherwise make: summarizing what someone else says, framing a quotation in one's own words, indicating the view that the writer is responding to, marking the shift from a source's view to the writer's own view, offering evidence for that view, entertaining and answering counterarguments, and explaining what is at stake in the first place. In showing students how to make such moves, templates do more than organize students' ideas; they help bring those ideas into existence.

OKAY, BUT TEMPLATES?

We are aware, of course, that some instructors may have reservations about templates. Some, for instance, may object that such formulaic devices represent a return to prescriptive forms of instruction that encourage passive learning or lead students to put their writing on automatic pilot.

This is an understandable reaction, we think, to kinds of rote instruction that have indeed encouraged passivity and drained writing of its creativity and dynamic relation to the social world. The trouble is that many students will never learn on their own to make the key intellectual moves that our templates represent. While seasoned writers pick up these moves unconsciously through their reading, many students do not. Consequently, we believe, students need to see these moves represented in the explicit ways that the templates provide.

The aim of the templates, then, is not to stifle critical thinking but to be direct with students about the key rhetorical moves that it comprises. Since we encourage students to modify and adapt the templates to the particularities of the arguments they are making, using such prefabricated formulas as learning tools need not result in writing and thinking that are themselves formulaic. Admittedly, no teaching tool can guarantee that students will engage in hard, rigorous thought. Our templates do, however, provide concrete prompts that can stimulate and shape such thought: What do "they say" about my topic? What would a naysayer say about my argument? What is my evidence? Do I need to qualify my point? Who cares?

In fact, templates have a long and rich history. Public orators from ancient Greece and Rome through the European Renaissance studied rhetorical *topoi* or "commonplaces," model passages and formulas that represented the different strategies available to public speakers. In many respects, our templates echo this classical rhetorical tradition of imitating established models.

The journal *Nature* requires aspiring contributors to follow a guideline that is like a template on the opening page of their manuscript: "Two or three sentences explaining what the main result [of their study] reveals in direct comparison with what was thought to be the case previously, or how the main result adds to previous knowledge." In the field of education, a form designed by the education theorist Howard Gardner asks postdoctoral fellowship applicants to complete the following template: "Most scholars in the field believe _____. As a result of my study, _____." That these two examples are geared toward post-doctoral fellows and veteran researchers shows that it is not only struggling undergraduates who can use help making these key rhetorical moves, but experienced academics as well.

Templates have even been used in the teaching of personal narrative. The literary and educational theorist Jane Tompkins devised the following template to help student writers make the often difficult move from telling a story to explaining what it means: "X tells a story about _____ to make the point that _____. My own experience with _____ yields a point that is similar/different/both similar and different. What I take away from my own experience with _____ is _____. As a result, I conclude _____." We especially like this template because it suggests that "they say/I say" argument need not be mechanical, impersonal, or dry, and that telling a story and making an argument are more compatible activities than many think.

WHY IT'S OKAY TO USE "I"

But wait—doesn't the "I" part of "they say / I say" flagrantly encourage the use of the first-person pronoun? Aren't we aware that some teachers prohibit students from using "I" or "we," on the grounds that these pronouns encourage ill-considered, subjective opinions rather than objective and reasoned arguments? Yes, we are aware of this first-person prohibition, but we think it has serious flaws. First, expressing ill-considered, subjective opinions is not necessarily the worst sin beginning writers can commit; it might be a starting point from which they can move on to more reasoned, less self-indulgent perspectives. Second, prohibiting students from using "I" is simply not an effective way of curbing students' subjectivity, since one can offer poorly argued, ill-supported opinions just as easily without it. Third and most important, prohibiting the first person tends to hamper students' ability not only to take strong positions but to differentiate their own positions from those of others, as we point out in Chapter 5. To be sure, writers can resort to various circumlocutions—"it will here be argued," "the evidence suggests," "the truth is"—and these may be useful for avoiding a monotonous series of "I believe" sentences. But except for avoiding such monotony, we see no good reason why "I" should be set aside in persuasive writing. Rather than prohibit "I," then, we think a better tactic is to give students practice at using it well and learning its use, both by supporting their claims with evidence and by attending closely to alternative perspectives—to what "they" are saying.

HOW THIS BOOK IS ORGANIZED

Because of its centrality, we have allowed the "they say / I say" format to dictate the structure of this book. So while Part 1 addresses the art of listening to others, Part 2 addresses how to offer one's own response. Part 1 opens with a chapter on

"Starting with What Others Are Saying" that explains why it is generally advisable to begin a text by citing others rather than plunging directly into one's own views. Subsequent chapters take up the arts of summarizing and quoting what these others have to say. Part 2 begins with a chapter on different ways of responding, followed by chapters on marking the shift between what "they say" and what "I say," on introducing and answering objections, and on answering the all-important questions: "so what?" and "who cares?" Part 3 offers strategies for "Tying It All Together," beginning with a chapter on connection and coherence; followed by a chapter on formal and informal language, arguing that academic discourse is often perfectly compatible with the informal language that students use outside school; and concluding with a chapter on the art of metacommentary, showing students how to guide the way readers understand a text. Part 4 offers guidance for entering conversations in specific academic contexts, with chapters on entering class discussions, writing online, reading, and writing in literature courses, the sciences, and social sciences. Finally, we provide five readings and an index of templates.

WHAT THIS BOOK DOESN'T DO

There are some things that this book does not try to do. We do not, for instance, cover logical principles of argument such as syllogisms, warrants, logical fallacies, or the differences between inductive and deductive reasoning. Although such concepts can be useful, we believe most of us learn the ins and outs of argumentative writing not by studying logical principles in the abstract, but by plunging into actual discussions and debates, trying out different patterns of response, and in this way getting a sense of what works to persuade different audiences and what doesn't. In our view, people learn more about arguing from hearing someone say, "You miss my point. What I'm saying is not _____, but _____," or "I agree with you that _____, and would even add that _____," than they do from studying the differences between inductive and deductive reasoning. Such formulas give students an immediate sense of what it feels like to enter a public conversation in a way that studying abstract warrants and logical fallacies does not.

ENGAGING WITH THE IDEAS OF OTHERS

One central goal of this book is to demystify academic writing by returning it to its social and conversational roots. Although writing may require some degree of quiet and solitude, the "they say / I say" model shows students that they can best develop their arguments not just by looking inward but by doing what they often do in a good conversation with friends and family— by listening carefully to what others are saying and engaging with other views.

This approach to writing therefore has an ethical dimension, since it asks writers not simply to keep proving and reasserting what they already believe but to stretch what they believe by putting it up against beliefs that differ, sometimes radically, from their own. In an increasingly diverse, global society, this ability to engage with the ideas of others is especially crucial to democratic citizenship.

Gerald Graff
Cathy Birkenstein

THIRD EDITION

"THEY SAY I SAY"

*The Moves That Matter
in Academic Writing*

INTRODUCTION

Entering the Conversation

—◻—

THINK ABOUT AN ACTIVITY that you do particularly well: cooking, playing the piano, shooting a basketball, even something as basic as driving a car. If you reflect on this activity, you'll realize that once you mastered it you no longer had to give much conscious thought to the various moves that go into doing it. Performing this activity, in other words, depends on your having learned a series of complicated moves—moves that may seem mysterious or difficult to those who haven't yet learned them.

The same applies to writing. Often without consciously realizing it, accomplished writers routinely rely on a stock of established moves that are crucial for communicating sophisticated ideas. What makes writers masters of their trade is not only their ability to express interesting thoughts but their mastery of an inventory of basic moves that they probably picked up by reading a wide range of other accomplished writers. Less experienced writers, by contrast, are often unfamiliar with these basic moves and unsure how to make them in their own writing. This book is intended as a short, user-friendly guide to the basic moves of academic writing.

One of our key premises is that these basic moves are so common that they can be represented in *templates* that you can use right away to structure and even generate your own writing. Perhaps the most distinctive feature of this book is its presentation of many such templates, designed to help you successfully enter not only the world of academic thinking and writing, but also the wider worlds of civic discourse and work.

Instead of focusing solely on abstract principles of writing, then, this book offers model templates that help you put those principles directly into practice. Working with these templates can give you an immediate sense of how to engage in the kinds of critical thinking you are required to do at the college level and in the vocational and public spheres beyond.

Some of these templates represent simple but crucial moves like those used to summarize some widely held belief.

▸ **Many Americans assume that _____ .**

Others are more complicated.

▸ **On the one hand, _____ . On the other hand, _____ .**

▸ **Author X contradicts herself. At the same time that she argues _____ , she also implies _____ .**

▸ **I agree that _____ .**

▸ **This is not to say that _____ .**

It is true, of course, that critical thinking and writing go deeper than any set of linguistic formulas, requiring that you question assumptions, develop strong claims, offer supporting reasons and evidence, consider opposing arguments, and so on. But these deeper habits of thought cannot be put into practice unless you have a language for expressing them in clear, organized ways.

STATE YOUR OWN IDEAS AS A
RESPONSE TO OTHERS

The single most important template that we focus on in this book is the "they say _____ ; I say _____" formula that gives our book its title. If there is any one point that we hope you will take away from this book, it is the importance not only of expressing your ideas ("I say") but of presenting those ideas as a *response to some other person or group* ("they say"). For us, the underlying structure of effective academic writing—and of responsible public discourse—resides not just in stating our own ideas but in listening closely to others around us, summarizing their views in a way that they will recognize, and responding with our own ideas in kind. Broadly speaking, academic writing is argumentative writing, and we believe that to argue well you need to do more than assert your own position. You need to enter a conversation, using what others say (or might say) as a launching pad or sounding board for your own views. For this reason, one of the main pieces of advice in this book is to write the voices of others into your text.

In our view, then, the best academic writing has one underlying feature: it is deeply engaged in some way with other people's views. Too often, however, academic writing is taught as a process of saying "true" or "smart" things in a vacuum, as if it were possible to argue effectively without being in conversation *with* someone else. If you have been taught to write a traditional five-paragraph essay, for example, you have learned how to develop a thesis and support it with evidence. This is good advice as far as it goes, but it leaves out the important fact that in the real world we don't make arguments without being provoked. Instead, we make arguments because someone has said or done something (or perhaps *not* said or done

something) and we need to respond: "I can't see why you like the Lakers so much"; "I agree: it was a great film"; "That argument is contradictory." If it weren't for other people and our need to challenge, agree with, or otherwise respond to them, there would be no reason to argue at all.

To make an impact as a writer, you need to do more than make statements that are logical, well supported, and consistent. You must also find a way of entering a conversation with others' views—with something "they say." If your own argument doesn't identify the "they say" that you're responding to, it probably won't make sense. As the figure above suggests, *what* you are saying may be clear to your audience, but *why* you are saying it won't be. For it is what others are saying and thinking that motivates our writing and gives it a reason for being. It follows, then, as the figure on the next page suggests, that your own argument—the thesis or "I say" moment of your text—should always be a response to the arguments of others.

Many writers make explicit "they say / I say" moves in their writing. One famous example is Martin Luther King Jr.'s "Letter

from Birmingham Jail," which consists almost entirely of King's eloquent responses to a public statement by eight clergymen deploring the civil rights protests he was leading. The letter—which was written in 1963, while King was in prison for leading a demonstration against racial injustice in Birmingham—is structured almost entirely around a framework of summary and response, in which King summarizes and then answers their criticisms. In one typical passage, King writes as follows.

> You deplore the demonstrations taking place in Birmingham. But your statement, I am sorry to say, fails to express a similar concern for the conditions that brought about the demonstrations.
>
> MARTIN LUTHER KING JR., "Letter from Birmingham Jail"

King goes on to agree with his critics that "It is unfortunate that demonstrations are taking place in Birmingham," yet he hastens to add that "it is even more unfortunate that the city's white power structure left the Negro community with no alternative." King's letter is so thoroughly conversational, in fact, that it could be rewritten in the form of a dialogue or play.

> King's critics:
> King's response:
> Critics:
> Response:

Clearly, King would not have written his famous letter were it not for his critics, whose views he treats not as objections to his already-formed arguments but as the motivating source of those arguments, their central reason for being. He quotes not only what his critics have said ("Some have asked: 'Why didn't you give the new city administration time to act?' "), but also things they *might* have said ("One may well ask: 'How can you advocate breaking some laws and obeying others?' ")—all to set the stage for what he himself wants to say.

A similar "they say / I say" exchange opens an essay about American patriotism by the social critic Katha Pollitt, who uses her own daughter's comment to represent the national fervor of post-9/11 patriotism.

> My daughter, who goes to Stuyvesant High School only blocks from the former World Trade Center, thinks we should fly the American flag out our window. Definitely not, I say: The flag stands for jingoism and vengeance and war. She tells me I'm wrong—the flag means standing together and honoring the dead and saying no to terrorism. In a way we're both right. . . .
>
> KATHA POLLITT, "Put Out No Flags"

As Pollitt's example shows, the "they" you respond to in crafting an argument need not be a famous author or someone known to your audience. It can be a family member like Pollitt's daughter, or a friend or classmate who has made a provocative claim. It can even be something an individual or a group might say—or a side of yourself, something you once believed but no longer do, or something you partly believe but also doubt. The important thing is that the "they" (or "you" or "she") represent some wider group with which readers might identify—in Pollitt's case, those who patriotically believe in flying the flag. Pollitt's example also shows that responding to the views of others need not always involve unqualified opposition. By agreeing and disagreeing with her daughter, Pollitt enacts what we call the "yes and no" response, reconciling apparently incompatible views.

See Chapter 4 for more on agreeing, but with a difference.

While King and Pollitt both identify the views they are responding to, some authors do not explicitly state their views but instead allow the reader to infer them. See, for instance, if you can identify the implied or unnamed "they say" that the following claim is responding to.

> I like to think I have a certain advantage as a teacher of literature because when I was growing up I disliked and feared books.
> GERALD GRAFF, "Disliking Books at an Early Age"

In case you haven't figured it out already, the phantom "they say" here is the common belief that in order to be a good teacher of literature, one must have grown up liking and enjoying books.

As you can see from these examples, many writers use the "they say / I say" format to agree or disagree with others, to challenge standard ways of thinking, and thus to stir up controversy. This point may come as a shock to you if you have always had the impression that in order to succeed academically you need to play it safe and avoid controversy in your writing, making statements that nobody can possibly disagree with. Though this view of writing may appear logical, it is actually a recipe for flat, lifeless writing and for writing that fails to answer what we call the "so what?" and "who cares?" questions. "William Shakespeare wrote many famous plays and sonnets" may be a perfectly true statement, but precisely because nobody is likely to disagree with it, it goes without saying and thus would seem pointless if said.

WAYS OF RESPONDING

Just because much argumentative writing is driven by disagreement, it does not follow that *agreement* is ruled out. Although argumentation is often associated with conflict and opposition, the type of conversational "they say / I say" argument that we focus on in this book can be just as useful when you agree as when you disagree.

▶ She argues _____ , and I agree because _____ .

▶ Her argument that _____ is supported by new research showing that _____ .

Nor do you always have to choose between either simply agreeing *or* disagreeing, since the "they say / I say" format also works to both agree and disagree at the same time, as Pollitt illustrates above.

▸ He claims that _____, and I have mixed feelings about it. On the one hand, I agree that _____. On the other hand, I still insist that _____.

This last option—agreeing and disagreeing simultaneously—is one we especially recommend, since it allows you to avoid a simple yes or no response and present a more complicated argument, while containing that complication within a clear "on the one hand / on the other hand" framework.

While the templates we offer in this book can be used to structure your writing at the sentence level, they can also be expanded as needed to almost any length, as the following elaborated "they say / I say" template demonstrates.

▸ In recent discussions of _____, a controversial issue has been whether _____. On the one hand, some argue that _____. From this perspective, _____. On the other hand, however, others argue that _____. In the words of _____, one of this view's main proponents, "_____." According to this view, _____. In sum, then, the issue is whether _____ or _____.

My own view is that _____. Though I concede that _____, I still maintain that _____. For example, _____. Although some might object that _____, I would reply that _____. The issue is important because _____.

If you go back over this template, you will see that it helps you make a host of challenging moves (each of which is taken up in forthcoming chapters in this book). First, the template helps you open your text by identifying an issue in some ongoing conversation or debate ("In recent discussions of _____, a controversial issue has been _____"), and then to map some of the voices in this controversy (by using the "on the one hand / on the other hand" structure). The template also helps you introduce a quotation ("In the words of"), to explain the quotation in your own words ("According to this view"), and—in a new paragraph—to state your own argument ("My own view is that"), to qualify your argument ("Though I concede that"), and then to support your argument with evidence ("For example"). In addition, the template helps you make one of the most crucial moves in argumentative writing, what we call "planting a naysayer in your text," in which you summarize and then answer a likely objection to your own central claim ("Although it might be objected that _____, I reply _____"). Finally, this template helps you shift between general, overarching claims ("In sum, then") and smaller-scale, supporting claims ("For example").

Again, none of us is born knowing these moves, especially when it comes to academic writing. Hence the need for this book.

DO TEMPLATES STIFLE CREATIVITY?

If you are like some of our students, your initial response to templates may be skepticism. At first, many of our students complain that using templates will take away their originality and creativity and make them all sound the same. "They'll turn us into writing robots," one of our students insisted. Another agreed, adding, "Hey, I'm a jazz musician. And we don't play by set forms. We create our own." "I'm in college now," another student asserted; "this is third-grade-level stuff."

In our view, however, the templates in this book, far from being "third-grade-level stuff," represent the stock in trade of sophisticated thinking and writing, and they often require a great deal of practice and instruction to use successfully. As for the belief that pre-established forms undermine creativity, we think it rests on a very limited vision of what creativity is all about. In our view, the above template and the others in this book will actually help your writing become *more* original and creative, not less. After all, even the most creative forms of expression depend on established patterns and structures. Most songwriters, for instance, rely on a time-honored verse-chorus-verse pattern, and few people would call Shakespeare uncreative because he didn't invent the sonnet or the dramatic forms that he used to such dazzling effect. Even the most avant-garde, cutting-edge artists (like improvisational jazz musicians) need to master the basic forms that their work improvises on, departs from, and goes beyond, or else their work will come across as uneducated child's play. Ultimately, then, creativity and originality lie not in the avoidance of established forms but in the imaginative use of them.

Furthermore, these templates do not dictate the *content* of what you say, which can be as original as you can make it, but only suggest a way of formatting *how* you say it. In addition, once you begin to feel comfortable with the templates in this book, you will be able to improvise creatively on them to fit new situations and purposes and find others in your reading. In other words, the templates offered here are learning tools to get you started, not structures set in stone. Once you get used to using them, you can even dispense with them altogether, for the rhetorical moves they model will be at your fingertips in an unconscious, instinctive way.

But if you still need proof that writing templates do not stifle creativity, consider the following opening to an essay on the fast-food industry that we've included at the back of this book.

If ever there were a newspaper headline custom-made for Jay Leno's monologue, this was it. Kids taking on McDonald's this week, suing the company for making them fat. Isn't that like middle-aged men suing Porsche for making them get speeding tickets? Whatever happened to personal responsibility?

I tend to sympathize with these portly fast-food patrons, though. Maybe that's because I used to be one of them.

DAVID ZINCZENKO, "Don't Blame the Eater"

Although Zinczenko relies on a version of the "they say / I say" formula, his writing is anything but dry, robotic, or uncreative. While Zinczenko does not explicitly use the words "they say" and "I say," the template still gives the passage its underlying structure: "*They say* that kids suing fast-food companies for making them fat is a joke; but *I say* such lawsuits are justified."

BUT ISN'T THIS PLAGIARISM?

"But isn't this plagiarism?" at least one student each year will usually ask. "Well, is it?" we respond, turning the question around into one the entire class can profit from. "We are, after all, asking you to use language in your writing that isn't your own—language that you 'borrow' or, to put it less delicately, steal from other writers."

Often, a lively discussion ensues that raises important questions about authorial ownership and helps everyone better understand the frequently confusing line between plagiarism and the legitimate use of what others say and how they say it. Students are quick to see that no one person owns a conventional formula like "on the one hand . . . on the other hand . . . " Phrases like "a controversial issue" are so commonly used and recycled that they are generic—community property that can be freely used without fear of committing plagiarism. It *is* plagiarism, however, if the words used to fill in the blanks of such formulas are borrowed from others without proper acknowledgment. In sum, then, while it is not plagiarism to recycle conventionally used formulas, it is a serious academic offense to take the substantive content from others' texts without citing the author and giving him or her proper credit.

PUTTING IN YOUR OAR

Though the immediate goal of this book is to help you become a better writer, at a deeper level it invites you to become a certain type of person: a critical, intellectual thinker who, instead of sitting passively on the sidelines, can participate in the debates and conversations of your world in an active and empowered way. Ultimately, this book invites you to become a critical thinker who can enter the types of conversations described eloquently by the philosopher Kenneth Burke in the following widely cited passage. Likening the world of intellectual exchange to a never-ending conversation at a party, Burke writes:

> You come late. When you arrive, others have long preceded you, and they are engaged in a heated discussion, a discussion too heated for them to pause and tell you exactly what it is about. . . . You listen for a while, until you decide that you have caught the tenor of the argument; then you put in your oar. Someone answers; you answer him; another comes to your defense; another aligns himself against you. . . . The hour grows late, you must depart. And you do depart, with the discussion still vigorously in progress.
>
> KENNETH BURKE, *The Philosophy of Literary Form*

What we like about this passage is its suggestion that stating an argument and "putting in your oar" can only be done in conversation with others; that we all enter the dynamic world of ideas not as isolated individuals but as social beings deeply connected to others who have a stake in what we say.

This ability to enter complex, many-sided conversations has taken on a special urgency in today's diverse, post-9/11 world, where the future for all of us may depend on our ability to put ourselves in the shoes of those who think very differently from us. The central piece of advice in this book—that we listen carefully to others, including those who disagree with us, and then engage with them thoughtfully and respectfully—can help us see beyond our own pet beliefs, which may not be shared by everyone. The mere act of crafting a sentence that begins "Of course, someone might object that _____" may not seem like a way to change the world; but it does have the potential to jog us out of our comfort zones, to get us thinking critically about our own beliefs, and perhaps even to change our minds.

Exercises

1. Read the following paragraph from an essay by Emily Poe, a student at Furman University. Disregarding for the moment what Poe says, focus your attention on the phrases she uses to structure what she says (italicized here). Then write a new paragraph using Poe's as a model but replacing her topic, vegetarianism, with one of your own.

   The term "vegetarian" tends to be synonymous with "tree-hugger" in many people's minds. *They see* vegetarianism as a cult that brainwashes its followers into eliminating an essential part of their daily diets for an abstract goal of "animal welfare." *However*, few vegetarians choose their lifestyle just to follow the crowd. *On the contrary*, many of these supposedly brainwashed people are actually independent thinkers, concerned citizens, and compassionate human beings. *For the truth is* that there are many very good reasons for giving up meat. Perhaps the best reasons are to improve the environment, to encourage humane treatment of livestock, or to enhance one's own health. *In this essay, then*, closely examining a vegetarian diet as compared to a meat-eater's diet will show that vegetarianism is clearly the better option for sustaining the Earth and all its inhabitants.

2. Write a short essay in which you first summarize our rationale for the templates in this book and then articulate your own position in response. If you want, you can use the template below to organize your paragraphs, expanding and modifying it as necessary to fit what you want to say.

In the Introduction to *"They Say / I Say": The Moves That Matter in Academic Writing*, Gerald Graff and Cathy Birkenstein provide templates designed to _____. Specifically, Graff and Birkenstein argue that the types of writing templates they offer _____. As the authors themselves put it, "_____." Although some people believe _____, Graff and Birkenstein insist that _____. In sum, then, their view is that _____.

I [agree/disagree/have mixed feelings]. In my view, the types of templates that the authors recommend _____. For instance, _____. In addition, _____. Some might object, of course, on the grounds that _____. Yet I would argue that _____. Overall, then, I believe _____ —an important point to make given _____.

15

1

"THEY SAY"

ONE

"THEY SAY"

Starting with What Others Are Saying

—◻—

NOT LONG AGO we attended a talk at an academic conference where the speaker's central claim seemed to be that a certain sociologist—call him Dr. X—had done very good work in a number of areas of the discipline. The speaker proceeded to illustrate his thesis by referring extensively and in great detail to various books and articles by Dr. X and by quoting long passages from them. The speaker was obviously both learned and impassioned, but as we listened to his talk we found ourselves somewhat puzzled: the argument—that Dr. X's work was very important—was clear enough, but why did the speaker need to make it in the first place? Did anyone dispute it? Were there commentators in the field who had argued against X's work or challenged its value? Was the speaker's interpretation of what X had done somehow novel or revolutionary? Since the speaker gave no hint of an answer to any of these questions, we could only wonder why he was going on and on about X. It was only after the speaker finished and took questions from the audience that we got a clue: in response to one questioner, he referred to several critics who had

The hypothetical audience in the figure on p. 4 reacts similarly.

vigorously questioned Dr. X's ideas and convinced many sociologists that Dr. X's work was unsound.

This story illustrates an important lesson: that to give writing the most important thing of all—namely, a point—a writer needs to indicate clearly not only what his or her thesis is, but also what larger conversation that thesis is responding to. Because our speaker failed to mention what others had said about Dr. X's work, he left his audience unsure about why he felt the need to say what he was saying. Perhaps the point was clear to other sociologists in the audience who were more familiar with the debates over Dr. X's work than we were. But even they, we bet, would have understood the speaker's point better if he'd sketched in some of the larger conversation his own claims were a part of and reminded the audience about what "they say."

This story also illustrates an important lesson about the *order* in which things are said: to keep an audience engaged, a writer needs to explain what he or she is responding to—either before offering that response or, at least, very early in the discussion. Delaying this explanation for more than one or two paragraphs in a very short essay or blog entry, three or four pages in a longer work, or more than ten or so pages in a book reverses the natural order in which readers process material—and in which writers think and develop ideas. After all, it seems very unlikely that our conference speaker first developed his defense of Dr. X and only later came across Dr. X's critics. As someone knowledgeable in his field, the speaker surely encountered the criticisms first and only then was compelled to respond and, as he saw it, set the record straight.

Therefore, when it comes to constructing an argument (whether orally or in writing), we offer you the following advice: remember that you are entering a conversation and therefore need to start with "what others are saying," as the title of this chapter recommends, and then introduce your own ideas as a response. Specifically, we suggest that you summarize what "they say" as soon as you can in your text, and remind readers of it at strategic points as your text unfolds. Though it's true that not all texts follow this practice, we think it's important for all writers to master it before they depart from it.

This is not to say that you must start with a detailed list of everyone who has written on your subject before you offer your own ideas. Had our conference speaker gone to the opposite extreme and spent most of his talk summarizing Dr. X's critics with no hint of what he himself had to say, the audience probably would have had the same frustrated "why-is-he-going-on-like-this?" reaction. What we suggest, then, is that as soon as possible you state your own position and the one it's responding to *together*, and that you think of the two as a unit. It is generally best to summarize the ideas you're responding to briefly, at the start of your text, and to delay detailed elaboration until later. The point is to give your readers a quick preview of what is motivating your argument, not to drown them in details right away.

Starting with a summary of others' views may seem to contradict the common advice that writers should lead with their own thesis or claim. Although we agree that you shouldn't keep readers in suspense too long about your central argument, we also believe that you need to present that argument as part of some larger conversation, indicating something about the arguments of others that you are supporting, opposing, amending, complicating, or qualifying. One added benefit of summarizing others' views as soon as you can: you let those others do some of the work of framing and clarifying the issue you're writing about.

Consider, for example, how George Orwell starts his famous essay "Politics and the English Language" with what others are saying.

Most people who bother with the matter at all would admit that the English language is in a bad way, but it is generally assumed that we cannot by conscious action do anything about it. Our civilization is decadent and our language—so the argument runs—must inevitably share in the general collapse. . . .

[But] the process is reversible. Modern English . . . is full of bad habits . . . which can be avoided if one is willing to take the necessary trouble.

GEORGE ORWELL, "Politics and the English Language"

Orwell is basically saying, "Most people assume that we cannot do anything about the bad state of the English language. But I say we can."

Of course, there are many other powerful ways to begin. Instead of opening with someone else's views, you could start with an illustrative quotation, a revealing fact or statistic, or—as we do in this chapter—a relevant anecdote. If you choose one of these formats, however, be sure that it in some way illustrates the view you're addressing or leads you to that view directly, with a minimum of steps.

In opening this chapter, for example, we devote the first paragraph to an anecdote about the conference speaker and then move quickly at the start of the second paragraph to the misconception about writing exemplified by the speaker. In the following opening, from an opinion piece in the *New York Times Book Review*, Christina Nehring also moves quickly from an anecdote illustrating something she dislikes to her own claim—that book lovers think too highly of themselves.

"I'm a reader!" announced the yellow button. "How about you?" I looked at its bearer, a strapping young guy stalking my town's Festival of Books. "I'll bet you're a reader," he volunteered, as though we were two geniuses well met. "No," I replied. "Absolutely not," I wanted to yell, and fling my Barnes & Noble bag at his feet. Instead, I mumbled something apologetic and melted into the crowd.

There's a new piety in the air: the self congratulation of book lovers.

CHRISTINA NEHRING, "Books Make You a Boring Person"

Nehring's anecdote is really a kind of "they say": book lovers keep telling themselves how great they are.

TEMPLATES FOR INTRODUCING WHAT "THEY SAY"

There are lots of conventional ways to introduce what others are saying. Here are some standard templates that we would have recommended to our conference speaker.

▶ **A number of sociologists have recently suggested <u>that X's work has several fundamental problems</u>.**

▶ **It has become common today to dismiss _____.**

▶ **In their recent work, Y and Z have offered harsh critiques of _____ for _____.**

TEMPLATES FOR INTRODUCING "STANDARD VIEWS"

The following templates can help you make what we call the "standard view" move, in which you introduce a view that has become so widely accepted that by now it is essentially the conventional way of thinking about a topic.

▸ **Americans have always believed that <u>individual effort can triumph over circumstances</u>.**

▸ **Conventional wisdom has it that _____ .**

▸ **Common sense seems to dictate that _____ .**

▸ **The standard way of thinking about topic X has it that _____ .**

▸ **It is often said that _____ .**

▸ **My whole life I have heard it said that _____ .**

▸ **You would think that _____ .**

▸ **Many people assume that _____ .**

These templates are popular because they provide a quick and efficient way to perform one of the most common moves that writers make: challenging widely accepted beliefs, placing them on the examining table, and analyzing their strengths and weaknesses.

TEMPLATES FOR MAKING WHAT "THEY SAY" SOMETHING *YOU* SAY

Another way to introduce the views you're responding to is to present them as your own. That is, the "they say" that you respond to need not be a view held by others; it can be one that you yourself once held or one that you are ambivalent about.

▸ **I've always believed that <u>museums are boring</u>.**

▸ **When I was a child, I used to think that _____ .**

▸ Although I should know better by now, I cannot help thinking that _____ .

▸ At the same time that I believe _____ , I also believe _____ .

TEMPLATES FOR INTRODUCING
SOMETHING IMPLIED OR ASSUMED

Another sophisticated move a writer can make is to summarize a point that is not directly stated in what "they say" but is implied or assumed.

▸ Although none of them have ever said so directly, my teachers have often given me the impression that <u>education will open doors</u>.

▸ One implication of X's treatment of _____ is that _____ .

▸ Although X does not say so directly, she apparently assumes that _____ .

▸ While they rarely admit as much, _____ often take for granted that _____ .

These are templates that can help you think analytically—to look beyond what others say explicitly and to consider their unstated assumptions, as well as the implications of their views.

TEMPLATES FOR INTRODUCING
AN ONGOING DEBATE

Sometimes you'll want to open by summarizing a debate that presents two or more views. This kind of opening demonstrates your awareness that there are conflicting ways to look at your subject, the clear mark of someone who knows the subject and therefore is likely to be a reliable, trustworthy guide. Furthermore, opening with a summary of a debate can help you explore the issue you are writing about before declaring your own view. In this way, you can use the writing process itself to help you discover where you stand instead of having to commit to a position before you are ready to do so.

Here is a basic template for opening with a debate.

▶ In discussions of X, one controversial issue has been _____. On the one hand, _____ argues _____. On the other hand, _____ contends _____. Others even maintain _____. My own view is _____.

The cognitive scientist Mark Aronoff uses this kind of template in an essay on the workings of the human brain.

Theories of how the mind/brain works have been dominated for centuries by two opposing views. One, rationalism, sees the human mind as coming into this world more or less fully formed— preprogrammed, in modern terms. The other, empiricism, sees the mind of the newborn as largely unstructured, a blank slate.

MARK ARONOFF, "Washington Slept Here"

Another way to open with a debate involves starting with a proposition many people agree with in order to highlight the point(s) on which they ultimately disagree.

▶ When it comes to the topic of _____, most of us will readily agree that _____. Where this agreement usually ends, however, is on the question of _____. Whereas some are convinced that _____, others maintain that _____.

The political writer Thomas Frank uses a variation on this move.

> That we are a nation divided is an almost universal lament of this bitter election year. However, the exact property that divides us—elemental though it is said to be—remains a matter of some controversy.
>
> THOMAS FRANK, "American Psyche"

KEEP WHAT "THEY SAY" IN VIEW

We can't urge you too strongly to keep in mind what "they say" as you move through the rest of your text. After summarizing the ideas you are responding to at the outset, it's very important to continue to keep those ideas in view. Readers won't be able to follow your unfolding response, much less any complications you may offer, unless you keep reminding them what claims you are responding to.

In other words, even when presenting your own claims, you should keep returning to the motivating "they say." The longer and more complicated your text, the greater the chance that readers will forget what ideas originally motivated it—no matter how clearly you lay them out at the beginning. At strategic moments throughout your text, we recommend that you include what we call "return sentences." Here is an example.

▸ In conclusion, then, as I suggested earlier, defenders of
_____ can't have it both ways. Their assertion that
_____ is contradicted by their claim that _____.

We ourselves use such return sentences at every opportunity in this book to remind you of the view of writing that our book questions—that good writing means making true or smart or logical statements about a given subject with little or no reference to what others say about it.

By reminding readers of the ideas you're responding to, return sentences ensure that your text maintains a sense of mission and urgency from start to finish. In short, they help ensure that your argument is a genuine response to others' views rather than just a set of observations about a given subject. The difference is huge. To be responsive to others and the conversation you're entering, you need to start with what others are saying and continue keeping it in the reader's view.

Exercises

1. The following is a list of arguments that lack a "they say"—any sense of who needs to hear these claims, who might think otherwise. Like the speaker in the cartoon on page 4 who declares that *The Sopranos* presents complex characters, these one-sided arguments fail to explain what view they are responding to—what view, in effect, they are trying to correct, add to, qualify, complicate, and so forth. Your job in this exercise is to provide each argument with such a counterview. Feel free to use any of the templates in this chapter that you find helpful.

a. Our experiments suggest that there are dangerous levels of chemical X in the Ohio groundwater.
b. Material forces drive history.
c. Proponents of Freudian psychology question standard notions of "rationality."
d. Male students often dominate class discussions.
e. The film is about the problems of romantic relationships.
f. I'm afraid that templates like the ones in this book will stifle my creativity.

2. Below is a template that we derived from the opening of David Zinczenko's "Don't Blame the Eater" (p. 241). Use the template to structure a passage on a topic of your own choosing. Your first step here should be to find an idea that you support that others not only disagree with but actually find laughable (or, as Zinczenko puts it, worthy of a Jay Leno monologue). You might write about one of the topics listed in the previous exercise (the environment, gender relations, the meaning of a book or movie) or any other topic that interests you.

If ever there was an idea custom-made for a Jay Leno monologue, this was it: _____. Isn't that like _____? Whatever happened to _____?

I happen to sympathize with _____, though, perhaps because _____.

TWO

"HER POINT IS"

The Art of Summarizing

—◻—

IF IT IS TRUE, as we claim in this book, that to argue persuasively you need to be in dialogue with others, then summarizing others' arguments is central to your arsenal of basic moves. Because writers who make strong claims need to map their claims relative to those of other people, it is important to know how to summarize effectively what those other people say. (We're using the word "summarizing" here to refer to any information from others that you present in your own words, including that which you paraphrase.)

Many writers shy away from summarizing—perhaps because they don't want to take the trouble to go back to the text in question and wrestle with what it says, or because they fear that devoting too much time to other people's ideas will take away from their own. When assigned to write a response to an article, such writers might offer their own views on the article's *topic* while hardly mentioning what the article itself argues or says. At the opposite extreme are those who do nothing *but* summarize. Lacking confidence, perhaps, in their own ideas, these writers so overload their texts with summaries of others' ideas that their own voice gets lost. And since these summaries are not animated by the writers' own interests, they often read like mere lists of things that X thinks or Y says—with no clear focus.

As a general rule, a good summary requires balancing what the original author is saying with the writer's own focus. Generally speaking, a summary must at once be true to what the original author says while also emphasizing those aspects of what the author says that interest you, the writer. Striking this delicate balance can be tricky, since it means facing two ways at once: both outward (toward the author being summarized) and inward (toward yourself). Ultimately, it means being respectful of others but simultaneously structuring how you summarize them in light of your own text's central argument.

ON THE ONE HAND, PUT YOURSELF IN *THEIR* SHOES

To write a really good summary, you must be able to suspend your own beliefs for a time and put yourself in the shoes of someone else. This means playing what the writing theorist Peter Elbow calls the "believing game," in which you try to inhabit the world-view of those whose conversation you are joining—and whom you are perhaps even disagreeing with—and try to see their argument from their perspective. This ability to temporarily suspend one's own convictions is a hallmark of good actors, who must convincingly "become" characters whom in real life they may detest. As a writer, when you play the believing game well, readers should not be able to tell whether you agree or disagree with the ideas you are summarizing.

If, as a writer, you cannot or will not suspend your own beliefs in this way, you are likely to produce summaries that are so obviously biased that they undermine your credibility with readers. Consider the following summary.

> David Zinczenko's article, "Don't Blame the Eater," is nothing more than an angry rant in which he accuses the fast-food companies of an evil conspiracy to make people fat. I disagree because these companies have to make money. . . .

If you review what Zinczenko actually says (pp. 241–43), you should immediately see that this summary amounts to an unfair distortion. While Zinczenko does argue that the practices of the fast-food industry have the *effect* of making people fat, his tone is never "angry," and he never goes so far as to suggest that the fast-food industry conspires to make people fat with deliberately evil intent.

Another tell-tale sign of this writer's failure to give Zinczenko a fair hearing is the hasty way he abandons the summary after only one sentence and rushes on to his own response. So eager is this writer to disagree that he not only caricatures what Zinczenko says but also gives the article a hasty, superficial reading. Granted, there are many writing situations in which, because of matters of proportion, a one- or two-sentence summary is precisely what you want. Indeed, as writing professor Karen Lunsford (whose own research focuses on argument theory) points out, it is standard in the natural and social sciences to summarize the work of others quickly, in one pithy sentence or phrase, as in the following example.

> Several studies (Crackle, 2012; Pop, 2007; Snap, 2006) suggest that these policies are harmless; moreover, other studies (Dick, 2011; Harry, 2007; Tom, 2005) argue that they even have benefits.

But if your assignment is to respond in writing to a single author like Zinczenko, you will need to tell your readers enough about his or her argument so they can assess its merits on their own, independent of you.

When a writer fails to provide enough summary or to engage in a rigorous or serious enough summary, he or she often falls prey to what we call "the closest cliché syndrome," in which what gets summarized is not the view the author in question has actually expressed but a familiar cliché that the writer *mistakes* for the author's view (sometimes because the writer believes it and mistakenly assumes the author must too). So, for example, Martin Luther King Jr.'s passionate defense of civil disobedience in "Letter from Birmingham Jail" might be summarized not as the defense of political protest that it actually is but as a plea for everyone to "just get along." Similarly, Zinczenko's critique of the fast-food industry might be summarized as a call for overweight people to take responsibility for their weight.

Whenever you enter into a conversation with others in your writing, then, it is extremely important that you go back to what those others have said, that you study it very closely, and that you not confuse it with something you already believe. A writer who fails to do this ends up essentially conversing with imaginary others who are really only the products of his or her own biases and preconceptions.

ON THE OTHER HAND, KNOW WHERE *YOU* ARE GOING

Even as writing an effective summary requires you to temporarily adopt the worldview of another, it does not mean ignoring your own view altogether. Paradoxically, at the same time that summarizing another text requires you to represent fairly what it says, it also requires that your own response exert a quiet influence. A good summary, in other words, has a focus or spin that allows the summary to fit with your own agenda while still being true to the text you are summarizing.

Thus if you are writing in response to the essay by Zinczenko, you should be able to see that an essay on the fast-food industry in general will call for a very different summary than will an essay on parenting, corporate regulation, or warning labels. If you want your essay to encompass all three topics, you'll need to subordinate these three issues to one of Zinczenko's general claims and then make sure this general claim directly sets up your own argument.

For example, suppose you want to argue that it is parents, not fast-food companies, who are to blame for children's obesity. To set up this argument, you will probably want to compose a summary that highlights what Zinczenko says about the fast-food industry *and parents*. Consider this sample.

In his article "Don't Blame the Eater," David Zinczenko blames the fast-food industry for fueling today's so-called obesity epidemic, not only by failing to provide adequate warning labels on its high-calorie foods but also by filling the nutritional void in children's lives left by their overtaxed working parents. With many parents working long hours and unable to supervise what their children eat, Zinczenko claims, children today are easily victimized by the low-cost, calorie-laden foods that the fast-food chains are all too eager to supply. When he was a young boy, for instance, and his single mother was away at work, he ate at Taco Bell, McDonald's, and other chains on a regular basis, and ended up overweight. Zinczenko's hope is that with the new spate of lawsuits against the food industry, other children with working parents will have healthier choices available to them, and that they will not, like him, become obese.

In my view, however, it is the parents, and not the food chains, who are responsible for their children's obesity. While it is true that many of today's parents work long hours, there are still several things that parents can do to guarantee that their children eat healthy foods. . . .

The summary in the first paragraph succeeds because it points in two directions at once—both toward Zinczenko's own text *and* toward the second paragraph, where the writer begins to establish her own argument. The opening sentence gives a sense of Zinczenko's general argument (that the fast-food chains are to blame for obesity), including his two main supporting claims (about warning labels and parents), but it ends with an emphasis on the writer's main concern: parental responsibility. In this way, the summary does justice to Zinczenko's arguments while also setting up the ensuing critique.

This advice—to summarize authors in light of your own arguments—may seem painfully obvious. But writers often summarize a given author on one issue even though their text actually focuses on another. To avoid this problem, you need to make sure that your "they say" and "I say" are well matched. In fact, aligning what they say with what you say is a good thing to work on when revising what you've written.

Often writers who summarize without regard to their own interests fall prey to what might be called "list summaries," summaries that simply inventory the original author's various points but fail to focus those points around any larger overall claim. If you've ever heard a talk in which the points were connected only by words like "and then," "also," and "in addition,"

THE EFFECT OF A TYPICAL LIST SUMMARY

you know how such lists can put listeners to sleep—as shown in the figure above. A typical list summary sounds like this.

> The author says many different things about his subject. *First* he says. . . . *Then* he makes the point that. . . . *In addition* he says. . . . *And then* he writes. . . . *Also* he shows that. . . . *And then* he says. . . .

It may be boring list summaries like this that give summaries in general a bad name and even prompt some instructors to discourage their students from summarizing at all.

In conclusion, writing a good summary means not just representing an author's view accurately, but doing so in a way that fits your own composition's larger agenda. On the one hand, it means playing Peter Elbow's believing game and doing justice to the source; if the summary ignores or misrepresents the source, its bias and unfairness will show. On the other hand, even as it does justice to the source, a summary has to have a slant or spin that prepares the way for your own claims. Once a summary enters your text, you should think of it as joint property—reflecting both the source you are summarizing and your own views.

SUMMARIZING SATIRICALLY

Thus far in this chapter we have argued that, as a general rule, good summaries require a balance between what someone else has said and your own interests as a writer. Now, however, we want to address one exception to this rule: the satiric summary, in which a writer deliberately gives his or her own spin to someone else's argument in order to reveal a glaring shortcoming in it. Despite our previous comments that well-crafted summaries generally strike a balance between heeding what someone else has said and your own independent interests, the satiric mode can at times be a very effective form of critique because it lets the summarized argument condemn itself without overt editorializing by you, the writer. If you've ever watched *The Daily Show*, you'll recall that it often merely summarizes silly things political leaders have said or done, letting their words or actions undermine themselves.

Consider another example. In September 2001, then-President George W. Bush in a speech to Congress urged the nation's "continued participation and confidence in the American economy" as a means of recovering from the terrorist attacks of 9/11. The journalist Allan Sloan criticized this proposal simply by summarizing it, observing that the president had equated "patriotism with shopping. Maxing out your credit cards at the mall wasn't self indulgence, it was a way to get back at Osama bin Laden." Sloan's summary leaves no doubt where he stands—he considers Bush's proposal ridiculous, or at least too simple.

USE SIGNAL VERBS THAT FIT THE ACTION

In introducing summaries, try to avoid bland formulas like "she says," or "they believe." Though language like this is sometimes serviceable enough, it often fails to reflect accurately what's been said. In some cases, "he says" may even drain the passion out of the ideas you're summarizing.

We suspect that the habit of ignoring the action in what we summarize stems from the mistaken belief we mentioned earlier that writing is about playing it safe and not making waves, a matter of piling up truths and bits of knowledge rather than a dynamic process of doing things to and with other people. People who wouldn't hesitate to *say* "X totally misrepresented," "attacked," or "loved" something when chatting with friends will in their writing often opt for far tamer and even less accurate phrases like "X said."

But the authors you summarize at the college level seldom simply "say" or "discuss" things; they "urge," "emphasize," and "complain about" them. David Zinczenko, for example, doesn't just *say* that fast-food companies contribute to obesity; he *complains* or *protests* that they do; he *challenges*, *chastises*, and *indicts* those companies. The Declaration of Independence doesn't just *talk about* the treatment of the colonies by the British; it *protests against* it. To do justice to the authors you cite, we recommend that when summarizing—or when introducing a quotation—you use vivid and precise signal verbs as often as possible. Though "he says" or "she believes" will sometimes be the most appropriate language for the occasion, your text will often be more accurate and lively if you tailor your verbs to suit the precise actions you're describing.

TEMPLATES FOR INTRODUCING SUMMARIES AND QUOTATIONS

▸ She advocates <u>a radical revision of the juvenile justice system</u>.

▸ They celebrate the fact that _____.

▸ _____, he admits.

VERBS FOR INTRODUCING SUMMARIES AND QUOTATIONS

VERBS FOR MAKING A CLAIM

argue	insist
assert	observe
believe	remind us
claim	report
emphasize	suggest

VERBS FOR EXPRESSING AGREEMENT

acknowledge	endorse
admire	extol
agree	praise

VERBS FOR EXPRESSING AGREEMENT

celebrate the fact that	reaffirm
corroborate	support
do not deny	verify

VERBS FOR QUESTIONING OR DISAGREEING

complain	qualify
complicate	question
contend	refute
contradict	reject
deny	renounce
deplore the tendency to	repudiate

VERBS FOR MAKING RECOMMENDATIONS

advocate	implore
call for	plead
demand	recommend
encourage	urge
exhort	warn

Exercises

1. To get a feel for Peter Elbow's "believing game," write a summary of some belief that you strongly disagree with. Then write a summary of the position that you actually hold on this topic. Give both summaries to a classmate or two, and see if they can tell which position you endorse. If you've succeeded, they won't be able to tell.

2. Write two different summaries of David Zinczenko's "Don't Blame the Eater" (pp. 241–43). Write the first one for an essay arguing that, contrary to what Zinczenko claims, there *are* inexpensive and convenient alternatives to fast-food restaurants. Write the second for an essay that questions whether being overweight is a genuine medical problem rather than a problem of cultural stereotypes. Compare your two summaries: though they are about the same article, they should look very different.

THREE

"AS HE HIMSELF PUTS IT"

The Art of Quoting

—◌—

A KEY PREMISE OF THIS BOOK is that to launch an effective argument you need to write the arguments of others into your text. One of the best ways to do so is by not only summarizing what "they say," as suggested in Chapter 2, but by quoting their exact words. Quoting someone else's words gives a tremendous amount of credibility to your summary and helps ensure that it is fair and accurate. In a sense, then, quotations function as a kind of proof of evidence, saying to readers: "Look, I'm not just making this up. She makes this claim and here it is in her exact words."

Yet many writers make a host of mistakes when it comes to quoting, not the least of which is the failure to quote enough in the first place, if at all. Some writers quote too little— perhaps because they don't want to bother going back to the original text and looking up the author's exact words, or because they think they can reconstruct the author's ideas from memory. At the opposite extreme are writers who so overquote that they end up with texts that are short on commentary of their own—maybe because they lack confidence in their ability to comment on the quotations, or because they don't fully understand what they've quoted and therefore have trouble explaining what the quotations mean.

But the main problem with quoting arises when writers assume that quotations speak for themselves. Because the meaning of a quotation is obvious to *them*, many writers assume that this meaning will also be obvious to their readers, when often it is not. Writers who make this mistake think that their job is done when they've chosen a quotation and inserted it into their text. They draft an essay, slap in a few quotations, and whammo, they're done.

Such writers fail to see that quoting means more than simply enclosing what "they say" in quotation marks. In a way, quotations are orphans: words that have been taken from their original contexts and that need to be integrated into their new textual surroundings. This chapter offers two key ways to produce this sort of integration: (1) by choosing quotations wisely, with an eye to how well they support a particular part of your text, and (2) by surrounding every major quotation with a frame explaining whose words they are, what the quotation means, and how the quotation relates to your own text. The point we want to emphasize is that quoting what "they say" must always be connected with what *you* say.

QUOTE RELEVANT PASSAGES

Before you can select appropriate quotations, you need to have a sense of what you want to do with them—that is, how they will support your text at the particular point where you insert them. Be careful not to select quotations just for the sake of demonstrating that you've read the author's work; you need to make sure they support your own argument.

However, finding relevant quotations is not always easy. In fact, sometimes quotations that were initially relevant to your argument, or to a key point in it, become less so as your text changes during the process of writing and revising. Given the evolving and messy nature of writing, you may sometimes think that you've found the perfect quotation to support your argument, only to discover later on, as your text develops, that your focus has changed and the quotation no longer works. It can be somewhat misleading, then, to speak of finding your thesis and finding relevant quotations as two separate steps, one coming after the other. When you're deeply engaged in the writing and revising process, there is usually a great deal of back-and-forth between your argument and any quotations you select.

FRAME EVERY QUOTATION

Finding relevant quotations is only part of your job; you also need to present them in a way that makes their relevance and meaning clear to your readers. Since quotations do not speak for themselves, you need to build a frame around them in which you do that speaking for them.

Quotations that are inserted into a text without such a frame are sometimes called "dangling" quotations for the way they're left dangling without any explanation. One teacher we've worked with, Steve Benton, calls these "hit-and-run" quotations, likening them to car accidents in which the driver speeds away and avoids taking responsibility for the dent in your fender or the smashed taillights, as in the figure that follows.

On the following page is a typical hit-and-run quotation by a writer responding to an essay by the feminist philosopher

DON'T BE A HIT-AND-RUN QUOTER.

Susan Bordo, who laments that media pressures on young women to diet are spreading to previously isolated regions of the world like the Fiji islands.

> Susan Bordo writes about women and dieting. "Fiji is just one example. Until television was introduced in 1995, the islands had no reported cases of eating disorders. In 1998, three years after programs from the United States and Britain began broadcasting there, 62 percent of the girls surveyed reported dieting."
> I think Bordo is right. Another point Bordo makes is that. . . .

Since this writer fails to introduce the quotation adequately or explain why he finds it worth quoting, readers will have a hard time reconstructing what Bordo argued. Besides neglecting to say who Bordo is or even that the quoted words are hers, the writer does not explain how her words connect with anything he is saying or even what she says that he thinks is so "right." He simply abandons the quotation in his haste to zoom on to another point.

To adequately frame a quotation, you need to insert it into what we like to call a "quotation sandwich," with the statement introducing it serving as the top slice of bread and the explanation following it serving as the bottom slice. The introductory or lead-in claims should explain who is speaking and set up what the quotation says; the follow-up statements should explain why you consider the quotation to be important and what you take it to say.

TEMPLATES FOR INTRODUCING QUOTATIONS

▸ X states, "<u>not all steroids should be banned from sports</u>."

▸ As the prominent philosopher X puts it, "_____."

▸ According to X, "_____."

▸ X himself writes, "_____."

▸ In her book, _____, X maintains that "_____."

▸ Writing in the journal *Commentary*, X complains that "_____."

▸ In X's view, "_____."

▸ X agrees when she writes, "_____."

▸ X disagrees when he writes, "_____."

▸ X complicates matters further when she writes, "_____."

TEMPLATES FOR EXPLAINING QUOTATIONS

The one piece of advice about quoting that our students say they find most helpful is to get in the habit of following every major quotation by explaining what it means, using a template like one of the ones below.

▸ **Basically, X is warning <u>that the proposed solution will only make the problem worse.</u>**

▸ **In other words, X believes _____ .**

▸ **In making this comment, X urges us to _____ .**

▸ **X is corroborating the age-old adage that _____ .**

▸ **X's point is that _____ .**

▸ **The essence of X's argument is that _____ .**

When offering such explanations, it is important to use language that accurately reflects the spirit of the quoted passage. It is quite serviceable to write "Bordo states" or "asserts" in introducing the quotation about Fiji. But given the fact that Bordo is clearly alarmed by the extension of the media's reach to Fiji, it is far more accurate to use language that reflects her alarm: "Bordo is alarmed that" or "is disturbed by" or "complains."

See pp. 39–40 for a list of action verbs for summarizing what others say.

Consider, for example, how the earlier passage on Bordo might be revised using some of these moves.

The feminist philosopher Susan Bordo deplores Western media's obsession with female thinness and dieting. Her basic complaint is that increasing numbers of women across the globe are being led to see themselves as fat and in need of a diet. Citing the islands of Fiji as a case in point, Bordo notes that "until television was introduced in 1995, the islands had no reported cases of eating disorders. In 1998, three years after programs from the United States and Britain began broadcasting there, 62 percent of the girls surveyed reported dieting" (149–50). Bordo's point is that the Western cult of dieting is spreading even to remote places across the globe. Ultimately, Bordo complains, the culture of dieting will find you, regardless of where you live.

Bordo's observations ring true to me because, now that I think about it, many women I know, regardless of where they are from, worry about their weight. . . .

This framing of the quotation not only better integrates Bordo's words into the writer's text, but also serves to demonstrate the writer's interpretation of what Bordo is saying. While "the feminist philosopher" and "Bordo notes" provide information that readers need to know, the sentences that follow the quotation build a bridge between Bordo's words and those of the writer. The reference to 62 percent of Fijian girls dieting is no longer an inert statistic (as it was in the flawed passage presented earlier) but a quantitative example of how "the Western cult of dieting is spreading . . . across the globe." Just as important, these sentences explain what Bordo is saying in the writer's own words—and thereby make clear that the quotation is being used purposefully to set up the writer's own argument and has not been stuck in just for padding the essay or the works-cited list.

BLEND THE AUTHOR'S WORDS
WITH YOUR OWN

The above framing material also works well because it accurately represents Bordo's words while giving those words the writer's own spin. Notice how the passage refers several times to the key concept of dieting, and how it echoes Bordo's references to "television" and to U.S. and British "broadcasting" by referring to "culture," which is further specified as "Western." Instead of simply repeating Bordo word for word, the follow-up sentences echo just enough of her language while still moving the discussion in the writer's own direction. In effect, the framing creates a kind of hybrid mix of Bordo's words and those of the writer.

CAN YOU OVERANALYZE A QUOTATION?

But is it possible to overexplain a quotation? And how do you know when you've explained a quotation thoroughly enough? After all, not all quotations require the same amount of explanatory framing, and there are no hard-and-fast rules for knowing how much explanation any quotation needs. As a general rule, the most explanatory framing is needed for quotations that may be hard for readers to process: quotations that are long and complex, that are filled with details or jargon, or that contain hidden complexities.

And yet, though the particular situation usually dictates when and how much to explain a quotation, we will still offer one piece of advice: when in doubt, go for it. It is better to risk being overly explicit about what you take a quotation to mean than to leave the quotation dangling and your readers in doubt. Indeed, we encourage you to provide such explanatory framing even when writing to an audience that you know to be familiar with the author being quoted and able to interpret your quotations on their own. Even in such cases, readers need to see how *you* interpret the quotation, since words—especially those of controversial figures—can be interpreted in various ways and used to support different, sometimes opposing, agendas. Your readers need to see what you make of the material you've quoted, if only to be sure that your reading of the material and theirs is on the same page.

HOW *NOT* TO INTRODUCE QUOTATIONS

We want to conclude this chapter by surveying some ways *not* to introduce quotations. Although some writers do so, you should not introduce quotations by saying something like "Orwell asserts an idea that" or "A quote by Shakespeare says." Introductory phrases like these are both redundant and misleading. In the first example, you could write either "Orwell asserts that" or "Orwell's assertion is that," rather than redundantly combining the two. The second example misleads readers, since it is the writer who is doing the quoting, not Shakespeare (as "a quote by Shakespeare" implies).

The templates in this book will help you avoid such mistakes. Once you have mastered templates like "as X puts it," or "in X's own words," you probably won't even have to think about them—and will be free to focus on the challenging ideas that templates help you frame.

Exercises

1. Find a published piece of writing that quotes something that "they say." How has the writer integrated the quotation into his or her own text? How has he or she introduced the quotation, and what, if anything, has the writer said to explain it and tie it to his or her own text? Based on what you've read in this chapter, are there any changes you would suggest?

2. Look at something you have written for one of your classes. Have you quoted any sources? If so, how have you integrated the quotation into your own text? How have you introduced it? Explained what it means? Indicated how it relates to *your* text? If you haven't done all these things, revise your text to do so, perhaps using the Templates for Introducing Quotations (p. 46) and Explaining Quotations (pp. 46–47). If you've not written anything with quotations, try revising some academic text you've written to do so.

2

—◻—

"I SAY"

FOUR

"YES / NO / OKAY, BUT"

Three Ways to Respond

THE FIRST THREE CHAPTERS of this book discuss the "they say" stage of writing, in which you devote your attention to the views of some other person or group. In this chapter we move to the "I say" stage, in which you offer your own argument as a response to what "they" have said.

Moving to the "I say" stage can be daunting in academia, where it often may seem that you need to be an expert in a field to have an argument at all. Many students have told us that they have trouble entering some of the high-powered conversations that take place in college or graduate school because they do not know enough about the topic at hand, or because, they say, they simply are not "smart enough." Yet often these same students, when given a chance to study in depth the contribution that some scholar has made in a given field, will turn around and say things like "I can see where she is coming from, how she makes her case by building on what other scholars have said. Perhaps had I studied the situation longer I could have come up with a similar argument." What these students came to realize is that good arguments are based not on knowledge that only a special class of experts has access to, but on everyday habits of mind that can be isolated, identified, and used by almost anyone. Though there's certainly no substitute for expertise and for knowing as much as possible about one's topic, the arguments that finally win the day are built, as the title of this chapter suggests, on some very basic rhetorical patterns that most of us use on a daily basis.

There are a great many ways to respond to others' ideas, but this chapter concentrates on the three most common and recognizable ways: agreeing, disagreeing, or some combination of both. Although each way of responding is open to endless variation, we focus on these three because readers come to any text needing to learn fairly quickly where the writer stands, and they do this by placing the writer on a mental map consisting of a few familiar options: the writer agrees with those he or she is responding to, disagrees with them, or presents some combination of both agreeing and disagreeing.

When writers take too long to declare their position relative to views they've summarized or quoted, readers get frustrated, wondering, "Is this guy agreeing or disagreeing? Is he *for* what this other person has said, *against* it, or what?" For this reason, this chapter's advice applies to reading as well as to writing. Especially with difficult texts, you need not only to find the position the writer is responding to—the "they say"—but also to determine whether the writer is agreeing with it, challenging it, or some mixture of the two.

ONLY *THREE* WAYS TO RESPOND?

Perhaps you'll worry that fitting your own response into one of these three categories will force you to oversimplify your argument or lessen its complexity, subtlety, or originality. This is certainly a serious concern for academics who are rightly skeptical of writing that is simplistic and reductive. We would argue, however, that the more complex and subtle your argument is, and the more it departs from the conventional ways people think, the more your readers will need to be able to place it on their mental map in order to process the complex details you present. That is, the complexity, subtlety, and originality of your response are more likely to stand out and be noticed if readers have a baseline sense of where you stand relative to any ideas you've cited. As you move through this chapter, we hope you'll agree that the forms of agreeing, disagreeing, and both agreeing and disagreeing that we discuss, far from being simplistic or one-dimensional, are able to accommodate a high degree of creative, complex thought.

It is always a good tactic to begin your response not by launching directly into a mass of details but by stating clearly whether you agree, disagree, or both, using a direct, no-nonsense formula such as: "I agree," "I disagree," or "I am of two minds. I agree that _____, but I cannot agree that _____." Once you have offered one of these straightforward statements (or one of the many variations discussed below), readers will have a strong grasp of your position and then be able to appreciate the complications you go on to offer as your response unfolds. See p. 21 for suggestions on previewing where you stand.

Still, you may object that these three basic ways of responding don't cover all the options—that they ignore interpretive or analytical responses, for example. In other words, you might think that when you interpret a literary work you don't necessarily agree or disagree with anything but simply explain the work's meaning, style, or structure. Many essays about literature and the arts, it might be said, take this form—they interpret a work's meaning, thus rendering matters of agreeing or disagreeing irrelevant.

We would argue, however, that the most interesting interpretations in fact tend to be those that agree, disagree, or
both—that instead of being offered solo, the best interpretations take strong stands relative to other interpretations. In fact,
there would be no reason to offer an interpretation of a work
of literature or art unless you were responding to the interpretations or possible interpretations of others. Even when you
point out features or qualities of an artistic work that others
have not noticed, you are implicitly disagreeing with what
those interpreters have said by pointing out that they missed
or overlooked something that, in your view, is important. In
any effective interpretation, then, you need not only to state
what you yourself take the work of art to mean but to do so
relative to the interpretations of other readers—be they professional scholars, teachers, classmates, or even hypothetical
readers (as in, "Although some readers might think that this
poem is about _____, it is in fact about _____").

DISAGREE—AND EXPLAIN WHY

Disagreeing may seem like one of the simpler moves a writer
can make, and it is often the first thing people associate with
critical thinking. Disagreeing can also be the easiest way to
generate an essay: find something you can disagree with in what
has been said or might be said about your topic, summarize
it, and argue with it. But disagreement in fact poses hidden
challenges. You need to do more than simply assert that you
disagree with a particular view; you also have to offer persuasive
reasons *why* you disagree. After all, disagreeing means more
than adding "not" to what someone else has said, more than
just saying, "Although they say women's rights are improving,

I say women's rights are *not* improving." Such a response merely contradicts the view it responds to and fails to add anything interesting or new. To turn it into an argument, you need to give reasons to support what you say: because another's argument fails to take relevant factors into account; because it is based on faulty or incomplete evidence; because it rests on questionable assumptions; or because it uses flawed logic, is contradictory, or overlooks what you take to be the real issue. To move the conversation forward (and, indeed, to justify your very act of writing), you need to demonstrate that you have something to contribute.

You can even disagree by making what we call the "duh" move, in which you disagree not with the position itself but with the assumption that it is a new or stunning revelation. Here is an example of such a move, used to open an essay on the state of American schools.

> According to a recent report by some researchers at Stanford University, high school students with college aspirations "often lack crucial information on applying to college and on succeeding academically once they get there."
>
> Well, duh. . . . It shouldn't take a Stanford research team to tell us that when it comes to "succeeding academically," many students don't have a clue.
>
> GERALD GRAFF, "Trickle-Down Obfuscation"

Like all of the other moves discussed in this book, the "duh" move can be tailored to meet the needs of almost any writing situation. If you find the expression "duh" too brash to use with your intended audience, you can always dispense with the term itself and write something like "It is true that _____ ; but we already knew that."

TEMPLATES FOR DISAGREEING, WITH REASONS

▶ **X is mistaken because she overlooks <u>recent fossil discoveries in the South</u>.**

▶ **X's claim that _____ rests upon the questionable assumption that _____.**

▶ **I disagree with X's view that _____ because, as recent research has shown, _____.**

▶ **X contradicts herself/can't have it both ways. On the one hand, she argues _____. On the other hand, she also says _____.**

▶ **By focusing on _____, X overlooks the deeper problem of _____.**

You can also disagree by making what we call the "twist it" move, in which you agree with the evidence that someone else has presented but show through a twist of logic that this evidence actually supports your own, contrary position. For example:

> X argues for stricter gun control legislation, saying that the crime rate is on the rise and that we need to restrict the circulation of guns. I agree that the crime rate is on the rise, but that's precisely why I oppose stricter gun control legislation. We need to own guns to protect ourselves against criminals.

In this example of the "twist it" move, the writer agrees with X's claim that the crime rate is on the rise but then argues that this increasing crime rate is in fact a valid reason for *opposing* gun control legislation.

At times you might be reluctant to express disagreement, for any number of reasons—not wanting to be unpleasant, to hurt someone's feelings, or to make yourself vulnerable to being disagreed with in return. One of these reasons may in fact explain why the conference speaker we described at the start of Chapter 1 avoided mentioning the disagreement he had with other scholars until he was provoked to do so in the discussion that followed his talk.

As much as we understand such fears of conflict and have experienced them ourselves, we nevertheless believe it is better to state our disagreements in frank yet considerate ways than to deny them. After all, suppressing disagreements doesn't make them go away; it only pushes them underground, where they can fester in private unchecked. Nevertheless, disagreements do not need to take the form of personal put-downs. Further-more, there is usually no reason to take issue with *every* aspect of someone else's views. You can single out for criticism only those aspects of what someone else has said that are troubling, and then agree with the rest—although such an approach, as we will see later in this chapter, leads to the somewhat more complicated terrain of both agreeing and disagreeing at the same time.

AGREE—BUT WITH A DIFFERENCE

Like disagreeing, agreeing is less simple than it may appear. Just as you need to avoid simply contradicting views you disagree with, you also need to do more than simply echo views you agree with. Even as you're agreeing, it's important to bring something new and fresh to the table, adding something that makes you a valuable participant in the conversation.

There are many moves that enable you to contribute something of your own to a conversation even as you agree with what someone else has said. You may point out some unnoticed evidence or line of reasoning that supports X's claims that X herself hadn't mentioned. You may cite some corroborating personal experience, or a situation not mentioned by X that her views help readers understand. If X's views are particularly challenging or esoteric, what you bring to the table could be an accessible translation—an explanation for readers not already in the know. In other words, your text can usefully contribute to the conversation simply by pointing out unnoticed implications or explaining something that needs to be better understood.

Whatever mode of agreement you choose, the important thing is to open up some difference or contrast between your position and the one you're agreeing with rather than simply parroting what it says.

TEMPLATES FOR AGREEING

▸ I agree that <u>diversity in the student body is educationally valuable</u> because my experience <u>at Central University</u> confirms it.

▸ X is surely right about _____ because, as she may not be aware, recent studies have shown that _____.

▸ X's theory of _____ is extremely useful because it sheds light on the difficult problem of _____.

▸ Those unfamiliar with this school of thought may be interested to know that it basically boils down to _____.

Some writers avoid the practice of agreeing almost as much as others avoid disagreeing. In a culture like America's that prizes originality, independence, and competitive individualism, writers sometimes don't like to admit that anyone else has made the same point, seemingly beating them to the punch. In our view, however, as long as you can support a view taken by someone else without merely restating what he or she has said, there is no reason to worry about being "unoriginal." Indeed, there is good reason to rejoice when you agree with others since those others can lend credibility to your argument. While you don't want to present yourself as a mere copycat of someone else's views, you also need to avoid sounding like a lone voice in the wilderness.

But do be aware that whenever you agree with one person's view, you are likely disagreeing with someone else's. It is hard to align yourself with one position without at least implicitly positioning yourself against others. The psychologist Carol Gilligan does just that in an essay in which she agrees with scientists who argue that the human brain is "hard-wired" for cooperation, but in so doing aligns herself against anyone who believes that the brain is wired for selfishness and competition.

> These findings join a growing convergence of evidence across the human sciences leading to a revolutionary shift in consciousness. . . . If cooperation, typically associated with altruism and self-sacrifice, sets off the same signals of delight as pleasures commonly associated with hedonism and self-indulgence; if the opposition between selfish and selfless, self vs. relationship biologically makes no sense, then a new paradigm is necessary to reframe the very terms of the conversation.
>
> CAROL GILLIGAN, "Sisterhood Is Pleasurable:
> A Quiet Revolution in Psychology"

In agreeing with some scientists that "the opposition between selfish and selfless . . . makes no sense," Gilligan implicitly disagrees with anyone who thinks the opposition *does* make sense. Basically, what Gilligan says could be boiled down to a template.

▸ I agree that _____, a point that needs emphasizing since so many people still believe _____ .

▸ If group X is right that _____, as I think they are, then we need to reassess the popular assumption that _____ .

What such templates allow you to do, then, is to agree with one view while challenging another—a move that leads into the domain of agreeing and disagreeing simultaneously.

AGREE AND DISAGREE SIMULTANEOUSLY

This last option is often our favorite way of responding. One thing we particularly like about agreeing and disagreeing simultaneously is that it helps us get beyond the kind of "is too" / "is not" exchanges that often characterize the disputes of young children and the more polarized shouting matches of talk radio and TV.

TEMPLATES FOR AGREEING
AND DISAGREEING SIMULTANEOUSLY

"Yes and no." "Yes, but . . . " "Although I agree up to a point, I still insist . . . " These are just some of the ways you can make your argument complicated and nuanced while maintaining a clear, reader-friendly framework. The parallel structure—"yes and no"; "on the one hand I agree, on the other I disagree"—enables readers to place your argument on that map of positions we spoke of earlier in this chapter while still keeping your argument sufficiently complex.

Another aspect we like about this option is that it can be tipped subtly toward agreement or disagreement, depending on where you lay your stress. If you want to stress the disagreement end of the spectrum, you would use a template like the one below.

▶ **Although I agree with X up to a point, I cannot accept his overriding assumption that <u>religion is no longer a major force today</u>.**

Conversely, if you want to stress your agreement more than your disagreement, you would use a template like this one.

▶ **Although I disagree with much that X says, I fully endorse his final conclusion that _____ .**

The first template above might be called a "yes, but . . . " move, the second a "no, but . . . " move. Other versions include the following.

▶ **Though I concede that _____ , I still insist that _____ .**

▶ **X is right that _____ , but she seems on more dubious ground when she claims that _____ .**

▶ **While X is probably wrong when she claims that _____ , she is right that _____ .**

▶ **Whereas X provides ample evidence that _____ , Y and Z's research on _____ and _____ convinces me that _____ instead.**

Another classic way to agree and disagree at the same time is to make what we call an "I'm of two minds" or a "mixed feelings" move.

▸ I'm of two minds about X's claim that _____. On the one hand, I agree that _____. On the other hand, I'm not sure if _____.

▸ My feelings on the issue are mixed. I do support X's position that _____, but I find Y's argument about _____ and Z's research on _____ to be equally persuasive.

This move can be especially useful if you are responding to new or particularly challenging work and are as yet unsure where you stand. It also lends itself well to the kind of speculative investigation in which you weigh a position's pros and cons rather than come out decisively either for or against. But again, as we suggest earlier, whether you are agreeing, disagreeing, or both agreeing and disagreeing, you need to be as clear as possible, and making a frank statement that you are ambivalent is one way to be clear.

IS BEING UNDECIDED OKAY?

Nevertheless, writers often have as many concerns about expressing ambivalence as they do about expressing disagreement or agreement. Some worry that by expressing ambivalence they will come across as evasive, wishy-washy, or unsure of themselves. Others worry that their ambivalence will end up confusing readers who require decisive clear-cut conclusions.

Three Ways to Respond

The truth is that in some cases these worries are legitimate. At times ambivalence can frustrate readers, leaving them with the feeling that you failed in your obligation to offer the guidance they expect from writers. At other times, however, acknowledging that a clear-cut resolution of an issue is impossible can demonstrate your sophistication as a writer. In an academic culture that values complex thought, forthrightly declaring that you have mixed feelings can be impressive, especially after having ruled out the one-dimensional positions on your issue taken by others in the conversation. Ultimately, then, how ambivalent you end up being comes down to a judgment call based on different readers' responses to your drafts, on your knowledge of your audience, and on the challenges of your particular argument and situation.

Exercises

1. Read one of the essays in the back of this book or on **theysayiblog.com**, identifying those places where the author agrees with others, disagrees, or both.

2. Write an essay responding in some way to the essay that you worked with in the preceding exercise. You'll want to summarize and/or quote some of the author's ideas and make clear whether you're agreeing, disagreeing, or both agreeing and disagreeing with what he or she says. Remember that there are templates in this book that can help you get started; see Chapters 1–3 for templates that will help you represent other people's ideas, and Chapter 4 for templates that will get you started with your response.

FIVE

"AND YET"

Distinguishing What You *Say*
from What They *Say*

———□———

IF GOOD ACADEMIC WRITING involves putting yourself into
dialogue with others, it is extremely important that readers be
able to tell at every point when you are expressing your own
view and when you are stating someone else's. This chapter
takes up the problem of moving from what *they* say to what
you say without confusing readers about who is saying what.

DETERMINE WHO IS SAYING WHAT
IN THE TEXTS YOU READ

Before examining how to signal who is saying what in your
own writing, let's look at how to recognize such signals when
they appear in the texts you read—an especially important skill
when it comes to the challenging works assigned in school.
Frequently, when students have trouble understanding difficult texts, it is not just because the texts contain unfamiliar
ideas or words, but because the texts rely on subtle clues to let

readers know when a particular view should be attributed to the writer or to someone else. Especially with texts that present a true dialogue of perspectives, readers need to be alert to the often subtle markers that indicate whose voice the writer is speaking in.

Consider how the social critic and educator Gregory Mantsios uses these "voice markers," as they might be called, to distinguish the different perspectives in his essay on America's class inequalities.

> "We are all middle-class," or so it would seem. Our national consciousness, as shaped in large part by the media and our political leadership, provides us with a picture of ourselves as a nation of prosperity and opportunity with an ever expanding middle-class life-style. As a result, our class differences are muted and our collective character is homogenized.
>
> Yet class divisions are real and arguably the most significant factor in determining both our very being in the world and the nature of the society we live in.
>
> GREGORY MANTSIOS, "Rewards and Opportunities:
> The Politics and Economics of Class in the U.S."

Although Mantsios makes it look easy, he is actually making several sophisticated rhetorical moves here that help him distinguish the common view he opposes from his own position.

In the opening sentence, for instance, the phrase "or so it would seem" shows that Mantsios does not necessarily agree with the view he is describing, since writers normally don't present views they themselves hold as ones that only "seem" to be true. Mantsios also places this opening view in quotation marks to signal that it is not his own. He then further distances himself from the belief being summarized in the opening paragraph by attributing it to "our national consciousness, as shaped in large part by the media and our political leadership," and then further attributing to this "consciousness" a negative, undesirable "result": one in which "our class differences" get "muted" and "our collective character" gets "homogenized," stripped of its diversity and distinctness. Hence, even before Mantsios has declared his own position in the second paragraph, readers can get a pretty solid sense of where he probably stands.

Furthermore, the second paragraph opens with the word "yet," indicating that Mantsios is now shifting to his own view (as opposed to the common view he has thus far been describing). Even the parallelism he sets up between the first and second paragraphs—between the first paragraph's claim that class differences do not exist and the second paragraph's claim that they do—helps throw into sharp relief the differences between the two voices. Finally, Mantsios's use of a direct, authoritative, declarative tone in the second paragraph also suggests a switch in voice. Although he does not use the words "I say" or "I argue," he clearly identifies the view he holds by presenting it not as one that merely *seems* to be true or that *others tell us* is true, but as a view that *is* true or, as Mantsios puts it, "real."

Paying attention to these voice markers is an important aspect of reading comprehension. Readers who fail to notice these markers often take an author's summaries of what someone else believes to be an expression of what the author himself or herself believes. Thus when we teach Mantsios's essay, some students invariably come away thinking that the statement "we are all middle-class" is Mantsios's own position rather than the perspective he is opposing, failing to see that in writing these words Mantsios acts as a kind of ventriloquist, mimicking what others say rather than directly expressing what he himself is thinking.

To see how important such voice markers are, consider what the Mantsios passage looks like if we remove them.

> We are all middle-class. . . . We are a nation of prosperity and opportunity with an ever expanding middle-class life-style. . . .
>
> Class divisions are real and arguably the most significant factor in determining both our very being in the world and the nature of the society we live in.

In contrast to the careful delineation between voices in Mantsios's original text, this unmarked version leaves it hard to tell where his voice begins and the voices of others end. With the markers removed, readers cannot tell that "We are all middle-class" represents a view the author opposes, and that "Class divisions are real" represents what the author himself believes. Indeed, without the markers, especially the "Yet," readers might well miss the fact that the second paragraph's claim that "Class divisions are real" contradicts the first paragraph's claim that "We are all middle-class."

TEMPLATES FOR SIGNALING WHO IS SAYING WHAT IN YOUR OWN WRITING

To avoid confusion in your own writing, make sure that at every point your readers can clearly tell who is saying what. To do so, you can use as voice-identifying devices many of the templates presented in previous chapters.

- **Although X makes the best possible case for <u>universal, government-funded health care</u>, I <u>am not persuaded</u>.**

- **My view, however, contrary to what X has argued, is that _____ .**

- **Adding to X's argument, I would point out that _____ .**

- **According to both X and Y, _____ .**

- **Politicians, X argues, should _____ .**

- **Most athletes will tell you that _____ .**

BUT I'VE BEEN TOLD NOT TO USE "I"

Notice that the first three templates above use the first-person "I" or "we," as do many of the templates in this book, thereby contradicting the common advice about avoiding the first person in academic writing. Although you may have been told that the "I" word encourages subjective, self-indulgent opinions rather than well-grounded arguments, we believe that texts using "I" can be just as well supported—or just as self-indulgent—as those that don't. For us, well-supported arguments are grounded in persuasive reasons and evidence, not in the use or nonuse of any particular pronouns.

Furthermore, if you consistently avoid the first person in your writing, you will probably have trouble making the key move addressed in this chapter: differentiating your views from those of others, or even offering your own views in the first place. But don't just take our word for it. See for yourself how freely the first person is used by the writers quoted in this book, and by the writers assigned in your courses.

Nevertheless, certain occasions may warrant avoiding the first person and writing, for example, that "she is correct" instead of "I think that she is correct." Since it can be monotonous to read an unvarying series of "I" statements ("I believe . . . I think . . . I argue"), it is a good idea to mix first-person assertions with ones like the following.

▸ **X is right that <u>certain common patterns can be found in the communities</u>.**

▸ **The evidence shows that _____ .**

▸ **X's assertion that _____ does not fit the facts.**

▸ **Anyone familiar with _____ should agree that _____ .**

One might even follow Mantsios's lead, as in the following template.

▸ **But _____ are real, and are arguably the most significant factor in _____ .**

On the whole, however, academic writing today, even in the sciences and social sciences, makes use of the first person fairly liberally.

See pp. 252–59 for an example of the way a physicist uses the first person.

ANOTHER TRICK FOR IDENTIFYING WHO IS SPEAKING

To alert readers about whose perspective you are describing at any given moment, you don't always have to use overt voice markers like "X argues" followed by a summary of the argument. Instead, you can alert readers about whose voice you're speaking in by *embedding* a reference to X's argument in your own sentences. Hence, instead of writing:

> Liberals believe that cultural differences need to be respected. I have a problem with this view, however.

you might write:

> I have a problem with *what liberals call cultural differences.*

> There is a major problem with the liberal doctrine of *so-called cultural differences.*

You can also embed references to something you yourself have previously said. So instead of writing two cumbersome sentences like:

> Earlier in this chapter we coined the term "voice markers." We would argue that such markers are extremely important for reading comprehension.

you might write:

> We would argue that "voice markers," as we identified them earlier, are extremely important for reading comprehension.

Embedded references like these allow you to economize your train of thought and refer to other perspectives without any major interruption.

TEMPLATES FOR EMBEDDING VOICE MARKERS

▸ **X overlooks what I consider an important point about <u>cultural differences</u>.**

▸ **My own view is that what X insists is a _____ is in fact a _____ .**

▸ **I wholeheartedly endorse what X calls _____ .**

▸ **These conclusions, which X discusses in _____ , add weight to the argument that _____ .**

When writers fail to use voice-marking devices like the ones discussed in this chapter, their summaries of others' views tend to become confused with their own ideas—and vice versa. When readers cannot tell if you are summarizing your own views or endorsing a certain phrase or label, they have to stop and think: "Wait. I thought the author disagreed with this claim. Has she actually been asserting this view all along?" or "Hmmm, I thought she would have objected to this kind of phrase. Is she actually endorsing it?" Getting in the habit of using voice markers will keep you from confusing your readers and help alert you to similar markers in the challenging texts you read.

Exercises

1. To see how one writer signals when she is asserting her own views and when she is summarizing those of someone else, read the following passage by the social historian Julie Charlip. As you do so, identify those spots where Charlip refers to the views of others and the signal phrases she uses to distinguish her views from theirs.

Marx and Engels wrote: "Society as a whole is more and more split-ting up into two great hostile camps, into two great classes directly facing each other—the bourgeoisie and the proletariat" (10). If only that were true, things might be more simple. But in late twentieth-century America, it seems that society is splitting more and more into a plethora of class factions—the working class, the working poor, lower-middle class, upper-middle class, lower uppers, and upper uppers. I find myself not knowing what class I'm from.

In my days as a newspaper reporter, I once asked a sociology pro-fessor what he thought about the reported shrinking of the middle class. Oh, it's not the middle class that's disappearing, he said, but the working class. His definition: if you earn thirty thousand dollars a year working in an assembly plant, come home from work, open a beer and watch the game, you are working class; if you earn twenty thousand dollars a year as a school teacher, come home from work to a glass of white wine and PBS, you are middle class.

How do we define class? Is it an issue of values, lifestyle, taste? Is it the kind of work you do, your relationship to the means of production? Is it a matter of how much money you earn? Are we allowed to choose? In this land of supposed classlessness, where we don't have the tradition of English society to keep us in our places, how do we know where we really belong? The average American will tell you he or she is "middle class." I'm sure that's what my father would tell you. But I always felt that we were in some no man's land, suspended between classes, sharing similari-ties with some and recognizing sharp, exclusionary differences from others. What class do I come from? What class am I in now? As an historian, I seek the answers to these questions in the specificity of my past.

JULIE CHARLIP, "A Real Class Act: Searching
for Identity in the Classless Society"

2. Study a piece of your own writing to see how many perspectives you account for and how well you distinguish your own voice from those you are summarizing. Consider the following questions:

   a. How many perspectives do you engage?
   b. What other perspectives might you include?
   c. How do you distinguish your views from the other views you summarize?
   d. Do you use clear voice-signaling phrases?
   e. What options are available to you for clarifying who is saying what?
   f. Which of these options are best suited for this particular text?

If you find that you do *not* include multiple views or clearly distinguish between others' views and your own, revise your text to do so.

SIX

"SKEPTICS MAY OBJECT"

Planting a Naysayer in Your Text

———⌐□⌐———

THE WRITER Jane Tompkins describes a pattern that repeats itself whenever she writes a book or an article. For the first couple of weeks when she sits down to write, things go relatively well. But then in the middle of the night, several weeks into the writing process, she'll wake up in a cold sweat, suddenly realizing that she has overlooked some major criticism that readers will surely make against her ideas. Her first thought, invariably, is that she will have to give up on the project, or that she will have to throw out what she's written thus far and start over. Then she realizes that "this moment of doubt and panic is where my text really begins." She then revises what she's written in a way that incorporates the criticisms she's anticipated, and her text becomes stronger and more interesting as a result.

This little story contains an important lesson for all writers, experienced and inexperienced alike. It suggests that even though most of us are upset at the idea of someone criticizing our work, such criticisms can actually work to our advantage. Although it's naturally tempting to ignore criticism of our ideas, doing so may in fact be a big mistake, since our writing improves when we not only listen to these objections but give them an explicit hearing in our writing. Indeed, no single device more quickly improves a piece of writing than planting a naysayer in the text—saying, for example, that "although some readers may object" to something in your argument, you "would reply that _____."

ANTICIPATE OBJECTIONS

But wait, you say. Isn't the advice to incorporate critical views a recipe for destroying your credibility and undermining your argument? Here you are, trying to say something that will hold up, and we want you to tell readers all the negative things someone might say against you?

Exactly. We *are* urging you to tell readers what others might say against you, but our point is that doing so will actually *enhance* your credibility, not undermine it. As we argue throughout this book, writing well does not mean piling up uncontroversial truths in a vacuum; it means engaging others in a dialogue or debate—not only by opening your text with a summary of what others *have* said, as we suggest in Chapter 1, but also by imagining what others *might* say against your argument as it unfolds. Once you see writing as an act of entering a conversation, you should also see how opposing arguments can work for you rather than against you.

Paradoxically, the more you give voice to your critics' objections, the more you tend to disarm those critics, especially if you go on to answer their objections in convincing ways. When you entertain a counterargument, you make a kind of preemptive strike, identifying problems with your argument before others can point them out for you. Furthermore, by entertaining counterarguments, you show respect for your readers, treating them not as gullible dupes who will believe anything you say but as independent, critical thinkers who are aware that your view is not the only one in town. In addition, by imagining what others might say against your claims, you come across as a generous, broad-minded person who is confident enough to open himself or herself to debate—like the writer in the figure on the following page.

Conversely, if you don't entertain counterarguments, you may very likely come across as closed-minded, as if you think your beliefs are beyond dispute. You might also leave important questions hanging and concerns about your arguments unaddressed. Finally, if you fail to plant a naysayer in your text, you may find that you have very little to say. Our own students often say that entertaining counterarguments makes it easier to generate enough text to meet their assignment's page-length requirements.

Planting a naysayer in your text is a relatively simple move, as you can see by looking at the following passage from a book by the writer Kim Chernin. Having spent some thirty pages complaining about the pressure on American women to be thin, Chernin inserts a whole chapter entitled "The Skeptic," opening it as follows.

At this point I would like to raise certain objections that have been inspired by the skeptic in me. She feels that I have been ignoring some of the most common assumptions we all make about our bodies and these she wishes to see addressed. For example: "You know perfectly well," she says to me, "that you feel better when you lose weight. You buy new clothes. You look at yourself more eagerly in the mirror. When someone invites you to a party you don't stop and ask yourself whether you want to go. You feel sexier. Admit it. You like yourself better."

KIM CHERNIN, *The Obsession:*
Reflections on the Tyranny of Slenderness

The remainder of Chernin's chapter consists of her answers to this inner skeptic. In the face of the skeptic's challenge to her book's central premise (that the pressure to diet seriously harms women's lives), Chernin responds neither by repressing the skeptic's critical voice nor by giving in to it and relinquishing her own position. Instead, she embraces that voice and writes it into her text. Note too that instead of dispatching this naysaying voice quickly, as many of us would be tempted to do, Chernin stays with it and devotes a full paragraph to it. By borrowing some of Chernin's language, we can come up with templates for entertaining virtually any objection.

TEMPLATES FOR ENTERTAINING OBJECTIONS

▸ **At this point I would like to raise some objections that have been inspired by the skeptic in me. She feels that I have been ignoring the complexities of the situation.**

▸ **Yet some readers may challenge my view by insisting that** _____.

▸ **Of course, many will probably disagree on the grounds that** _____.

Note that the objections in the above templates are attributed not to any specific person or group, but to "skeptics," "readers," or "many." This kind of nameless, faceless naysayer is perfectly appropriate in many cases. But the ideas that motivate arguments and objections often can—and, where possible, should—be ascribed to a specific ideology or school of thought (for example, liberals, Christian fundamentalists, neopragmatists) rather than to anonymous anybodies. In other words, naysayers can be labeled, and you can add precision and impact to your writing by identifying what those labels are.

TEMPLATES FOR NAMING YOUR NAYSAYERS

▸ Here many *feminists* would probably object that <u>gender does influence language</u>.

▸ But *social Darwinists* would certainly take issue with the argument that _____.

▸ *Biologists*, of course, may want to question whether _____.

▸ Nevertheless, both *followers and critics of Malcolm X* will probably suggest otherwise and argue that _____.

To be sure, some people dislike such labels and may even resent having labels applied to themselves. Some feel that labels put individuals in boxes, stereotyping them and glossing over what makes each of us unique. And it's true that labels can be used inappropriately, in ways that ignore individuality and promote stereotypes. But since the life of ideas, including many of our most private thoughts, is conducted through groups and types rather than solitary individuals, intellectual exchange requires labels to give definition and serve as a convenient shorthand. If you categorically reject all labels, you give up an important resource and even mislead readers by presenting yourself and others as having no connection to anyone else. You also miss an opportunity to generalize the importance and relevance of your work to some larger conversation. When you attribute a position you are summarizing to liberalism, say, or historical materialism, your argument is no longer just about your own solitary views but about the intersection of broad ideas and habits of mind that many readers may already have a stake in.

The way to minimize the problem of stereotyping, then, is not to categorically reject labels but to refine and qualify their use, as the following templates demonstrate.

▶ Although not all *Christians* think alike, some of them will probably dispute my claim that _____.

▶ *Non-native English speakers* are so diverse in their views that it's hard to generalize about them, but some are likely to object on the grounds that _____.

Another way to avoid needless stereotyping is to qualify labels carefully, substituting "pro bono lawyers" for "lawyers" in general, for example, or "quantitative sociologists" for all "social scientists," and so on.

TEMPLATES FOR INTRODUCING OBJECTIONS INFORMALLY

Objections can also be introduced in more informal ways. For instance, you can frame objections in the form of questions.

▶ But is my proposal realistic? What are the chances of its actually being adopted?

▶ Yet is it necessarily true that _____? Is it always the case, as I have been suggesting, that _____?

▶ However, does the evidence I've cited prove conclusively that _____?

You can also let your naysayer speak directly.

▸ **"Impossible," some will say. "You must be reading the research selectively."**

Moves like this allow you to cut directly to the skeptical voice itself, as the singer-songwriter Joe Jackson does in the following excerpt from a *New York Times* article complaining about the restrictions on public smoking in New York City bars and restaurants.

> I like a couple of cigarettes or a cigar with a drink, and like many other people, I only smoke in bars or nightclubs. Now I can't go to any of my old haunts. Bartenders who were friends have turned into cops, forcing me outside to shiver in the cold and curse under my breath. . . . It's no fun. Smokers are being demonized and victimized all out of proportion.
>
> "Get over it," say the anti-smokers. "You're the minority." I thought a great city was a place where all kinds of minorities could thrive. . . . "Smoking kills," they say. As an occasional smoker with otherwise healthy habits, I'll take my chances. Health consciousness is important, but so are pleasure and freedom of choice.
>
> JOE JACKSON, "Want to Smoke? Go to Hamburg"

Jackson could have begun his second paragraph, in which he shifts from his own voice to that of his imagined naysayer, more formally, as follows: "Of course anti-smokers will object that since we smokers are in the minority, we should simply stop complaining and quietly make the sacrifices we are being called on to make for the larger social good." Or "Anti-smokers might insist, however, that the smoking minority should submit to the non-smoking majority." We think, though, that Jackson gets the job done in a far more lively way with the more colloquial form he chooses. Borrowing a standard move of playwrights and novelists, Jackson cuts directly to the objectors' view and then to his own retort, then back to the objectors' view and then to his own retort again, thereby creating a kind of dialogue or miniature play within his own text. This move works well for Jackson, but only because he uses quotation marks and other voice markers to make clear at every point whose voice he is in.

See Chapter 5 for more advice on using voice markers.

REPRESENT OBJECTIONS FAIRLY

Once you've decided to introduce a differing or opposing view into your writing, your work has only just begun, since you still need to represent and explain that view with fairness and generosity. Although it is tempting to give opposing views short shrift, to hurry past them, or even to mock them, doing so is usually counterproductive. When writers make the best case they can for their critics (playing Peter Elbow's "believing game"), they actually bolster their credibility with readers rather than undermine it. They make readers think, "This is a writer I can trust."

See pp. 31–32 for more on the believing game.

We recommend, then, that whenever you entertain objections in your writing, you stay with them for several sentences or even paragraphs and take them as seriously as possible. We also recommend that you read your summary of opposing views with an outsider's eye: put yourself in the shoes of someone who disagrees with you and ask if such a reader would recognize himself in your summary. Would that reader think you have taken his views seriously, as beliefs that reasonable people might hold? Or would he detect a mocking tone or an oversimplification of his views?

There will always be certain objections, to be sure, that you believe do not deserve to be represented, just as there will be objections that seem so unworthy of respect that they inspire ridicule. Remember, however, that if you do choose to mock a view that you oppose, you are likely to alienate those readers who don't already agree with you—likely the very readers you want to reach. Also be aware that in mocking another's view you may contribute to a hostile argument culture in which someone may ridicule you in return.

ANSWER OBJECTIONS

Do be aware that when you represent objections successfully, you still need to be able to answer those objections persuasively. After all, when you write objections into a text, you take the risk that readers will find those objections more convincing than the argument you yourself are advancing. In the editorial quoted above, for example, Joe Jackson takes the risk that readers will identify more with the anti-smoking view he summarizes than with the pro-smoking position he endorses.

This is precisely what Benjamin Franklin describes happening to himself in *The Autobiography of Benjamin Franklin* (1793), when he recalls being converted to Deism (a religion that exalts reason over spirituality) by reading *anti*-Deist books. When he encountered the views of Deists being negatively summarized by authors who opposed them, Franklin explains, he ended up finding the Deist position more persuasive. To avoid having this kind of unintentional reverse effect on

readers, you need to do your best to make sure that any counterarguments you address are not more convincing than your own
claims. It is good to address objections in your writing, but only
if you are able to overcome them.

One surefire way to *fail* to overcome an objection is to dismiss it out of hand—saying, for example, "That's just wrong."
The difference between such a response (which offers no supporting reasons whatsoever) and the types of nuanced responses
we're promoting in this book is the difference between bullying
your readers and genuinely persuading them.

Often the best way to overcome an objection is not to try
to refute it completely but to agree with part of it while challenging only the part you dispute. In other words, in answering counterarguments, it is often best to say "yes, but" or "yes
and no," treating the counterview as an opportunity to
revise and refine your own position. Rather than build
your argument into an impenetrable fortress, it is often
best to make concessions while still standing your ground, as
Kim Chernin does in the following response to the counterargument quoted above. While in the voice of the "skeptic,"
Chernin writes: "Admit it. You like yourself better when you've
lost weight." In response, Chernin replies as follows.

See pp. 61–64
for more on
agreeing, with
a difference.

Can I deny these things? No woman who has managed to lose
weight would wish to argue with this. Most people feel better about
themselves when they become slender. And yet, upon reflection,
it seems to me that there is something precarious about this wellbeing. After all, 98 percent of people who lose weight gain it back.
Indeed, 90 percent of those who have dieted "successfully" gain
back more than they ever lost. Then, of course, we can no longer
bear to look at ourselves in the mirror.

In this way, Chernin shows how you can use a counterview to improve and refine your overall argument by making a concession. Even as she concedes that losing weight feels good in the short run, she argues that in the long run the weight always returns, making the dieter far more miserable.

TEMPLATES FOR MAKING CONCESSIONS WHILE STILL STANDING YOUR GROUND

► Although I grant that <u>the book is poorly organized</u>, I still maintain that <u>it raises an important issue</u>.

► Proponents of X are right to argue that _____ . But they exaggerate when they claim that _____ .

► While it is true that _____ , it does not necessarily follow that _____ .

► On the one hand, I agree with X that _____ . But on the other hand, I still insist that _____ .

Templates like these show that answering naysayers' objections does not have to be an all-or-nothing affair in which you either definitively refute your critics or they definitively refute you. Often the most productive engagements among differing views end with a combined vision that incorporates elements of each one.

But what if you've tried out all the possible answers you can think of to an objection you've anticipated and you *still* have a nagging feeling that the objection is more convincing than your argument itself? In that case, the best remedy is to go back and make some fundamental revisions to your argument, even reversing your position completely if need be. Although finding out late in the game that you aren't fully convinced by your own argument can be painful, it can actually make your final text more intellectually honest, challenging, and serious. After all, the goal of writing is not to keep proving that whatever you initially said is right, but to stretch the limits of your thinking. So if planting a strong naysayer in your text forces you to change your mind, that's not a bad thing. Some would argue that that is what the academic world is all about.

Exercises

1. Read the following passage by the cultural critic Eric Schlosser. As you'll see, he hasn't planted any naysayers in this text. Do it for him. Insert a brief paragraph stating an objection to his argument and then responding to the objection as he might.

The United States must declare an end to the war on drugs. This war has filled the nation's prisons with poor drug addicts and small-time drug dealers. It has created a multibillion-dollar black market, enriched organized crime groups and promoted the corruption of government officials throughout the world. And it has not stemmed the widespread use of illegal drugs. By any rational measure, this war has been a total failure.

We must develop public policies on substance abuse that are guided not by moral righteousness or political expediency but by common sense. The United States should immediately decriminalize the cultivation and possession of small amounts of marijuana for personal use. Marijuana should no longer be classified as a Schedule I narcotic, and those who seek to use marijuana as medicine should no longer face criminal sanctions. We must shift our entire approach to drug abuse from the criminal justice system to the public health system. Congress should appoint an independent commission to study the harm-reduction policies that have been adopted in Switzerland, Spain, Portugal, and the Netherlands. The commission should recommend policies for the United States based on one important criterion: what works.

In a nation where pharmaceutical companies advertise powerful antidepressants on billboards and where alcohol companies run amusing beer ads during the Super Bowl, the idea of a "drug-free society" is absurd. Like the rest of American society, our drug policy would greatly benefit from less punishment and more compassion.

ERIC SCHLOSSER, "A People's Democratic Platform"

2. Look over something you've written that makes an argument. Check to see if you've anticipated and responded to any objections. If not, revise your text to do so. If so, have you anticipated all the likely objections? Who if anyone have you attributed the objections to? Have you represented the objections fairly? Have you answered them well enough, or do you think you now need to qualify your own argument? Could you use any of the language suggested in this chapter? Does the introduction of a naysayer strengthen your argument? Why, or why not?

SEVEN

"SO WHAT? WHO CARES?"

Saying Why It Matters

—⊡—

BASEBALL IS THE NATIONAL PASTIME. Bernini was the best sculptor of the baroque period. All writing is conversational. So what? Who cares? Why does any of this matter?

How many times have you had reason to ask these questions? Regardless of how interesting a topic may be to you as a writer, readers always need to know what is at stake in a text and why they should care. All too often, however, these questions are left unanswered—mainly because writers and speakers assume that audiences will know the answers already or will figure them out on their own. As a result, students come away from lectures feeling like outsiders to what they've just heard, just as many of us feel left hanging after talks we've attended. The problem is not necessarily that the speakers lack a clear, well-focused thesis or that the thesis is inadequately supported with evidence. Instead, the problem is that the speakers don't address the crucial question of why their arguments matter.

That this question is so often left unaddressed is unfortunate since the speakers generally *could* offer interesting, engaging answers. When pressed, for instance, most academics will tell you that their lectures and articles matter because they address some belief that needs to be corrected or updated—and because their arguments have important, real-world consequences. Yet many academics fail to identify these reasons and consequences explicitly in what they say and write. Rather than assume that audiences will know why their claims matter, all writers need to answer the "so what?" and "who cares?" questions up front. Not everyone can claim to have a cure for cancer or a solution to end poverty. But writers who fail to show that others *should* care or already *do* care about their claims will ultimately lose their audiences' interest.

This chapter focuses on various moves that you can make to answer the "who cares?" and "so what?" questions in your own writing. In one sense, the two questions get at the same thing: the relevance or importance of what you are saying. Yet they get at this significance in different ways. Whereas "who cares?" literally asks you to identify a person or group who cares about your claims, "so what?" asks about the real-world applications and consequences of those claims—what difference it would make if they were accepted. We'll look first at ways of making clear who cares.

"WHO CARES?"

To see how one writer answers the "who cares?" question, consider the following passage from the science writer Denise Grady. Writing in the *New York Times*, she explains some of the latest research into fat cells.

> Scientists used to think body fat and the cells it was made of were pretty much inert, just an oily storage compartment. But within the past decade research has shown that fat cells act like chemical factories and that body fat is potent stuff: a highly active

tissue that secretes hormones and other substances with profound and sometimes harmful effects. . . .

In recent years, biologists have begun calling fat an "endocrine organ," comparing it to glands like the thyroid and pituitary, which also release hormones straight into the bloodstream.

DENISE GRADY, "The Secret Life of a Potent Cell"

Notice how Grady's writing reflects the central advice we give in this book, offering a clear claim and also framing that claim as a response to what someone else has said. In so doing, Grady immediately identifies at least one group with a stake in the new research that sees fat as "active," "potent stuff": namely, the scientific community, which formerly believed that body fat is inert. By referring to these scientists, Grady implicitly acknowledges that her text is part of a larger conversation and shows who besides herself has an interest in what she says.

Consider, however, how the passage would read had Grady left out what "scientists used to think" and simply explained the new findings in isolation.

Within the past few decades research has shown that fat cells act like chemical factories and that body fat is potent stuff: a highly active tissue that secretes hormones and other substances. In recent years, biologists have begun calling fat an "endocrine organ," comparing it to glands like the thyroid and pituitary, which also release hormones straight into the bloodstream.

Though this statement is clear and easy to follow, it lacks any indication that anyone needs to hear it. Okay, one nods while reading this passage, fat is an active, potent thing. Sounds plausible enough; no reason to think it's not true. But does anyone really care? Who, if anyone, is interested?

TEMPLATES FOR INDICATING WHO CARES

To address "who cares?" questions in your own writing, we suggest using templates like the following, which echo Grady in refuting earlier thinking.

▸ <u>Parents</u> used to think <u>spanking was necessary</u>. But recently [or within the past few decades] <u>experts</u> suggest that <u>it can be counterproductive</u>.

▸ This interpretation challenges the work of those critics who have long assumed that _____.

▸ These findings challenge the work of earlier researchers, who tended to assume that _____.

▸ Recent studies like these shed new light on _____, which previous studies had not addressed.

Grady might have been more explicit by writing the "who cares?" question directly into her text, as in the following template.

▸ But who really cares? Who besides me and a handful of recent researchers has a stake in these claims? At the very least, the researchers who formerly believed _____ should care.

To gain greater authority as a writer, it can help to name specific people or groups who have a stake in your claims and to go into some detail about their views.

▸ Researchers have long assumed that _____. For instance, one eminent scholar of cell biology, _____, assumed in _____, her seminal work on cell structures and functions, that fat cells _____. As _____ herself put it, "_____" (2012). Another leading scientist, _____, argued that fat cells "_____" (2011). Ultimately, when it came to the nature of fat, the basic assumption was that _____.

But a new body of research shows that fat cells are far more complex and that _____.

In other cases, you might refer to certain people or groups who *should* care about your claims.

▸ If sports enthusiasts stopped to think about it, many of them might simply assume that the most successful athletes _____. However, new research shows _____.

▸ These findings challenge neoliberals' common assumption that _____.

▸ At first glance, teenagers might say _____. But on closer inspection _____.

As these templates suggest, answering the "who cares?" question involves establishing the type of contrast between what others say and what you say that is central to this book. Ultimately, such templates help you create a dramatic tension or clash of views in your writing that readers will feel invested in and want to see resolved.

"SO WHAT?"

Although answering the "who cares?" question is crucial, in many cases it is not enough, especially if you are writing for general readers who don't necessarily have a strong investment in the particular clash of views you are setting up. In the case of Grady's argument about fat cells, such readers may still wonder why it matters that some researchers think fat cells are active, while others think they're inert. Or, to move to a different field of study, American literature, *so what* if some scholars disagree about Huck Finn's relationship with the runaway slave Jim in Mark Twain's *Adventures of Huckleberry Finn*? Why should anyone besides a few specialists in the field care about such disputes? What, if anything, hinges on them?

The best way to answer such questions about the larger consequences of your claims is to appeal to something that your audience already figures to care about. Whereas the "who cares?" question asks you to identify an interested person or group, the "so what?" question asks you to link your argument to some larger matter that readers already deem important. Thus in analyzing *Huckleberry Finn*, a writer could argue that seemingly narrow disputes about the hero's relationship with Jim actually shed light on whether Twain's canonical, widely read novel is a critique of racism in America or is itself marred by it.

Let's see how Grady invokes such broad, general concerns in her article on fat cells. Her first move is to link researchers' interest in fat cells to a general concern with obesity and health.

> Researchers trying to decipher the biology of fat cells hope to find new ways to help people get rid of excess fat or, at least, prevent obesity from destroying their health. In an increasingly obese world, their efforts have taken on added importance.

Further showing why readers should care, Grady's next move is to demonstrate the even broader relevance and urgency of her subject matter.

> Internationally, more than a billion people are overweight. Obesity and two illnesses linked to it, heart disease and high blood pressure, are on the World Health Organization's list of the top 10 global health risks. In the United States, 65 percent of adults weigh too much,

compared with about 56 percent a decade ago, and government researchers blame obesity for at least 300,000 deaths a year.

What Grady implicitly says here is "Look, dear reader, you may think that these questions about the nature of fat cells I've been pursuing have little to do with everyday life. In fact, however, these questions are extremely important—particularly in our 'increasingly obese world' in which we need to prevent obesity from destroying our health."

Notice that Grady's phrase "in an increasingly _____ world" can be adapted as a strategic move to address the "so what?" question in other fields as well. For example, a sociologist ana‑lyzing back‑to‑nature movements of the past thirty years might make the following statement.

> In a world increasingly dominated by cellphones and sophisticated computer technologies, these attempts to return to nature appear futile.

This type of move can be readily applied to other disciplines because no matter how much disciplines may differ from one another, the need to justify the importance of one's concerns is common to them all.

TEMPLATES FOR ESTABLISHING WHY YOUR CLAIMS MATTER

▸ *Huckleberry Finn* matters/is important because <u>it is one of the most widely taught novels in the American school system.</u>

▸ Although X may seem trivial, it is in fact crucial in terms of today's concern over _____.

▸ Ultimately, what is at stake here is _____ .

▸ These findings have important implications for the broader domain of _____ .

▸ If we are right about _____, then major consequences follow for _____ .

▸ These conclusions/This discovery will have significant applications in _____ as well as in _____ .

Finally, you can also treat the "so what?" question as a related aspect of the "who cares?" question.

▸ Although X may seem of concern to only a small group of _____, it should in fact concern anyone who cares about _____ .

All these templates help you hook your readers. By suggesting the real-world applications of your claims, the templates not only demonstrate that others care about your claims but also tell your readers why *they* should care. Again, it bears repeating that simply stating and proving your thesis isn't enough. You also need to frame it in a way that helps readers care about it.

WHAT ABOUT READERS WHO ALREADY KNOW WHY IT MATTERS?

At this point, you might wonder if you need to answer the "who cares?" and "so what?" questions in *everything* you write. Is it really necessary to address these questions if you're proposing something so obviously consequential as, say, a treatment for autism or a program to eliminate illiteracy? Isn't it obvious that everyone cares about such problems? Does it really need to be spelled out? And what about when you're writing for audiences who you know are already interested in your claims and who understand perfectly well why they're important? In other words, do you always need to address the "so what?" and "who cares?" questions?

As a rule, yes—although it's true that you can't keep answering them forever and at a certain point must say enough is enough. Although a determined skeptic can infinitely ask why something matters—"Why should I care about earning a salary? And why should I care about supporting a family?"—you have to stop answering at some point in your text. Nevertheless, we urge you to go as far as possible in answering such questions. If you take it for granted that readers will somehow intuit the answers to "so what?" and "who cares?" on their own, you may make your work seem less interesting than it actually is, and you run the risk that readers will dismiss your text as irrelevant and unimportant. By contrast, when you are careful to explain who cares and why, it's a little like bringing a cheerleading squad into your text. And though some expert readers might already know why your claims matter, even they need to be reminded. Thus the safest move is to be as explicit as possible in answering the "so what?" question, even for those already in the know. When you step back from the text and explain why it matters, you are urging your audience to keep reading, pay attention, and care.

Exercises

1. Find several texts (scholarly essays, newspaper articles, emails, memos, blogs, etc.) and see whether they answer

the "so what?" and "who cares?" questions. Probably some do, some don't. What difference does it make whether they do or do not? How do the authors who answer these questions do so? Do they use any strategies or techniques that you could borrow for your own writing? Are there any strategies or techniques recommended in this chapter, or that you've found or developed on your own, that you'd recommend to these authors?

2. Look over something you've written yourself. Do you indicate "so what?" and "who cares"? If not, revise your text to do so. You might use the following template to get started.

My point here (that _____) should interest those who _____. Beyond this limited audience, however, my point should speak to anyone who cares about the larger issue of _____.

3

TYING IT ALL TOGETHER

EIGHT

"AS A RESULT"

Connecting the Parts

———⊡———

WE ONCE HAD A STUDENT named Bill, whose characteristic sentence pattern went something like this.

Spot is a good dog. He has fleas.

"Connect your sentences," we urged in the margins of Bill's papers. "What does Spot being good have to do with his fleas?" "These two statements seem unrelated. Can you connect them in some logical way?" When comments like these yielded no results, we tried inking in suggested connections for him.

Spot is a good dog, *but* he has fleas.
Spot is a good dog, *even though* he has fleas.

But our message failed to get across, and Bill's disconnected sentence pattern persisted to the end of the semester.

And yet Bill did focus well on his subjects. When he mentioned Spot the dog (or Plato, or any other topic) in one sentence, we could count on Spot (or Plato) being the topic of the following sentence as well. This was not the case with some of Bill's classmates, who sometimes changed topic from sentence to sentence or even from clause to clause within a single sentence. But because Bill neglected to mark his connections, his writing was as frustrating to read as theirs. In all these cases, we had to struggle to figure out on our own how the sentences and paragraphs connected or failed to connect with one another.

What makes such writers so hard to read, in other words, is that they never gesture back to what they have just said or forward to what they plan to say. "Never look back" might be their motto, almost as if they see writing as a process of thinking of something to say about a topic and writing it down, then thinking of something else to say about the topic and writing that down too, and on and on until they've filled the assigned number of pages and can hand the paper in. Each sentence basically starts a new thought, rather than growing out of or extending the thought of the previous sentence.

When Bill talked about his writing habits, he acknowledged that he never went back and read what he had written. Indeed, he told us that, other than using his computer software to check for spelling errors and make sure that his tenses were all aligned, he never actually reread what he wrote before turning it in. As Bill seemed to picture it, writing was something one did while sitting at a computer, whereas reading was a separate activity generally reserved for an easy chair, book in hand. It had never occurred to Bill that to write a good sentence he had to think about how it connected to those that came before and after; that he had to think hard about how that sentence fit into the sentences that surrounded it. Each sentence for Bill existed in a sort of tunnel isolated from every other sentence on the page. He never bothered to fit all the parts of his essay together because he apparently thought of writing as a matter of piling up information or observations rather than building a sustained argument. What we suggest in this chapter, then, is that you converse not only with others in your writing but with yourself: that you establish clear relations between one statement and the next by connecting those statements.

This chapter addresses the issue of how to connect all the parts of your writing. The best compositions establish a sense of momentum and direction by making explicit connections among their different parts, so that what is said in one sentence (or paragraph) both sets up what is to come and is clearly informed by what has already been said. When you write a sentence, you create an expectation in the reader's mind that the next sentence will in some way echo and extend it, even if—*especially if*—that next sentence takes your argument in a new direction.

It may help to think of each sentence you write as having arms that reach backward and forward, as the figure below suggests. When your sentences reach outward like this, they establish connections that help your writing flow smoothly in a way readers appreciate. Conversely, when writing lacks such connections and moves in fits and starts, readers repeatedly have to go back over the sentences and guess at the connections on their own. To prevent such disconnection and make your writing flow, we advise

YOUR SENTENCE

YOUR
LAST
SENTENCE

YOUR
NEXT
SENTENCE

following a "do it yourself" principle, which means that it is your job as a writer to do the hard work of making the connections rather than, as Bill did, leaving this work to your readers.

This chapter offers several strategies you can use to put this principle into action: (1) using transition terms (like "therefore" and "as a result"); (2) adding pointing words (like "this" or "such"); (3) developing a set of key terms and phrases for each text you write; and (4) repeating yourself, but with a difference—a move that involves repeating what you've said, but with enough variation to avoid being redundant. All these moves require that you always look back and, in crafting any one sentence, think hard about those that precede it.

Notice how we ourselves have used such connecting devices thus far in this chapter. The second paragraph of this chapter, for example, opens with the transitional "And yet," signaling a change in direction, while the opening sentence of the third includes the phrase "in other words," telling you to expect a restatement of a point we've just made. If you look through this book, you should be able to find many sentences that contain some word or phrase that explicitly hooks them back to something said earlier, to something about to be said, or both. And many sentences in *this* chapter repeat key terms related to the idea of connection: "connect," "disconnect," "link," "relate," "forward," and "backward."

USE TRANSITIONS

For readers to follow your train of thought, you need not only to connect your sentences and paragraphs to each other, but also to mark the kind of connection you are making. One of the easiest ways to make this move is to use *transitions* (from the Latin root *trans*, "across"), which help you cross from one point to another in your text. Transitions are usually placed at or near the start of sentences so they can signal to readers where your text is going: in the same direction it has been moving, or in a new direction. More specifically, transitions tell readers whether your text is echoing a previous sentence or paragraph ("in other words"), adding something to it ("in addition"), offering an example of it ("for example"), generalizing from it ("as a result"), or modifying it ("and yet").

The following is a list of commonly used transitions, categorized according to their different functions.

ADDITION

also	indeed
and	in fact
besides	moreover
furthermore	so too
in addition	

ELABORATION

actually	to put it another way
by extension	to put it bluntly
in other words	to put it succinctly
in short	ultimately
that is	

EXAMPLE

after all	for instance
as an illustration	specifically
consider	to take a case in point
for example	

CAUSE AND EFFECT

accordingly	so
as a result	then
consequently	therefore
hence	thus
since	

COMPARISON

along the same lines	likewise
in the same way	similarly

CONTRAST

although	nevertheless
but	nonetheless
by contrast	on the contrary
conversely	on the other hand
despite	regardless
even though	whereas
however	while yet
in contrast	

CONCESSION

admittedly	naturally
although it is true	of course
granted	to be sure

CONCLUSION

as a result	in sum
consequently	therefore
hence	thus
in conclusion	to sum up
in short	to summarize

Ideally, transitions should operate so unobtrusively in a piece of writing that they recede into the background and readers do not even notice that they are there. It's a bit like what happens when drivers use their turn signals before turning right or left: just as other drivers recognize such signals almost unconsciously, readers should process transition terms with a minimum of thought. But even though such terms should function unobtrusively in your writing, they can be among the most powerful tools in your vocabulary. Think how your heart sinks when someone, immediately after praising you, begins a sentence with "but" or "however." No matter what follows, you know it won't be good.

Notice that some transitions can help you not only to move from one sentence to another, but to combine two or more sentences into one. Combining sentences in this way helps prevent the choppy, staccato effect that arises when too many short sentences are strung together, one after the other. For instance, to combine Bill's two choppy sentences ("Spot is a good dog. He has fleas.") into one, better-flowing sentence, we suggested that he rewrite them as "Spot is a good dog, *even though* he has fleas."

Transitions like these not only guide readers through the twists and turns of your argument but also help ensure that you *have* an argument in the first place. In fact, we think of words like "but," "yet," "nevertheless," "besides," and others as argument words, since it's hard to use them without making some kind of argument. The word "therefore," for instance, commits you to making sure that the claims preceding it lead logically to the conclusion that it introduces. "For example" also assumes an argument, since it requires the material you are introducing to stand as an instance or proof of some preceding generalization. As a result, the more you use transitions, the more you'll be able not only to connect the parts of your text but also to construct a strong argument in the first place. And if you draw on them frequently enough, using them should eventually become second nature.

To be sure, it is possible to overuse transitions, so take time to read over your drafts carefully and eliminate any transitions that are unnecessary. But following the maxim that you need to learn the basic moves of argument before you can deliberately depart from them, we advise you not to forgo explicit transition terms until you've first mastered their use. In all our years of teaching, we've read countless essays that suffered from having few or no transitions, but cannot recall one in which the transitions were overused. Seasoned writers sometimes omit explicit transitions, but only because they rely heavily on the other types of connecting devices that we turn to in the rest of this chapter.

Before doing so, however, let us warn you about inserting transitions without really thinking through their meanings—using "therefore," say, when your text's logic actually requires "nevertheless" or "however." So beware. Choosing transition terms should involve a bit of mental sweat, since the whole point of using them is to make your writing *more* reader-friendly, not less. The only thing more frustrating than reading Bill-style passages like "Spot is a good dog. He has fleas" is reading misconnected sentences like "Spot is a good dog. For example, he has fleas."

USE POINTING WORDS

Another way to connect the parts of your argument is by using pointing words—which, as their name implies, point or refer backward to some concept in the previous sentence. The most common of these pointing words include "this," "these," "that," "those," "their," and "such" (as in "these pointing words" near the start of this sentence) and simple pronouns like "his," "he," "her," "she," "it," and "their." Such terms help you create the flow we spoke of earlier that enables readers to move effortlessly through your text. In a sense, these terms are like an invisible hand reaching out of your sentence, grabbing what's needed in the previous sentences and pulling it along.

Like transitions, however, pointing words need to be used carefully. It's dangerously easy to insert pointing words into your text that don't refer to a clearly defined object, assuming that because the object you have in mind is clear to you it will also be clear to your readers. For example, consider the use of "this" in the following passage.

> Alexis de Tocqueville was highly critical of democratic societies, which he saw as tending toward mob rule. At the same time, he accorded democratic societies grudging respect. *This* is seen in Tocqueville's statement that . . .

When "this" is used in such a way it becomes an ambiguous or free-floating pointer, since readers can't tell if it refers to Tocqueville's critical attitude toward democratic societies, his grudging respect for them, or some combination of both. "This what?" readers mutter as they go back over such passages and try to figure them out. It's also tempting to try to cheat with pointing words, hoping that they will conceal or make up for conceptual confusions that may lurk in your argument. By referring to a fuzzy idea as "this" or "that," you might hope the fuzziness will somehow come across as clearer than it is.

You can fix problems caused by a free-floating pointer by making sure there is one and only one possible object in the vicinity that the pointer could be referring to. It also often helps to name the object the pointer is referring to at the same time that you point to it, replacing the bald "this" in the example above with a more precise phrase like "this ambivalence toward democratic societies" or "this grudging respect."

REPEAT KEY TERMS AND PHRASES

A third strategy for connecting the parts of your argument is to develop a constellation of key terms and phrases, including their synonyms and antonyms, that you repeat throughout your text. When used effectively, your key terms should be items that readers could extract from your text in order to get a solid sense of your topic. Playing with key terms also can be a good way to come up with a title and appropriate section headings for your text.

Notice how often Martin Luther King Jr. uses the key words "criticism," "statement," "answer," and "correspondence" in the opening paragraph of his famous "Letter from Birmingham Jail."

Dear Fellow Clergymen:

While confined here in the Birmingham city jail, I came across your recent *statement* calling my present activities "unwise and untimely." Seldom do I pause to *answer criticism* of my work and ideas. If I sought to *answer* all the *criticisms* that cross my desk, my secretaries would have little time for anything other than *such correspondence* in the course of the day, and I would have no time for constructive work. But since I feel that you are men of genuine good will and that your *criticisms* are sincerely set forth, I want to try to *answer* your *statement* in what I hope will be patient and reasonable terms.

MARTIN LUTHER KING JR., "Letter from Birmingham Jail"

Even though King uses the terms "criticism" and "answer" three times each and "statement" twice, the effect is not overly repetitive. In fact, these key terms help build a sense of momentum in the paragraph and bind it together.

For another example of the effective use of key terms, consider the following passage, in which the historian Susan Douglas develops a constellation of sharply contrasting key terms around the concept of "cultural schizophrenics": women like herself who, Douglas claims, have mixed feelings about the images of ideal femininity with which they are constantly bombarded by the media.

In a variety of ways, the mass media helped make us the cultural schizophrenics we are today, women who rebel against yet submit to prevailing images about what a desirable, worthwhile woman should be. . . . [T]he mass media has engendered in many women a kind of cultural identity crisis. We are ambivalent toward femininity on the one hand and feminism on the other. Pulled in opposite directions—told we were equal, yet told we were subordinate; told we could change history but told we were trapped by history—we got the bends at an early age, and we've never gotten rid of them.

When I open *Vogue*, for example, I am simultaneously infuriated and seduced. . . . I adore the materialism; I despise the materialism. . . . I want to look beautiful; I think wanting to look beautiful is about the most dumb-ass goal you could have. The magazine stokes my desire; the magazine triggers my bile. And this doesn't only happen when I'm reading *Vogue*; it happens all the time. . . . On the one hand, on the other hand—that's not just me—that's what it means to be a woman in America.

To explain this schizophrenia . . .

SUSAN DOUGLAS, Where the Girls Are:
Growing Up Female with the Mass Media

In this passage, Douglas establishes "schizophrenia" as a key concept and then echoes it through synonyms like "identity crisis," "ambivalent," "the bends"—and even demonstrates it through a series of contrasting words and phrases:

> rebel against / submit
> told we were equal / told we were subordinate
> told we could change history / told we were trapped by history
> infuriated / seduced
> I adore / I despise
> I want / I think wanting . . . is about the most dumb-ass goal
> stokes my desire / triggers my bile
> on the one hand / on the other hand

These contrasting phrases help flesh out Douglas's claim that women are being pulled in two directions at once. In so doing, they bind the passage together into a unified whole that, despite its complexity and sophistication, stays focused over its entire length.

REPEAT YOURSELF—BUT WITH A DIFFERENCE

The last technique we offer for connecting the parts of your text involves repeating yourself, but with a difference—which basically means saying the same thing you've just said, but in a slightly different way that avoids sounding monotonous. To effectively connect the parts of your argument and keep it moving forward, be careful not to leap from one idea to a different idea or introduce new ideas cold. Instead, try to build bridges between your ideas by echoing what you've just said while simultaneously moving your text into new territory.

Several of the connecting devices discussed in this chapter are ways of repeating yourself in this special way. Key terms, pointing terms, and even many transitions can be used in a way that not only brings something forward from the previous sentence but in some way alters it. When Douglas, for instance, uses the key term "ambivalent" to echo her earlier reference to schizophrenics, she is repeating herself with a difference—repeating the same concept, but with a different word that adds new associations.

In addition, when you use transition phrases like "in other words" and "to put it another way," you repeat yourself with a difference, since these phrases help you restate earlier claims but in a different register. When you open a sentence with "in other words," you are basically telling your readers that in case they didn't fully understand what you meant in the last sentence, you are now coming at it again from a slightly different angle, or that since you're presenting a very important idea, you're not going to skip over it quickly but will explore it further to make sure your readers grasp all its aspects.

We would even go so far as to suggest that after your first sentence, almost every sentence you write should refer back to previous statements in some way. Whether you are writing a "furthermore" comment that adds to what you have just said or a "for example" statement that illustrates it, each sentence should echo at least one element of the previous sentence in some discernible way. Even when your text changes direction and requires transitions like "in contrast," "however," or "but," you still need to mark that shift by linking the sentence to the one just before it, as in the following example.

Cheyenne loved basketball. Nevertheless, she feared her height would put her at a disadvantage.

These sentences work because even though the second sentence changes course and qualifies the first, it still echoes key concepts from the first. Not only does "she" echo "Cheyenne," since both refer to the same person, but "feared" echoes "loved" by establishing the contrast mandated by the term "nevertheless." "Nevertheless," then, is not an excuse for changing subjects radically. It too requires repetition to help readers shift gears with you and follow your train of thought.

Repetition, in short, is the central means by which you can move from point A to point B in a text. To introduce one last analogy, think of the way experienced rock climbers move up a steep slope. Instead of jumping or lurching from one handhold to the next, good climbers get a secure handhold on the position they have established before reaching for the next ledge. The same thing applies to writing. To move smoothly from point to point in your argument, you need to firmly ground what you say in what you've already said. In this way, your writing remains focused while simultaneously moving forward.

"But hold on," you may be thinking. "Isn't repetition precisely what sophisticated writers should avoid, on the grounds that it will make their writing sound simplistic—as if they are belaboring the obvious?" Yes and no. On the one hand, writers certainly can run into trouble if they merely repeat themselves and nothing more. On the other hand, repetition is key to creating continuity in writing. It is impossible to stay on track in a piece of writing if you don't repeat your points throughout the length of the text. Furthermore, writers would never make an impact on readers if they didn't repeat their main points often enough to reinforce those points and make them stand out above subordinate points. The trick therefore is not to avoid repeating yourself but to repeat yourself in varied and interesting enough ways that you advance your argument without sounding tedious.

Exercises

1. Read the following opening to Chapter 2 of *The Road to Wigan Pier*, by George Orwell. Annotate the connecting devices by underlining the transitions, circling the key terms, and putting boxes around the pointing terms.

Our civilisation . . . is founded on coal, more completely than one realises until one stops to think about it. The machines that keep us alive, and the machines that make the machines, are all directly or indirectly dependent upon coal. In the metabolism of the Western world the coal-miner is second in importance only to the man who ploughs the soil. He is a sort of grimy caryatid upon whose shoulders nearly everything that is not grimy is supported. For this reason the actual process by which coal is extracted is well worth watching, if you get the chance and are willing to take the trouble.

When you go down a coal-mine it is important to try and get to the coal face when the "fillers" are at work. This is not easy, because when the mine is working visitors are a nuisance and are not encouraged, but if you go at any other time, it is possible to come away with a totally wrong impression. On a Sunday, for instance, a mine seems almost peaceful. The time to go there is when the machines are roaring and the air is black with coal dust, and when you can actually see what the miners have to do. At those times the place is like hell, or at any rate like my own mental picture of hell. Most of the things one imagines in hell are there—heat, noise, confusion, darkness, foul air, and, above all, unbearably cramped space. Everything except the fire, for there is no fire down there except the feeble beams of Davy lamps and electric torches which scarcely penetrate the clouds of coal dust.

When you have finally got there—and getting there is a job in itself: I will explain that in a moment—you crawl through the last line of pit props and see opposite you a shiny black wall three or four feet high. This is the coal face. Overhead is the smooth ceiling made by the rock from which the coal has been cut; underneath is the rock again, so that the gallery you are in is only as high as the ledge of coal itself, probably not much more than a yard. The first impression of all, overmastering everything else for a while, is the frightful, deafening din from the conveyor belt which carries the coal away. You cannot see very far, because the fog of coal dust throws back the beam of your lamp, but you can see on either side of you the line of half-naked kneeling men, one to every four or five yards, driving their shovels under the fallen coal and flinging it swiftly over their left shoulders. . . .

GEORGE ORWELL, *The Road to Wigan Pier*

2. Read over something you've written with an eye for the devices you've used to connect the parts. Underline all the transitions, pointing terms, key terms, and repetition. Do you see any patterns? Do you rely on certain devices more than others? Are there any passages that are hard to follow—and if so, can you make them easier to read by trying any of the other devices discussed in this chapter?

NINE

"AIN'T SO / IS NOT"

Academic Writing Doesn't Always Mean Setting Aside Your Own Voice

—◻—

HAVE YOU EVER gotten the impression that writing well in college means setting aside the kind of language you use in everyday conversation? That to impress your instructors you need to use big words, long sentences, and complex sentence structures? If so, then we're here to tell you that it ain't necessarily so. On the contrary, academic writing can—and in our view *should*—be relaxed, easy to follow, and even a little bit fun. Although we don't want to suggest that you avoid using sophisticated, academic terms in your writing, we encourage you to draw upon the kinds of expressions and turns of phrase that you use every day when texting or conversing with family and friends. In this chapter, we want to show you how you can write effective academic arguments while holding on to some of your own voice.

This point is important, since you may well become turned off from writing if you think your everyday language practices have to be checked at the classroom door. You may end up feeling like a student we know who, when asked how she felt about the writing she does in college, answered, "I do it because I have to, but it's just not me!"

This is not to suggest that *any* language you use among friends has a place in academic writing. Nor is it to suggest that you may fall back on colloquial usage as an excuse for not learning more rigorous forms of expression. After all, learning these more rigorous forms of expression and developing a more intellectual self is a major reason for getting an education. We do, however, wish to suggest that relaxed, colloquial language can often enliven academic writing and even enhance its rigor and precision. Such informal language also helps you connect with readers in a personal as well as an intellectual way. In our view, then, it is a mistake to assume that the academic and the everyday are completely separate languages that can never be used together.

MIX ACADEMIC AND COLLOQUIAL STYLES

Many successful writers blend academic, professional language with popular expressions and sayings. Consider, for instance, the following passage from a scholarly article about the way teachers respond to errors in student writing.

> Marking and judging formal and mechanical errors in student papers is one area in which composition studies seems to have a multiple-personality disorder. On the one hand, our mellow, student-centered, process-based selves tend to condemn marking formal errors at all. Doing it represents the Bad Old Days. Ms. Fidditch and Mr. Flutesnoot with sharpened red pencils, spilling innocent blood across the page. Useless detail work. Inhumane, perfectionist standards, making our students feel stupid, wrong,

trivial, misunderstood. Joseph Williams has pointed out how arbitrary and context-bound our judgments of formal error are. And certainly our noting of errors on student papers gives no one any great joy; as Peter Elbow says, English is most often associated *either* with grammar or with high literature—"two things designed to make folks feel most out of it."

ROBERT CONNORS AND ANDREA LUNSFORD,
"Frequency of Formal Errors in Current College Writing,
or Ma and Pa Kettle Do Research"

This passage blends writing styles in several ways. First, it places informal, relaxed expressions like "mellow," "the Bad Old Days," and "folks" alongside more formal, academic phrases like "multiple-personality disorder," "student-centered," "process-based," and "arbitrary and context-bound." Even the title of the piece, "Frequency of Formal Errors in Current College Writing, or Ma and Pa Kettle Do Research," blends formal, academic usage on the left side of the comma with a popular-culture reference to the fictional movie characters Ma and Pa Kettle on the right. Second, to give vivid, concrete form to their discussion of grading disciplinarians, Connors and Lunsford conjure up such archetypal, imaginary figures as the stuffy, old-fashioned taskmasters Ms. Fidditch and Mr. Flutesnoot. Through such imaginative uses of language, Connors and Lunsford inject greater force into what might otherwise have been dry, scholarly prose.

Formal/informal mixings like this can be found in countless other texts, though more frequently in the humanities than the sciences, and more frequently still in journalism. Notice how the food industry critic Eric Schlosser describes some changes in the city of Colorado Springs in his best-selling book on fast foods in the United States.

> The loopiness once associated with Los Angeles has come full
> blown to Colorado Springs—the strange, creative energy that crops
> up where the future's consciously being made, where people walk
> the fine line separating a visionary from a total nutcase.
>
> ERIC SCHLOSSER, Fast Food Nation

Schlosser could have played it safe and referred not to the
"loopiness" but to the "eccentricity" associated with Los Angeles, or to "the fine line separating a visionary from a lunatic"
instead of " . . . a total nutcase." His decision, however, to go
with the more adventuresome, colorful terms gives a liveliness
to his writing that would have been lacking with the more
conventional terms.

Another example of writing that blends the informal with
the formal comes from an essay on the American novelist Willa
Cather by the literary critic Judith Fetterley. Discussing "how
very successful Cather has been in controlling how we think
about her," Fetterley, building on the work of another scholar,
writes as follows.

> As Merrill Skaggs has put it, "She is neurotically controlling and
> self-conscious about her work, but she knows at all points what she
> is doing. Above all else, she is self-conscious."
>
> Without question, Cather was a control freak.
>
> JUDITH FETTERLEY, "Willa Cather and the
> Question of Sympathy: The Unofficial Story"

This passage demonstrates not only that specialized phrases
from psychology like "self-conscious" and "neurotically controlling" are compatible with everyday, popular expressions like
"control freak," but also that translating the one type of language into the other, the specialized into the everyday, can help

drive home a point. By translating Skaggs's polysyllabic See p. 244 for an essay that mixes colloquial and academic styles. description of Cather as "neurotically controlling and self-conscious" into the succinct, if blunt, claim that "Without question, Cather was a control freak," Fetterley suggests that one need not choose between rarified, academic ways of talking and the everyday language of casual conversation. Indeed, her passage offers a simple recipe for blending the high and the low: first make your point in the language of a professional field, and then make it again in everyday language—a great trick, we think, for underscoring a point.

While one effect of blending languages like this is to give your writing more punch, another is to make a political statement—about the way, for example, society unfairly overvalues some dialects and devalues others. For instance, in the titles of two of her books, *Talkin and Testifyin: The Language of Black America* and *Black Talk: Words and Phrases from the Hood to the Amen Corner*, the language scholar Geneva Smitherman mixes African American vernacular phrases with more scholarly language in order to suggest, as she explicitly argues in these books, that black English vernacular is as legitimate a variety of language as "standard" English. Here are three typical passages.

In Black America, the oral tradition has served as a fundamental vehicle for gittin ovuh. That tradition preserves the Afro-American heritage and reflects the collective spirit of the race.

Blacks are quick to ridicule "educated fools," people who done gone to school and read all dem books and still don't know nothin!

. . . it is a socially approved verbal strategy for black rappers to talk about how bad they is.

GENEVA SMITHERMAN, *Talkin and Testifyin:*
The Language of Black America

In these examples, Smitherman blends the standard written English of phrases like "oral tradition" and "fundamental vehicle" with black oral vernacular like "gittin ovuh," "dem books," and "how bad they is." Indeed, she even blends standard English spelling with that of black English variants like "dem" and "ovuh," thus mimicking what some black English vernacular actually sounds like. Although some scholars might object to these unconventional practices, this is precisely Smitherman's point: that our habitual language practices need to be opened up, and that the number of participants in the academic conversation needs to be expanded.

Along similar lines, the writer and activist Gloria Anzaldúa mixes standard English with Tex-Mex, a hybrid blend of English, Castilian Spanish, a North Mexican dialect, and the Indian language Nahuatl, to make a political point about the suppression of the Spanish language in the United States.

> From this racial, ideological, cultural, and biological cross-pollinization, an "alien" consciousness is presently in the making—a new *mestiza* consciousness, *una conciencia de mujer.*
>
> GLORIA ANZALDÚA,
> *Borderlands / La Frontera: The New Mestiza*

Like Smitherman, Anzaldúa gets her point across not only through what she says but through the way she says it, literally showing that the new hybrid, or *mestiza*, consciousness that she describes is, as she puts it, "presently in the making." Ultimately, these passages suggest that blending languages—what Vershawn Ashanti Young calls "code meshing"—can call into question the very idea that the languages are distinct and separate.

WHEN TO MIX STYLES?
CONSIDER YOUR AUDIENCE AND PURPOSE

Because there are so many options in writing, you should never feel limited in your choice of words, as if such choices are set in stone. You can always experiment with your language and improve it. You can always dress it up, dress it down, or some combination of both. In dressing down your language, for example, you can make the claim that somebody "failed to notice" something by saying instead that it "flew under the radar." Or you can state that the person was "unaware" of something by saying that he was "out to lunch." You could even recast the title of this book, "*They Say / I Say*," as a teenager might say it: "She Goes / I'm Like."

But how do you know when it is better to play things straight and stick to standard English, and when to be more adventuresome and mix things up? When, in other words, should you write "failed to notice" and when is it okay (or more effective) to write "flew under the radar"? Is it *always* appropriate to mix styles? And when you do so, how do you know when enough is enough?

In all situations, think carefully about your audience and purpose. When you write a letter applying for a job, for instance, or submit a grant proposal, where your words will be weighed by an official screening body, using language that's too colloquial or slangy may well jeopardize your chances of success. On such occasions, it is usually best to err on the safe side, conforming as closely as possible to the conventions of standard written English. In other situations for other audiences, however, there is room to be more creative—in this book, for example. Ultimately, your judgments about the appropriate language for the situation should always take into account your likely audience and your purpose in writing.

Although it may have been in the past, academic writing in most disciplines today is no longer the linguistic equivalent of a black-tie affair. To succeed as a writer in college, then, you need not always limit your language to the strictly formal. Although academic writing does rely on complex sentence patterns and on specialized, disciplinary vocabularies, it is surprising how often such writing draws on the languages of the street, popular culture, our ethnic communities, and home. It is by blending these languages that what counts as "standard" English changes over time and the range of possibilities open to academic writers continues to grow.

Exercises

1. Take a paragraph from this book and dress it down, rewriting it in informal colloquial language. Then rewrite the same paragraph again by dressing it up, making it much more formal. Then rewrite the paragraph one more time in a way that blends the two styles. Share your paragraphs with a classmate, and discuss which versions are most effective and why.

2. Find something you've written for a course, and study it to see whether you've used any of your own everyday expressions, any words or structures that are not "academic." If by chance you don't find any, see if there's a place or two where shifting into more casual or unexpected language would help you make a point, get your reader's attention, or just add liveliness to your text. Be sure to keep your audience and purpose in mind, and use language that will be appropriate to both.

TEN

"BUT DON'T GET ME WRONG"

The Art of Metacommentary

—◫—

WHEN WE TELL PEOPLE that we are writing a chapter on the art of metacommentary, they often give us a puzzled look and tell us that they have no idea what "metacommentary" is. "We know what commentary is," they'll sometimes say, "but what does it mean when it's *meta*?" Our answer is that whether or not they know the term, they practice the art of metacommentary on a daily basis whenever they make a point of explaining something they've said or written: "What I meant to say was _____," "My point was not _____, but _____," or "You're probably not going to like what I'm about to say, but _____." In such cases, they are not offering new points but telling an audience how to interpret what they have already said or are about to say. In short, then, metacommentary is a way of commenting on your claims and telling others how—and how not—to think about them.

It may help to think of metacommentary as being like the chorus in a Greek play that stands to the side of the drama unfolding on the stage and explains its meaning to the audience—or like a voice-over narrator who comments on and explains the action in a television show or movie. Think of metacommentary as a sort of second text that stands alongside your main text and explains what it means. In the main text you say something; in the metatext you guide your readers in interpreting and processing what you've said.

What we are suggesting, then, is that you think of your text as two texts joined at the hip: a main text in which you make your argument and another in which you "work" your ideas, distinguishing your views from others they may be confused with, anticipating and answering objections, connecting one point to another, explaining why your claim might be controversial, and so forth. The figure below demonstrates what we mean.

THE MAIN TEXT SAYS SOMETHING, THE METATEXT TELLS READERS HOW—AND HOW NOT—TO THINK ABOUT IT.

USE METACOMMENTARY TO CLARIFY
AND ELABORATE

But why do you need metacommentary to tell readers what you mean and guide them through your text? Can't you just clearly say what you mean up front? The answer is that, no matter how clear and precise your writing is, readers can still fail to understand it in any number of ways. Even the best writers can provoke reactions in readers that they didn't intend, and even good readers can get lost in a complicated argument or fail to see how one point connects with another. Readers may also fail to see what follows from your argument, or they may follow your reasoning and examples yet fail to see the larger conclusion you draw from them. They may fail to see your argument's overall significance, or mistake what you are saying for a related argument that they have heard before but that you want to distance yourself from. As a result, no matter how straightforward a writer you are, readers still need you to help them grasp what you really mean. Because the written word is prone to so much mischief and can be interpreted in so many different ways, we need metacommentary to keep misinterpretations and other communication misfires at bay.

Another reason to master the art of metacommentary is that it will help you develop your ideas and generate more text. If you have ever had trouble producing the required number of pages for a writing project, metacommentary can help you add both length and depth to your writing. We've seen many students who try to produce a five-page paper sputter to a halt at two or three pages, complaining they've said everything they can think of about their topic. "I've stated my thesis and presented my reasons and evidence," students have told us. "What else is there to do?" It's almost as if such writers have generated a thesis and don't know what to do with it. When these students learn to use metacommentary, however, they get more out of their ideas and write longer, more substantial texts. In sum, metacommentary can help you extract the full potential from your ideas, drawing out important implications, explaining ideas from different perspectives, and so forth.

So even when you may think you've said everything possible in an argument, try inserting the following types of metacommentary.

▶ In other words, <u>she doesn't realize how right she is.</u>

▶ What _____ really means is _____.

▶ My point is not _____ but _____.

▶ Ultimately, then, my goal is to demonstrate that _____.

Ideally, such metacommentary should help you recognize some implications of your ideas that you didn't initially realize were there.

Let's look at how the cultural critic Neil Postman uses metacommentary in the following passage describing the shift in American culture when it began to move from print and reading to television and movies.

> *It is my intention in this book to show* that a great . . . shift has taken place in America, with the result that the content of much of our public discourse has become dangerous nonsense. *With this in view, my task in the chapters ahead is* straightforward. *I must, first, demonstrate* how, under the governance of the printing press, discourse in America was different from what it is now—generally coherent, serious and rational; *and then* how, under the

governance of television, it has become shriveled and absurd. *But to avoid the possibility that my analysis will be interpreted as* standard-brand academic whimpering, a kind of elitist complaint against "junk" on television, *I must first explain that . . .* I appreciate junk as much as the next fellow, *and I know full well that* the printing press has generated enough of it to fill the Grand Canyon to overflowing. Television is not old enough to have matched printing's output of junk.

NEIL POSTMAN, *Amusing Ourselves to Death:*
Public Discourse in the Age of Show Business

To see what we mean by metacommentary, look at the phrases above that we have italicized. With these moves, Postman essentially stands apart from his main ideas to help readers follow and understand what he is arguing.

> He previews what he will argue: *It is my intention in this book to show . . .*

> He spells out how he will make his argument: *With this in view, my task in these chapters . . . is. . . . I must, first, demonstrate . . . and then . . .*

> He distinguishes his argument from other arguments it may easily be confused with: *But to avoid the possibility that my analysis will be interpreted as . . . I must first explain that . . .*

TITLES AS METACOMMENTARY

Even the title of Postman's book, *Amusing Ourselves to Death: Public Discourse in the Age of Show Business*, functions as a form of metacommentary since, like all titles, it stands apart from the text itself and tells readers the book's main point: that the very pleasure provided by contemporary show business is destructive.

Titles, in fact, are one of the most important forms of metacommentary, functioning rather like carnival barkers telling passersby what they can expect if they go inside. Subtitles, too, function as metacommentary, further explaining or elaborating on the main title. The subtitle of this book, for example, not only explains that it is about "the moves that matter in academic writing," but indicates that "they say / I say" is one of these moves. Thinking of a title as metacommentary can actually help you develop sharper titles, ones that, like Postman's, give readers a hint of what your argument will be. Contrast such titles with unhelpfully open-ended ones like "Shakespeare" or "Steroids" or "English Essay," or essays with no titles at all. Essays with vague titles (or no titles) send the message that the writer has simply not bothered to reflect on what he or she is saying and is uninterested in guiding or orienting readers.

USE OTHER MOVES AS METACOMMENTARY

Many of the other moves covered in this book function as metacommentary: entertaining objections, adding transitions, framing quotations, answering "so what?" and "who cares?" When you entertain objections, you stand outside of your text and imagine what a critic might say; when you add transitions, you essentially explain the relationship between various claims. And when you answer the "so what?" and "who cares?" questions, you look beyond your central argument and explain who should be interested in it and why.

TEMPLATES FOR INTRODUCING METACOMMENTARY

TO WARD OFF POTENTIAL MISUNDERSTANDINGS

The following moves help you differentiate certain views from ones they might be mistaken for.

- **Essentially, I am arguing not that <u>we should give up the policy</u>, but that we should monitor effects far more closely.**

- **This is not to say _____, but rather _____.**

- **X is concerned less with _____ than with _____.**

TO ELABORATE ON A PREVIOUS IDEA

The following moves elaborate on a previous point, saying to readers: "In case you didn't get it the first time, I'll try saying the same thing in a different way."

- **In other words, _____.**

- **To put it another way, _____.**

- **What X is saying here is that _____.**

TO PROVIDE A ROADMAP TO YOUR TEXT

This move orients readers, clarifying where you have been and where you are going—and making it easier for them to process and follow your text.

- **Chapter 2 explores _____, while Chapter 3 examines _____.**

- **Having just argued that _____, I want now to complicate the point by _____.**

TO MOVE FROM A GENERAL CLAIM TO A SPECIFIC EXAMPLE

These moves help you explain a general point by providing a concrete example that illustrates what you're saying.

▶ For example, _____ .

▶ _____ , for instance, demonstrates _____ .

▶ Consider _____ , for example.

▶ To take a case in point, _____ .

TO INDICATE THAT A CLAIM IS MORE, LESS, OR EQUALLY IMPORTANT

The following templates help you give relative emphasis to the claim that you are introducing, showing whether that claim is of more or less weight than the previous one, or equal to it.

▶ Even more important, _____ .

▶ But above all, _____ .

▶ Incidentally, we will briefly note, _____ .

▶ Just as important, _____ .

▶ Equally, _____ .

▶ Finally, _____ .

TO EXPLAIN A CLAIM WHEN YOU ANTICIPATE OBJECTIONS

Here's a template to help you anticipate and respond to possible objections.

▶ Although some readers may object that _____ , I would answer that _____ .

TO GUIDE READERS TO YOUR MOST GENERAL POINT

These moves show that you are wrapping things up and tying up various subpoints previously made.

Chapter 6 has more templates for anticipating objections.

▶ In sum, then, _____ .

▶ My conclusion, then, is that _____ .

▶ In short, _____ .

In this chapter we have tried to show that the most persuasive writing often doubles back and comments on its own claims in ways that help readers negotiate and process them. Instead of simply piling claim upon claim, effective writers are constantly "stage managing" how their claims will be recieved. It's true of course that to be persuasive a text has to have strong claims to argue in the first place. But even the strongest arguments will flounder unless writers use metacommentary to prevent potential misreadings and make their arguments shine.

Exercises

1. Read an essay or article and annotate it to indicate the different ways the author uses metacommentary. Use the templates on pp. 135–37 as your guide. For example, you may want to circle transitional phrases and write "trans" in the margins, to put brackets around sentences that elaborate on earlier sentences and mark them "elab," or underline sentences in which the author sums up what he or she has been saying, writing "sum" in the margins.

    How does the author use metacommentary? Does the author follow any of the templates provided in this book word for word? Did you find any forms of metacommentary not discussed in this chapter? If so, can you identify them, name them, and perhaps devise templates based on them for use in your own writing? And finally, how do you think the author's use of metacommentary enhances (or harms) his or her writing?

2. Complete each of the following metacommentary templates in any way that makes sense.

▶ In making a case for the medical use of marijuana, I am not saying that _____.

▶ But my argument will do more than prove that one particular industrial chemical has certain toxic properties. In this article, I will also _____.

▶ My point about the national obsessions with sports reinforces the belief held by many _____ that _____.

▶ I believe, therefore, that the war is completely unjustified. But let me back up and explain how I arrived at this conclusion: _____. In this way, I came to believe that this war is a big mistake.

ELEVEN

"HE ~~SAYS~~ CONTENDS"

Using the Templates to Revise

—⌐◻⌐—

ONE OF THE MOST IMPORTANT stages of the writing process is revision, when you look at a draft with an eye for how well you've made your argument and what you need to do to make it better. The challenge is to figure out what needs work—and then what exactly you need to do.

Sometimes you'll have specific comments and suggestions from a teacher, noting that you need to state your position more explicitly, that your point is unclear, that you've misunderstood an author you're summarizing, and so forth. But what if you don't have any such guidance, or aren't sure what to do with it? The list of guidelines below offers help and points you back to relevant advice and templates in this book.

Do you present your argument as a response to what others say? Do you make reference to other views besides your own? Do you use voice markers to distinguish clearly for readers between your views and those of others? In order to make your argument as convincing as possible, would it help to add more concessions to opposing views, using "yes but" templates?

Asking yourself these large-scale revision questions will help you see how well you've managed the "they say / I say" framework and this in turn should help you see where further revisions are needed. The checklist below follows the order of chapters in this book.

How Do You Represent What Others Say?

Do you start with what others say? If not, try revising to do so. See pp. 23–26 for templates that can help.

Do you summarize or paraphrase what they've said? If so, have you represented their views accurately—and adequately?

Do you quote others? Do you frame each quotation successfully, integrating it into your text? Does the quotation support your argument? Have you introduced each quotation adequately, naming the person you're quoting (and saying who that person is if your readers won't know)? Do you explain in your own words what the quotation means? Do you then clearly indicate how the quotation bears on your own argument? See pp. 44–46 for tips on creating a "quotation sandwich."

Check the verbs you use to introduce any summaries and quotations: do they express accurately what was said? If you've used common signal phrases such as "X said" or "Y believes," is there a verb that reflects more accurately what was said? See pp. 39–40 for a list of verbs for introducing summaries and quotations.

Have you documented all summaries and quotations, both with parenthetical documentation in your text and a references or works cited list?

Do you remind readers of what others say at various points throughout your text? If not, see pp. 27–28 for help revising in order to do so.

What Do *You* Say?

Do you agree, disagree, or both with those you're responding to? Have you said so explicitly?

If you disagree, do you give reasons why you disagree? If you agree, what more have you added to the conversation? If you both agree and disagree, do you do so without confusing readers or seeming evasive?

Have you stated your position and the one it responds to as a connected unit?

What reasons and evidence do you offer to support your "I say"? In other words, do your argument and the argument you are responding to—your "I say" and "they say"—address the same topic or issue, or does a switch occur that takes you on a tangent that will confuse readers? One way to ensure that your "I say" and "they say" are aligned rather than seeming like ships passing in the night is to use the same key terms in both. See Chapter 8 for tips on how to do so.

Will readers be able to distinguish what you say from what others say? See Chapter 5 for advice about using voice markers to make that distinction clear, especially at moments when you are moving from your view to someone else's view or back.

Have You Introduced Any Naysayers?

Have you acknowledged likely objections to your argument? If so, have you represented these views fairly—and responded to them persuasively? See Chapter 6 for tips on how to do so.

If not, think about what other perspectives exist on your topic, and incorporate them into your draft.

Have You Used Metacommentary to Clarify What You Do or Don't Mean?

No matter how clearly you've explained your points, it's a good idea to explain what you mean—or *don't* mean—with phrases like "in other words" or "don't get me wrong." See Chapter 10 for examples of how to do so.

Do you have a title? If so, does it tell readers what your main point or issue is, and does it do so in a lively manner? Should you add a subtitle to elaborate on the title?

Have You Tied It All Together?

Can readers follow your argument from one sentence and paragraph to the next and see how each successive point supports your overall argument?

Check your use of transitions, words like "however" and "therefore." Such words make clear how your ideas relate to one another; if you need to add transitions, see pp. 109–10 for a complete list.

Check your use of pointing words. Do you use common pointers like "this" and "that," which help lead readers from one sentence to the next? If so, is it always clear what "this" and "that" refer to, or do you need to add nouns in order to avoid ambiguity? See pp. 112–14 for help working with pointing words.

Have you used what we call "repetition with a difference" to help connect parts of your argument? See pp. 114–18 for examples of how to do so.

Have You Shown Why Your Argument Matters?

Don't assume that readers will see why your argument is important—or why they should care. Be sure that you have told them why. See Chapter 7 if you need help.

A REVISED STUDENT ESSAY

Here is an example of how one student, Antonia Peacocke, used this book to revise an essay. Starting with an article she'd written for her high school newspaper, Peacocke then followed the advice in our book as she turned her article into a college level academic essay. Her original article was a brief account of why she liked *Family Guy*, and her first step in revising was to open with a "they say" and an "I say," previewing her overall argument in brief form at the essay's beginning. While her original version had acknowledged that many find the show "objectionable," she hadn't named these people or indicated why they didn't like the show. In her revised version, after doing further research, Peacocke identified those with whom she disagreed and responded to them at length, as the essay itself illustrates.

In addition, Peacocke strengthened existing transitions, added new ones, and clarified the stakes of her argument, saying more explicitly why readers should care about whether *Family Guy* is good or bad. In making these revisions she gave her own spin to several templates in this book.

We've annotated Peacocke's essay in the margins to point out particular rhetorical moves discussed in our book and the chapters in which those discussions appear. We hope studying her essay and our annotations will suggest how you might craft and revise your own writing.

Antonia Peacocke wrote this essay in the summer between high school and her first year at Harvard. She is now a PhD student in philosophy at the University of California at Berkeley.

Family Guy and Freud: Jokes and Their Relation to the Unconscious

ANTONIA PEACOCKE

WHILE SLOUCHING in front of the television after a long day, you probably don't think a lot about famous psychologists of the twentieth century. Somehow, these figures don't come up often in prime-time—or even daytime—TV programming. Whether you're watching *Living Lohan* or the *NewsHour*, the likelihood is that you are not thinking of Sigmund Freud, even if you've heard of his book *Jokes and Their Relation to the Unconscious*. I say that you should be.

What made me think of Freud in the first place, actually, was *Family Guy*, the cartoon created by Seth MacFarlane. (Seriously—stay with me here.) Any of my friends can tell you that this program holds endless fascination for me; as a matter of fact, my high school rag-sheet "perfect mate" was the baby Stewie Griffin, a character on the show (see Fig. 1). Embarrassingly enough, I have almost reached the point at which I can perform

> Starts with what others are saying (Chapter 1)

> Responds to what they say (Chapter 4)

> Metacommentary wards off potential skepticism (Chapter 10)

one-woman versions of several episodes. I know every
website that streams the show for free, and I still refuse to
return the five *Family Guy* DVDs a friend lent me in 2006.
Before I was such a devotee, however, I was adamantly
opposed to the program for its particular brand of humor.

It will come as no surprise that I was not alone in this
view; many still denounce *Family Guy* as bigoted and crude.
New York Times journalist Stuart Elliott claimed just this
year that "the characters on the Fox television series *Family
Guy* . . . purposely offen[d] just about every group of people

> Quotes and
> summarizes
> what others
> say (Chapters
> 2 and 3)

Fig 1. Peter and Stewie Griffin (Everett Collection)

you could name." Likewise Stephen Dubner, co-author of *Freakonomics,* called *Family Guy* "a cartoon comedy that packs more gags per minute about race, sex, incest, bestiality, etc. than any other show [he] can think of." Comparing its level of offense to that of Don Imus's infamous comments about the Rutgers women's basketball team in the same year, comments that threw the popular CBS radio talk-show host off the air, Dubner said he wondered why Imus couldn't get away with as much as *Family Guy* could.

Dubner did not know about all the trouble *Family Guy* has had. In fact, it must be one of the few television shows in history that has been canceled not just once, but twice. After its premiere in April 1999, the show ran until August 2000, but was besieged by so many complaints, some of them from MacFarlane's old high school headmaster, Rev. Richardson W. Schell, that Fox shelved it until July 2001 (Weinraub). Still afraid of causing a commotion, though, Fox had the cartoon censored and irregularly scheduled; as a result, its ratings fell so low that 2002 saw its second cancellation (Weinraub). But then it came back with a vengeance—I'll get into that later.

Family Guy has found trouble more recently, too. In 2007, comedian Carol Burnett sued Fox for 6 million dollars, claiming that the show's parody of the Charwoman, a character that she had created for *The Carol Burnett Show,* not only violated copyright but also besmirched the character's name in revenge for Burnett's refusal to grant permission to use her theme song ("Carol Burnett Sues over *Family Guy* Parody"). The suit came after MacFarlane had made the Charwoman into a cleaning woman for a pornography store in one episode of *Family Guy*. Burnett lost, but U.S. district judge Dean Pregerson agreed that he could "fully appreciate how distasteful and offensive the segment [was] to Ms. Burnett" (qtd. in Grossberg).

I must admit, I can see how parts of the show might seem offensive if taken at face value. Look, for example, at the mock fifties instructional video that features in the episode "I Am Peter, Hear Me Roar."

> Represents a naysayer's objections fairly (Chapter 6)

[*The screen becomes black and white. Vapid music plays in the background. The screen reads* "WOMEN IN THE WORKPLACE *ca.* 1956," *then switches to a shot of an office with various women working on typewriters. A businessman speaks to the camera.*]

BUSINESSMAN: Irrational and emotionally fragile by nature, female coworkers are a peculiar animal. They are very insecure about their appearance. Be sure to tell them how good they look every day, even if they're homely and unkempt. [*He turns to an unattractive female typist.*] You're doing a great job, Muriel, and you're prettier than Mamie van Doren! [*She smiles. He grins at the camera, raising one eyebrow knowingly, and winks.*]

And remember, nothing says "Good job!" like a firm open-palm slap on the behind. [*He walks past a woman bent over a file cabinet and demonstrates enthusiastically. She smiles, looking flattered. He grins at the camera again as the music comes to an end.*]

Laughing at something so blatantly sexist could cause anyone a pang of guilt, and before I thought more about the show this seemed to be a huge problem. I agreed with Dubner, and I failed to see how anyone could laugh at such jokes without feeling at least slightly ashamed.

> Agrees, but with a difference (Chapter 4)

Soon, though, I found myself forced to give *Family Guy* a chance. It was simply everywhere: my brother and many of my friends watched it religiously, and its devoted fans relentlessly proselytized for it. In case you have any doubts about its immense popularity, consider these facts. On Facebook, the universal forum for my generation, there are currently 23 separate *Family Guy* fan groups with a combined membership of 1,669 people (compared with only 6 groups protesting against *Family Guy*, with 105 members total). Users of the well-respected Internet Movie Database rate the show 8.8 out of 10. The box-set DVDs were the best-selling television DVDs of 2003 in the United States (Moloney). Among the public and within the industry, the show receives fantastic acclaim; it has won eight awards, including three prime-time Emmys (IMDb). Most importantly, each time it was cancelled fans provided the brute force necessary to get it

> Anticipates a naysayer's skepticism (Chapter 6)

back on the air. In 2000, online campaigns did the trick; in 2002, devotees demonstrated outside Fox Studios, refused to watch the Fox network, and boycotted any companies that advertised on it (Moloney). Given the show's high profile, both with my friends and family and in the world at large, it would have been more work for me to avoid the Griffin family than to let myself sink into their animated world.

With more exposure, I found myself crafting a more positive view of *Family Guy*. Those who don't often watch the program, as Dubner admits he doesn't, could easily come to think that the cartoon takes pleasure in controversial humor just for its own sake. But those who pay more attention and think about the creators' intentions can see that *Family Guy* intelligently satirizes some aspects of American culture.

> Distinguishes between what others say and what she says (Chapter 5)

Some of this satire is actually quite obvious. Take, for instance, a quip Brian the dog makes about Stewie's literary choices in a fourth-season episode, "PTV." (Never mind that a dog and a baby can both read and hold lengthy conversations.)

> Mixes academic and colloquial styles (Chapter 9)

[*The Griffins are in their car. Brian turns to Stewie, who sits reading in his car seat.*]

> Uses a quotation sandwich to explicate this excerpt (Chapter 3)

BRIAN: *East of Eden*? So you, you, you pretty much do whatever Oprah tells you to, huh?
STEWIE: You know, this book's been around for fifty years. It's a classic.

> BRIAN: But you just got it last week. And there's a giant Oprah sticker on the front.
>
> STEWIE: Oh—oh—oh, is that what that is? Oh, lemme just peel that right off.
>
> BRIAN: So, uh, what are you gonna read after that one?
>
> STEWIE: Well, she hasn't told us yet—damn!

Brian and Stewie demonstrate insightfully and comically how Americans are willing to follow the instructions of a celebrity blindly—and less willing to admit that they are doing so.

The more off-color jokes, though, those that give *Family Guy* a bad name, attract a different kind of viewer. Such viewers are not "rats in a behaviorist's maze," as *Slate* writer Dana Stevens labels modern American television consumers in her article "Thinking Outside the Idiot Box." They are conscious and critical viewers, akin to the "screenagers" identified by Douglas Rushkoff in an essay entitled "Bart Simpson: Prince of Irreverence" (294). They are not—and this I cannot stress enough, self-serving as it may seem—immoral or easily manipulated people.

Rushkoff's piece analyzes the humor of *The Simpsons*, a show criticized for many of the same reasons as *Family Guy*. "The people I call 'screenagers,'" Rushkoff explains, ". . . speak the media language better than their parents do and they see through clumsy attempts to program them into submission" (294). He claims that gaming technology has

> Distinguishes what others say from what she says (Chapter 5)

made my generation realize that television is programmed for us with certain intentions; since we can control characters in the virtual world, we are more aware that characters on TV are similarly controlled. "Sure, [these 'screenagers'] might sit back and watch a program now and again," Rushkoff explains, "but they do so voluntarily, and with full knowledge of their complicity. It is not an involuntary surrender" (294). In his opinion, our critical eyes and our unwillingness to be programmed by the programmers make for an entirely new relationship with the shows we watch. Thus we enjoy *The Simpsons'* parodies of mass media culture since we are skeptical of it ourselves.

Rushkoff's argument about *The Simpsons* actually applies to *Family Guy* as well, except in one dimension: Rushkoff writes that *The Simpsons'* creators do "not comment on social issues as much as they [do on] the media imagery around a particular social issue" (296). MacFarlane and company seem to do the reverse. Trusting in their viewers' ability to analyze what they are watching, the creators of *Family Guy* point out the weaknesses and defects of U.S. society in a mocking and sometimes intolerant way.

Taken in this light, the "instructional video" quoted above becomes not only funny but also insightful. In its satire, viewers can recognize the sickly sweet and falsely sensitive sexism of the 1950s in observing just how conveniently

> Uses transitions to connect the parts (Chapter 8)

self-serving the speaker of the video appears. The message of the clip denounces and ridicules sexism rather than condoning it. It is an excerpt that perfectly exemplifies the bold-faced candor of the show, from which it derives a lot of its appeal.

Making such comically outrageous remarks on the air also serves to expose certain prejudiced attitudes as outrageous themselves. Taking these comments at face value would be as foolish as taking Jonathan Swift's "Modest Proposal" seriously. Furthermore, while they put bigoted words into the mouths of their characters, the show's writers cannot be accused of portraying these characters positively. Peter Griffin, the "family guy" of the show's title, probably says and does the most offensive things of all—but as a lazy, overweight, and insensitive failure of a man, he is hardly presented as someone to admire. Nobody in his or her right mind would observe Peter's behavior and deem it worth emulation.

Family Guy has its own responses to accusations of crudity. In the episode "PTV," Peter sets up his own television station broadcasting from home and the Griffin family finds itself confronting the Federal Communications Commission directly (see Fig. 2 for a picture of the whole family). The episode makes many tongue-in-cheek jabs at the FCC, some of which are sung in a rousing musical number, but also sneaks in some of the creator's own

Fig 2. The Griffin family watches TV. (Everett Collection)

opinions. The plot comes to a climax when the FCC begins to censor "real life" in the town of Quahog; officials place black censor bars in front of newly showered Griffins and blow foghorns whenever characters curse. MacFarlane makes an important point: that no amount of television censorship will ever change the harsh nature of reality— and to censor reality is mere folly. Likewise, he puts explicit arguments about censorship into lines spoken by his characters, as when Brian says that "responsibility lies with the parents [and] there are plenty of things that are much worse for children than television."

It must be said too that not all of *Family Guy's* humor could be construed as offensive. Some of its jokes are more tame and insightful, the kind you might expect from *The New Yorker*. The following light commentary on the usefulness of high school algebra from "When You Wish Upon a Weinstein" could hardly be accused of upsetting anyone—except, perhaps, a few high school math teachers.

> [*Shot of Peter on the couch and his son Chris lying at his feet and doing homework.*]
>
> CHRIS: Dad, can you help me with my math? [My teacher] says if I don't learn it, I won't be able to function in the real world.
>
> [*Shot of Chris standing holding a map in a run-down gas station next to an attendant in overalls and a trucker cap reading "PUMP THIS." The attendant speaks with a Southern accent and gestures casually to show the different road configurations.*]
>
> ATTENDANT: Okay, now what you gotta do is go down the road past the old Johnson place, and you're gonna find two roads, one parallel and one perpendicular. Now keep going until you come to a highway that

bisects it at a 45-degree angle. [*Crosses his arms.*] Solve for x.

[*Shot of Chris lying on the ground next to the attendant in fetal position, sucking his thumb. His map lies abandoned near him.*]

In fact, *Family Guy* does not aim to hurt, and its creators take certain measures to keep it from hitting too hard. In an interview on *Access Hollywood*, Seth MacFarlane plainly states that there are certain jokes too upsetting to certain groups to go on the air. Similarly, to ensure that the easily misunderstood show doesn't fall into the hands of those too young to understand it, Fox will not license *Family Guy* rights to any products intended for children under the age of fourteen (Elliott).

However, this is not to say that MacFarlane's mission is corrective or noble. It is worth remembering that he wants only to amuse, a goal for which he was criticized by several of his professors at the Rhode Island School of Design (Weinraub). For this reason, his humor can be dangerous. On the one hand, I don't agree with George Will's reductive and generalized statement in his article "Reality Television: Oxymoron" that "entertainment seeking a mass audience is ratcheting up the violence, sexuality, and degradation, becoming increasingly coarse and trying to be . . . shocking in an unshockable society." I believe *Family Guy*

> **Uses transitions to connect the parts (Chapter 8)**

> **Agrees and disagrees; makes concessions while standing her ground (Chapters 4 and 6)**

has its intelligent points, and some of its seemingly "coarse" scenes often have hidden merit. I must concede, though, that a few of the show's scenes seem to be doing just what Will claims; sometimes the creators do seem to cross—or, perhaps, eagerly race past—the line of indecency. In one such crude scene, an elderly dog slowly races a paraplegic and Peter, who has just been hit by a car, to get to a severed finger belonging to Peter himself ("Whistle While Your Wife Works"). Nor do I find it particularly funny when Stewie physically abuses Brian in a bloody fight over gambling money ("Patriot Games").

Thus, while *Family Guy* can provide a sort of relief by breaking down taboos, we must still wonder whether or not these taboos exist for a reason. An excess of offensive jokes, especially those that are often misconstrued, can seem to grant tacit permission to think offensively if it's done for comedy— and laughing at others' expense can be cruel, no matter how funny. Jokes all have their origins, and the funniest ones are those that hit home the hardest; if we listen to Freud, these are the ones that let our animalistic and aggressive impulses surface from the unconscious. The distinction between a shamelessly candid but insightful joke and a merely shameless joke is a slight but important one. While I love *Family Guy* as much as any fan, it's important not to lose sight of what's truly unfunny in real life—even as we appreciate what is hilarious in fiction.

> Concludes by showing who cares and why her argument matters (Chapter 7)

Works Cited

"Carol Burnett Sues over *Family Guy* Parody." *CBC.com.*
    Canadian Broadcasting Centre, 16 Mar. 2007. Web.
    14 July 2008.

Dubner, Stephen J. "Why Is *Family Guy* Okay When Imus
    Wasn't?" Web log post. *Freakonomics: The Hidden
    Side of Everything*, 3 Dec. 2007. Web. 14 July 2008.

Elliott, Stuart. "Crude? So What? These Characters Still
    Find Work in Ads." *New York Times*. New York
    Times, 18 June 2008. Web. 14 July 2008.

Facebook. Search for *Family Guy* under "Groups." 14 July
    2008.

Freud, Sigmund. *Jokes and Their Relation to the
    Unconscious*. 1905. Trans. James Strachey. New York:
    Norton, 1989. Print.

Grossberg, Josh. "Carol Burnett Can't Stop Stewie."
    E! Online. E! Entertainment Television, 5 June 2007.
    Web. 14 Jul. 2008.

"I Am Peter, Hear Me Roar." *Family Guy*. Prod. Seth
    MacFarlane. Twentieth Century Fox. 28 Mar. 2000.
    Web. 14 July 2008.

Internet Movie Database. *Family Guy*. Ed. unknown. Last
    update date unknown. Web. 14 July 2008.

MacFarlane, Seth. Interview. *Access Hollywood*. Online
    posting on YouTube. 8 May 2007. Web. 14 July 2008.

Moloney, Ben Adam. "*Family Guy*—The TV Series." British Broadcasting Corporation. 30 Sept. 2004. Web. 14 Jul. 2008.

"Patriot Games." *Family Guy*. Prod. Seth MacFarlane. Twentieth Century Fox. 29 Jan. 2006. Web. 22 July 2008.

"PTV." *Family Guy*. Prod. Seth MacFarlane. Twentieth Century Fox. 6 Nov. 2005. Web. 14 July 2008.

Rushkoff, Douglas. "Bart Simpson: Prince of Irreverence." *Leaving Springfield: The Simpsons and the Possibility of Oppositional Culture*. Ed. John Alberti. Detroit: Wayne State UP, 2004. 292–301. Print.

Stevens, Dana. "Thinking Outside the Idiot Box." *Slate*. Slate, 25 Mar. 2005. Web. 14 Jul. 2008.

Weinraub, Bernard. "The Young Guy of 'Family Guy': A 30-Year-Old's Cartoon Hit Makes an Unexpected Comeback." *New York Times*. New York Times, 7 Jul. 2004. Web. 14 July 2008.

"When You Wish Upon a Weinstein." *Family Guy*. Prod. Seth MacFarlane. Twentieth Century Fox. 9 Nov. 2003. Web. 22 July 2008.

"Whistle While Your Wife Works." *Family Guy*. Prod. Seth MacFarlane. Twentieth Century Fox. 12 Nov. 2006. Web. 14 July 2008.

Will, George F. "Reality Television: Oxymoron." *Washington Post* 21 June 2001: A25. Print.

4

IN SPECIFIC
ACADEMIC CONTEXTS

"I TAKE YOUR POINT"

Entering Class Discussions

HAVE YOU EVER been in a class discussion that feels less like a genuine meeting of the minds than like a series of discrete, disconnected monologues? You make a comment, say, that seems provocative to you, but the classmate who speaks after you makes no reference to what you said, instead going off in an entirely different direction. Then, the classmate who speaks next makes no reference either to you or to anyone else, making it seem as if everyone in the conversation is more interested in their own ideas than in actually conversing with anyone else.

We like to think that the principles this book advances can help improve class discussions, which increasingly include various forms of online communication. Particularly important for class discussion is the point that our own ideas become more cogent and powerful the more responsive we are to others, and the more we frame our claims not in isolation but as responses to what others before us have said. Ultimately, then, a good face-to-face classroom discussion (or online communication) doesn't just happen spontaneously. It requires the same sorts of disciplined moves and practices used in many writing situations, particularly that of identifying to what and to whom you are responding.

FRAME YOUR COMMENTS AS A RESPONSE
TO SOMETHING THAT HAS ALREADY BEEN SAID

The single most important thing you need to do when joining a class discussion is to link what you are about to say to something that has already been said.

▸ I really liked Aaron's point about <u>the two sides being closer than they seem</u>. I'd add that <u>both seem rather moderate</u>.

▸ I take your point, Nadia, that _____ . Still . . .

▸ Though Sheila and Ryan seem to be at odds about _____, they may actually not be all that far apart.

In framing your comments this way, it is usually best to name both the person and the idea you're responding to. If you name the person alone ("I agree with Aaron because _____"), it may not be clear to listeners what part of what Aaron said you are referring to. Conversely, if you only summarize what Aaron said without naming him, you'll probably leave your classmates wondering whose comments you're referring to.

But won't you sound stilted and deeply redundant in class if you try to restate the point your classmate just made? After all, in the case of the first template above, the entire class will have just heard Aaron's point about the two sides being closer than they seem. Why then would you need to restate it?

We agree that in oral situations, it does often sound artificial to restate what others just said precisely because they just said it. It would be awkward if, on being asked to pass the salt at lunch, one were to reply: "If I understand you correctly, you have asked me to pass the salt. Yes, I can, and here it is." But in oral discussions about complicated issues that are open to multiple interpretations, we usually do need to resummarize what others have said to make sure that everyone is on the same page. Since Aaron may have made several points when he spoke and may have been followed by other commentators, the class will probably need you to summarize which point of his you are referring to. And even if Aaron made only one point, restating that point is helpful, not only to remind the group what his point was (since some may have missed or forgotten it) but also to make sure that he, you, and others have interpreted his point in the same way.

TO CHANGE THE SUBJECT,
INDICATE EXPLICITLY THAT YOU ARE DOING SO

It is fine to try to change the conversation's direction. There's just one catch: you need to make clear to listeners that this is what you are doing. For example:

▸ So far we have been talking about <u>the characters in the film</u>. But isn't the real issue here <u>the cinematography</u>?

▸ I'd like to change the subject to one that hasn't yet been addressed.

You can try to change the subject without indicating that you are doing so. But you risk that your comment will come across as irrelevant rather than as a thoughtful contribution that moves the conversation forward.

BE EVEN MORE EXPLICIT
THAN YOU WOULD BE IN WRITING

Because listeners in an oral discussion can't go back and reread what you just said, they are more easily overloaded than are readers of a print text. For this reason, in a class discussion you will do well to take some extra steps to help listeners follow your train of thought. (1) When you make a comment, limit yourself to one point only though you can elaborate on this point, fleshing it out with examples and evidence. If you feel you must make two points, either unite them under one larger umbrella point, or make one point first and save the other for later. Trying to bundle two or more claims into one comment can result in neither getting the attention it deserves. (2) Use metacommentary to highlight your key point so that listeners can readily grasp it.

▸ In other words, what I'm trying to get at here is _____.

▸ My point is this: _____.

▸ My point, though, is not _____, but _____.

▸ This distinction is important because _____.

"IMHO"

Is Digital Communication Good or Bad—or Both?

———————

YOU MAY WONDER what our advice in this book about enter-ing conversations and debates has to do with one of the major innovations in our society, the online technologies through which we now do much of our reading and writing. You may have heard parents and journalists complain that smartphones, iPads, and other electronic devices that seem almost wired into our brains are destroying our ability to think, communicate, and interact with others. At the same time, you've also prob-ably heard counterarguments to the effect that, on the con-trary, these digital technologies actually stretch the mind, bring people together, and even make us better writers.

These arguments are part of a set of interrelated debates that are taking place today, sometimes in the blogosphere itself, among journalists, academic researchers, and other commenta-tors. In some of these debates, those who extol their virtues argue that today's new online technologies make us smarter by exposing us to a wide range of perspectives and giving us instant access to massive stores of new information. Whereas once we would have had to spend hours burrowing through dusty library shelves to find the information we need, today we can access the same information with a click of a mouse in the comfort of our homes. Thanks to the internet, our potential knowledge is now thousands of times greater than ever before. How could such a development not be a huge plus for any writer?

The critics, however, retort that, far from making us smarter, online technologies are actually making us dumber, even in our capacity as writers. According to these critics, many online researchers end their investigations at the first entry that comes up in a Google search (often in Wikipedia), and the constraints of email, text messaging, and tweeting force us to communicate in reductive sound bites and inane abbreviations (OMG! LOL! IMHO!). The critics also charge that the very volume of new information that the web makes so easily available overwhelms us and prevents us from thinking clearly. So much comes at us so fast from electronic sources that we can no longer think straight or organize our thoughts into clear writing. The greater the mountain of information we have at our fingertips, say the critics, the less chance there is that we will find the fraction of it that is most valuable and useful to focus on and respond to. As a result, according to one critic, researcher Clifford Nass, the multitasking encouraged by the web and other digital technologies is making student writers less able to sustain a "big idea" in an essay and more prone to write in "little bursts and snippets" (Nass).

Yet many challenge this pessimistic view. Rhetoric and composition professor Andrea Lunsford rejects the notion that "Google is making us stupid," that "Facebook is frying our brains," and that the web is depriving students of the ability to express ideas (qtd. in Haven). According to Lunsford, reporting on a five-year research project, the Stanford Study of Writing, student writers today are remarkably "adept at crafting messages that will reach their intended audience *because* of their constant use of social media" (Lunsford). That is, today's students are proficient "at what rhetoricians call *kairos*—assessing their audience and adapting their tone and technique to best get their point across" (Thompson).

There is also disagreement over whether online technologies create or undermine genuine conversation and community. On the one hand, some praise the web for its ability to bring people from distant places together who otherwise would remain strangers, enabling them to interact more easily with others through such mediums as email, blogs, videochat, and social networking sites. Those who make this argument might claim that our advice in this book to present your ideas as a response to the ideas of others lends itself well to online communication. After all, the internet allows us to post something and then get quick, even instantaneous responses. It also allows us more easily to access multiple perspectives on any topic and then directly insert the voices of others into our text in links that readers can click on.

Critics, on the other hand, question the quality of the conversations that take place online, arguing that these conversations are rarely genuine meetings of minds and noting that online writers often speak past rather than to or with one another. Because online writers can hit "send" before reflecting, as writers more likely would using slower and more deliberate print media, these critics charge that true debate in which the various parties really listen to one another is exceedingly rare on the web. In other words, communicating online tends to undermine true conversation because writers can too easily dismiss or ignore other points of view, and thus are more likely to engage in egotistical monologues in which they use what others say as a pretext for expounding their own already established opinions.

So go some of the arguments pro and con about the impact of online technologies on our thinking and our communicative habits, including our writing. Though we agree that the internet has given us access to previously unimaginable stores of information and greatly expanded our range of communication—and that it potentially broadens our perspectives—we think the critics have a point in noting that many conversations on the web are not exchanges so much as monologues in which writers pass one another without intersecting. We ourselves have been dismayed when our own online articles have drawn comments that begin, "I haven't read Graff and Birkenstein's article, but in my opinion. . . ." In our view, the best remedy for such failures of communication is to improve the listening and summarizing skills we emphasize in this book, whether these skills are practiced online, offline, or even on a stone tablet.

As for how these digital technologies have influenced student writing, our own view, based on the writing we have seen in our combined seventy years of teaching, is that that this influence is neither disastrous, as the critics fear, nor wonderfully revolutionary, as the proponents claim. Contrary to Nass, student writers found it challenging to sustain a "big idea" long before the advent of the worldwide web, and, contrary to Lunsford, we see no evidence that tweeting and posting have made writers more adept at reaching audiences. As we see it, online technologies only recycle any difficulties writers have reaching audiences; if a writer has trouble reaching audiences in one medium, he or she will have it in another. A student of ours, for example, writing to an audience of his classmates on a course listserv, began a post in the following way:

"Going off what Meg said, I would argue..."

His audience was mystified, since nobody, including Meg herself, could remember what she had said. As this incident illustrates, the immediacy of online writing—not just in course listservs, but in emails, social media, and so forth—makes it appear so much like oral communication that we are seduced into forgetting that it is still a form of writing and therefore very often requires the mastery of formal conventions, in this case that of summarizing what has previously been said. It is hard to imagine any writer, as we have already suggested, who does not struggle with the rhetorical moves of argument, from summarizing, explaining, and quoting what others say to responding to what they say, and the myriad other competencies covered in this book.

Our purpose in this brief chapter, however, is not to try to settle these debates, but to invite *you* to think about how digital technologies affect your work as a reader and writer. Do these technologies make it easier to join conversations? Do they improve or degrade your thinking and writing? What is your opinion and why? To help you answer these questions, we conclude, then, with a couple of exercises that invite you to pick up where we have left off—and, as Kenneth Burke said, to put in your own oar.

WORKS CITED

Haven, Cynthia. "The New Literacy: Stanford Study Finds Richness and Complexity in Students' Writing." *Stanford Report*. Stanford University, 12 Oct. 2009. Web. 14 Nov. 2013.

Lunsford, Andrea. "Everyone's an Author." Presentation to Norton travelers, Park City. 6 Aug. 2012. Lecture.

Nass, Clifford. Interview. *Frontline*. PBS. WGBH, Boston, 1 Dec. 2009. Web. 14 Nov. 2013.

Thompson, Clive. "Clive Thompson on the New Literacy." *Wired*. Condé Nast, 24 Aug. 2009. Web. 14 Nov. 2013.

Exercises

1. Have we formulated the debatable issues above in a useful way? Have we left out anything important? Write an essay in which you summarize some of our commentary as your "they say" and offer your own response, whether to disagree, agree with a difference, or reframe the issues in some way.

2. As a test case for thinking about the questions raised in this chapter, go to the blog that accompanies this book, **theysayiblog.com**. Examine some of the exchanges that appear there and evaluate the quality of the responses. For example, how well do the participants in these exchanges summarize one another's claims before making their own responses? How would you characterize any discussion? Is there a true meeting of the minds or are writers sometimes caricatured or treated as straw men? How do these online discussions compare with the face-to-face discussions you have in class? What advantages does each offer? Go to other blogs on topics that interest you and ask these same questions.

FOURTEEN

"WHAT'S MOTIVATING THIS WRITER?"

Reading for the Conversation

———

"WHAT IS THE AUTHOR'S ARGUMENT? What is he or she trying to say?" For many years, these were the first questions we would ask our classes in a discussion of an assigned reading. The discussion that resulted was often halting, as our students struggled to get a handle on the argument, but eventually, after some awkward silences, the class would come up with something we could all agree was an accurate summary of the author's main thesis. Even after we'd gotten over that hurdle, however, the discussion would often still seem forced, and would limp along as we all struggled with the question that naturally arose next: Now that we had determined what the author was saying, what did we ourselves have to say?

For a long time we didn't worry much about these halting discussions, justifying them to ourselves as the predictable result of assigning difficult, challenging readings. Several years ago, however, as we started writing this book and began thinking about writing as the art of entering conversations, we latched onto the idea of leading with some different questions: "What other argument(s) is the writer responding to?" "Is the writer disagreeing or agreeing with something, and if so what?" "What is motivating the writer's argument?" "Are there other ideas that you have encountered in this class or elsewhere that might be pertinent?" The results were often striking. The discussions that followed tended to be far livelier and to draw in a greater number of students. We were still asking students to look for the main argument, but we were now asking them to see that argument as a response to some other argument that provoked it, gave it a reason for being, and helped all of us see why we should care about it.

What had happened, we realized, was that by changing the opening question, we changed the way our students approached reading, and perhaps the way they thought about academic work in general. Instead of thinking of the argument of a text as an isolated entity, they now thought of that argument as one that responded to and provoked other arguments. Since they were now dealing not with *one* argument but at least *two* (the author's argument and the one[s] he or she was responding to), they now had alternative ways of seeing the topic at hand. This meant that, instead of just trying to understand the view presented by the author, they were more able to question that view intelligently and engage in the type of discussion and debate that is the hallmark of a college education. In our discussions, animated debates often arose between students who found the author's argument convincing and others who were more convinced by the view it was challenging. In the best of these debates, the binary positions would be questioned by other students, who suggested each was too simple, that both might be right or that a third alternative was possible. Still other students might object that the discussion thus far had missed the author's real point and suggest that we all go back to the text and pay closer attention to what it actually said.

We eventually realized that the move from reading for the author's argument in isolation to reading for how the author's argument is in conversation with the arguments of others helps readers become active, critical readers rather than passive recipients of knowledge. On some level, reading for the conversation is more rigorous and demanding than reading for what one author says. It asks that you determine not only what the author thinks, but how what the author thinks fits with what others think, and ultimately with what you yourself think. Yet on another level, reading this way is a lot simpler and more familiar than reading for the thesis alone, since it returns writing to the familiar, everyday act of communicating with other people about real issues.

DECIPHERING THE CONVERSATION

We suggest, then, that when assigned a reading, you imagine the author not as sitting alone in an empty room hunched over a desk or staring at a screen, but as sitting in a crowded coffee shop talking to others who are making claims that he or she is engaging with. In other words, imagine the author as participating in an ongoing, multisided conversation in which everyone is trying to persuade others to agree or at least to take his or her position seriously.

The trick in reading for the conversation is to figure out *what views the author is responding to* and *what the author's own argument is*—or, to put it in the terms used in this book, to determine the "they say" and how the author responds to it.

One of the challenges in reading for the "they say" and "I say" can be figuring out which is which, since it may not be obvious when writers are summarizing others and when they are speaking for themselves. Readers need to be alert for any changes in voice that a writer might make, since instead of using explicit road-mapping phrases like "although many believe," authors may simply summarize the view that they want to engage with and indicate only subtly that it is not their own.

Consider again the opening to the selection by David Zinczenko on p. 241.

> If ever there were a newspaper headline custom made for Jay Leno's monologue, this was it. Kids taking on McDonald's this week, suing the company for making them fat. Isn't that like middle-aged men suing Porsche for making them get speeding tickets? Whatever happened to personal responsibility?
>
> I tend to sympathize with these portly fast-food patrons, though. Maybe that's because I used to be one of them.
>
> DAVID ZINCZENKO, "Don't Blame the Eater"

Whenever we teach this passage, some students inevitably assume that Zinczenko must be espousing the view expressed in his first paragraph: that suing McDonald's is ridiculous. When their reading is challenged by their classmates, these students point to the page and reply, "Look. It's right here on the page. This is what Zinczenko wrote. These are his exact words." The assumption these students are making is that if something appears on the page, the author must endorse it. In fact, however, we ventriloquize views that we don't believe in, and may in fact passionately disagree with, all the time. The central clues that Zinczenko disagrees with the view expressed in his opening

See Chapter 6 for more discussion of naysayers.

paragraph come in the second paragraph, when he finally offers a first-person declaration and uses a contrastive transition, "though," thereby resolving any questions about where he stands.

WHEN THE "THEY SAY" IS UNSTATED

Another challenge can be identifying the "they say" when it is not explicitly identified. Whereas Zinczenko offers an up-front summary of the view he is responding to, other writers assume that their readers are so familiar with these views that they need not name or summarize them. In such cases, you the reader have to reconstruct the unstated "they say" that is motivating the text through a process of inference.

See, for instance, if you can reconstruct the position that Tamara Draut is challenging in the opening paragraph of her essay "The Growing College Gap."

> "The first in her family to graduate from college." How many times have we heard that phrase, or one like it, used to describe a successful American with a modest background? In today's United States, a four-year degree has become the all-but-official ticket to middle-class security. But if your parents don't have much money or higher education in their own right, the road to college—and beyond—looks increasingly treacherous. Despite a sharp increase in the proportion of high school graduates going on to some form of postsecondary education, socio-economic status continues to exert a powerful influence on college admission and completion; in fact, gaps in enrollment by class and race, after declining in the 1960s and 1970s, are once again as wide as they were thirty years ago, and getting wider, even as college has become far more crucial to lifetime fortunes.
>
> TAMARA DRAUT, "The Growing College Gap"

You might think that the "they say" here is embedded in the third sentence: They say (or we all think) that a four-year degree is "the all-but-official ticket to middle-class security," and you might assume that Draut will go on to disagree.

If you read the passage this way, however, you would be mistaken. Draut is not questioning whether a college degree has become "the ticket to middle-class security," but whether most Americans can obtain that ticket, whether college is within the financial reach of most American families. You may have been thrown off by the "but" following the statement that college has become a prerequisite for middle-class security. However, unlike the "though" in Zinczenko's opening, this "but" does not signal that Draut will be disagreeing with the view she has just summarized, a view that in fact she takes as a given. What Draut disagrees with is that this ticket to middle-class security is still readily available to the middle and working classes.

Were one to imagine Draut in a room talking with others with strong views on this topic, one would need to picture her challenging not those who think college is a ticket to financial security (something she agrees with and takes for granted), but those who think the doors of college are open to anyone willing to put forth the effort to walk through them. The view that Draut is challenging, then, is not summarized in her opening. Instead, she assumes that readers are already so familiar with this view that it need not be stated.

Draut's example suggests that in texts where the central "they say" is not immediately identified, you have to construct it yourself based on the clues the text provides. You have to start by locating the writer's thesis and then imagine some of the arguments that might be made against it. What would it look like to disagree with this view? In Draut's case, it is relatively easy to construct a counterargument: it is the familiar faith in the

American Dream of equal opportunity when it comes to access to college. Figuring out the counterargument not only reveals what motivated Draut as a writer but helps you respond to her essay as an active, critical reader. Constructing this counterargument can also help you recognize how Draut challenges your own views, questioning opinions that you previously took for granted.

WHEN THE "THEY SAY" IS ABOUT SOMETHING "NOBODY HAS TALKED ABOUT"

Another challenge in reading for the conversation is that writers sometimes build their arguments by responding to a *lack* of discussion. These writers build their case not by playing off views that can be identified (like faith in the American Dream or the idea that we are responsible for our body weight), but by pointing to something others have overlooked. As the writing theorists John M. Swales and Christine B. Feak point out, one effective way to "create a research space" and "establish a niche" in the academic world is "by indicating a gap in . . . previous research." Much research in the sciences and humanities takes this "Nobody has noticed X" form.

In such cases, the writer may be responding to scientists, for example, who have overlooked an obscure plant that offers insights into global warming, or to literary critics who have been so busy focusing on the lead character in a play that they have overlooked something important about the minor characters.

READING PARTICULARLY CHALLENGING TEXTS

Sometimes it is difficult to figure out the views that writers are responding to not because these writers do not identify those views but because their language and the concepts they are dealing with are particularly challenging. Consider, for instance, the first two sentences of *Gender Trouble: Feminism and the Subversion of Identity*, a book by the feminist philosopher and literary theorist Judith Butler, thought by many to be a particularly difficult academic writer.

> Contemporary feminist debates over the meaning of gender lead time and again to a certain sense of trouble, as if the indeterminacy of gender might eventually culminate in the failure of feminism. Perhaps trouble need not carry such a negative valence.
>
> JUDITH BUTLER, *Gender Trouble: Feminism and the Subversion of Identity*

There are many reasons readers may stumble over this relatively short passage, not the least of which is that Butler does not explicitly indicate where her own view begins and the view she is responding to ends. Unlike Zinczenko, Butler does not use the first-person "I" or a phrase such as "in my own view" to show that the position in the second sentence is her own. Nor does Butler offer a clear transition such as "but" or "however" at the start of the second sentence to indicate, as Zinczenko does with "though," that in the second sentence she is questioning the argument she has summarized in the first. And finally, like many academic writers, Butler uses abstract, unfamiliar words that many readers may need to look up, like "gender" (sexual identity, male or female), "indeterminacy" (the quality of being impossible to define or pin down), "culminate" (finally result in), and "negative valence" (a term borrowed from chemistry, roughly denoting "negative significance" or "meaning"). For all these reasons, we can imagine many readers feeling intimidated before they reach the third sentence of Butler's book.

But readers who break down this passage into its essential parts will find that it is actually a lucid piece of writing that conforms to the classic "they say / I say" pattern. Though it can be difficult to spot the clashing arguments in the two sentences, close analysis reveals that the first sentence offers a way of looking at a certain type of "trouble" in the realm of feminist politics that is being challenged in the second.

To understand difficult passages of this kind, you need to translate them into your own words—to build a bridge, in effect, between the passage's unfamiliar terms and ones more familiar to you. Building such a bridge should help you connect what you already know to what the author is saying—and will then help you move from reading to writing, providing you with some of the language you will need to summarize the text. One major challenge in translating the author's words into your own, however, is to stay true to what the author is actually saying, avoiding what we call "the closest cliché syndrome," in which one mistakes a commonplace idea for an author's more complex one (mistaking Butler's critique of the concept of "woman," for instance, for the common idea that women must have equal rights). The work of complex writers like Butler, who frequently challenge conventional thinking, cannot always be collapsed into the types of ideas most of us are already familiar with. Therefore, when you translate, do not try to fit the ideas of such writers into your preexisting beliefs, but instead allow your own views to be challenged. In building a bridge to the writers you read, it is often necessary to meet those writers more than halfway.

For more on the closest cliché syndrome, see Chapter 2.

So what, then, does Butler's opening say? Translating Butler's words into terms that are easier to understand, we can see that the first sentence says that for many feminists today, "the indeterminacy of gender"—the inability to define the essence of sexual identity—spells the end of feminism; that for many feminists the inability to define "gender," presumably the building block of the feminist movement, means serious "trouble" for feminist politics. In contrast, the second sentence suggests that this same "trouble" need not be thought of in such "negative" terms, that the inability to define femininity, or "gender trouble" as Butler calls it in her book's title, may not be such a bad thing—and, as she goes on to argue in the pages that follow, may even be something that feminist activists can profit from. In other words, Butler suggests, highlighting uncertainties about masculinity and femininity can be a powerful feminist tool.

Pulling all these inferences together, then, the opening sentences can be translated as follows: "While many contemporary feminists believe that uncertainty about what it means to be a woman will undermine feminist politics, I, Judith Butler, believe that this uncertainty can actually help strengthen feminist politics." Translating Butler's point into our own book's basic move: "They say that if we cannot define 'woman,' feminism is in big trouble. But I say that this type of trouble is precisely what feminism needs." Despite its difficulty, then, we hope you agree that this initially intimidating passage does make sense if you stay with it.

We hope it is clear that critical reading is a two-way street. It is just as much about being open to the way that writers can challenge you, maybe even transform you, as it is about questioning those writers. And if you translate a writer's argument into your own words as you read, you should allow the text to take you outside the ideas that you already hold and to introduce you to new terms and concepts. Even if you end up disagreeing with an author, you first have to show that you have really listened to what he or she is saying, have fully grasped his or her arguments, and can accurately summarize those arguments. Without such deep, attentive listening, any critique you make will be superficial and decidedly *uncritical*. It will be a critique that says more about you than about the writer or idea you're supposedly responding to.

In this chapter we have tried to show that reading for the conversation means looking not just for the thesis of a text in isolation but for the view or views that motivate that thesis—the "they say." We have also tried to show that reading for the conversation means being alert for the different strategies writers use to engage the view(s) that are motivating them, since not all writers engage other perspectives in the same way. Some writers explicitly identify and summarize a view they are responding to at the outset of their text and then return to it frequently as their text unfolds. Some refer only obliquely to a view that is motivating them, assuming that readers will be able to reconstruct that view on their own. Other writers may not explicitly distinguish their own view from the views they are questioning in ways that all of us find clear, leaving some readers to wonder whether a given view is the writer's own or one that he or she is challenging. And some writers push off against the "they say" that is motivating them in a challenging academic language that requires readers to translate what they are saying into more accessible, everyday terms. In sum, then, though most persuasive writers do follow a conversational "they say / I say" pattern, they do so in a great variety of ways. What this means for readers is that they need to be armed with various strategies for detecting the conversations in what they read, even when those conversations are not self-evident.

FIFTEEN

"ON CLOSER EXAMINATION"

Entering Conversations about Literature

——————

IN CHINUA ACHEBE'S NOVEL *Things Fall Apart*, Okonkwo, the main character, is a tragic hero.

So what? Who cares?

Why does this typical way of opening an essay on a literary work leave readers wondering, "Why are you telling me this?" Because, in our view, such statements leave it unclear who would say otherwise. Would anyone deny that the main character of Achebe's novel is a tragic hero? Is there some other view of the subject that this writer is responding to? Since no such alternative interpretation is indicated, the reader thinks, "OK, Okonkwo is a tragic hero—as opposed to what?"

Now compare this opening with another possible one:

> Several members of our class have argued that Okonkwo, the main character of *Things Fall Apart*, is a hateful villain. My own view, however, is that, while it is true that Okonkwo commits villainous acts, he is ultimately a tragic hero—a flawed but ultimately sympathetic figure.

We hope you agree that the second version, which responds to what someone else says about Okonkwo, makes for more engaging writing than the first. Since the first version fails to present itself as a response to any alternative view of its subject, it comes at readers out of the blue, leaving them wondering why it needs to be said at all.

As we stress in this book, it is the views of others and our desire to respond to these views that gives our writing its underlying motivation and helps readers see why what we say matters, why others should care, and why we need to say it in the first place. In this chapter we suggest that this same principle applies to writing about literature. Literary critics, after all, don't make assertions about literary works out of the blue. Rather, they contribute to discussions and debates about the meaning and significance of literary works, some of which may continue for years and even centuries.

Indeed, this commitment to discussion animates most literature courses, in which students discuss and debate assigned works in class before writing papers about them. The premise is that engaging with classmates and teachers enables us to make discoveries about the work that we might not arrive at in simply reading the work alone.

We suggest that you think of writing about literature as a natural extension of such in-class discussions, listening carefully to others and using what they say to set up and motivate what you have to say.

START WITH WHAT OTHERS ARE SAYING

But in writing about literature, where do views to respond to— "they says"—come from? Many sources. Published literary criticism is perhaps the most obvious:

▸ Critic X complains that Author Y's story is compromised by his _____ perspective. While there's some truth to this critique, I argue that Critic X overlooks _____.

▸ According to Critic A, novel X suggests _____. I agree, but would add that _____.

But the view that you respond to in writing about literature can be far closer to home than published literary criticism. As our opening example illustrates, it can be something said about the literary work by a classmate or teacher:

▸ Several members of our class have suggested that the final message of play X is _____. I agree up to a point, but I still think that _____.

Another tactic is to start with something you yourself thought about the work that on second thought you now want to revise:

▸ On first reading play Z, I thought it was an uncritical celebration of _____. After rereading the play and discussing it in class, however, I see that it is more critical of _____ than I originally thought.

You can even respond to something that hasn't actually been said about the work, but might hypothetically be said:

▸ It might be said that poem Y is chiefly about _____. But the problem with this reading, in my view, is _____.

▸ Though religious readers might be tempted to analyze poem X as a parable about _____, a closer examination suggests that the poem is in fact _____.

Sometimes, the "they say" that you respond to in writing about a literary work can be found in the work itself, as distinct from what some critic or other reader has said *about* the work. Much great literary criticism responds directly to the literary work, summarizing some aspect of the work's form or content and then assessing it, in much the same way you can do in response to a persuasive essay:

▸ Ultimately, as I read it, *The Scarlet Letter* seems to say
_____. I have trouble accepting this proposition, however, on the grounds that _____.

One of the more powerful ways of responding to a literary work is to address any contradictions or inconsistencies:

▸ At the beginning of the poem, we encounter the generalization, seemingly introducing the poem's message, that "_____."
But this statement is then contradicted by the suggestion made later in the poem that "_____." This opens up a significant inconsistency in the text: is it suggesting _____ or, on the contrary, _____?

▸ At several places in novel X, Author Y leads us to understand that the story's central point is that _____. Yet elsewhere the text suggests _____, indicating that Y may be ambivalent on this issue.

If you review the above templates, you'll notice that each does what a good discussion, lecture, or essay does: it makes an argument about some aspect of a work that can be interpreted in various ways. Instead of just making a claim about the work in isolation—character X is a tragic hero; sonnet Y is about the loss of a loved one—these templates put one claim as a response to another, making clear what motivated the argument to begin with. They thus act as conversation starters that can invite or even provoke other readers to respond with their own interpretations and judgments.

FIGURING OUT
WHAT A LITERARY WORK "MEANS"

In order to enter conversations and debates about literature, you need to meet the time-honored challenge of being able to read and make sense of literary works, understanding and analyzing what the text says. On the one hand, like the types of persuasive essays we focus on throughout this book, literary works make arguments their authors want to convey, things they are for and against, ideas they want to endorse or condemn. On the other hand, discovering "the argument" of a literary work— what it's "saying"—can be a special challenge because, unlike persuasive essays, literary works usually do not spell out their arguments explicitly. Though poets, novelists, and playwrights may have the same level of conviction as persuasive writers, rarely do they step out from behind the pages of their texts and say, "Okay, folks, this is what it all means. What I'm trying to say in a nutshell is _____." That is, since literary texts do not include an explicit thesis statement identifying their main point, it's left up to us as readers to figure it out.

Because literary works tend to avoid such explicitness, their meanings often need to be teased out from the clues they provide: from the dialogue between characters, the plot, the imagery and symbolism, and the kind of language the author uses. In fact, it is this absence of overt argument that makes literature so endlessly debatable—and explains why scholars and critics argue so much about what literary works mean in ways similar to the classroom discussions that you have likely participated in as a student.

The Elusive Literary Author

Indeed, not even the use of the first person "I" in a literary work is an indication that you have located the author's own position or stance, as it usually is in an essay. When David Zinczenko, for example, in his essay "Don't Blame the Eater" (pp. 241–43) writes "I tend to sympathize with these portly fast-food patrons" who file lawsuits against the fast food industry, we can be confident that the "I" is Zinczenko himself, and that the position he expresses is his own and informs everything else in his essay. But we cannot assume that the "I" who addresses us in a work of fiction or poetry is necessarily the author, for he or she is a fictional character—and one who may be unreliable and untrustworthy.

Take, for example, the first sentence of Edgar Allan Poe's short story "The Cask of Amontillado":

> The thousand injuries of Fortunato I had borne as best I could, but when he ventured upon insult I vowed revenge.

As soon becomes clear in the story, the "I" who speaks as the narrator here is not Poe himself but an insanely vengeful murderer whose words must be seen through to get at the point of Poe's story.

Instead of a readily identifiable position, literary works often present the perspectives of a number of different characters and leave it to readers to determine which if any speaks for the author. Thus when we encounter the seemingly eloquent lines in *Hamlet*, "To thine own self be true / And thou shalt not be false to any man," we can't assume, as we might if we encountered this statement in an essay, that it represents the author's own view. For these words are uttered by Polonius, a character whom Shakespeare presents as a tedious, cliché-spouting bore—not someone he leads us to trust. After all, part of Hamlet's problem is that it's not clear to him what being "true" to his own self would require him to do.

This elusive quality of literary texts helps explain why some of our students complain about the challenge of finding the "hidden meaning," as they sometimes call it, let alone summarizing that meaning in the way assignments often require. Sure, some students say, they enjoy reading literature for pleasure. But analyzing literature in school for its "meaning" or "symbolism"—that's another matter. Some even say that the requirement that they hunt for meanings and symbols robs literature of its fun.

In fact, as most students come to recognize, analyzing meanings, symbols, and other elements should enhance rather than stifle the pleasure we get from reading literature. But it can indeed be hard to figure out what literary works mean. How do we determine the point of a story or poem when the author, unlike an essayist like Zinczenko, does not tell us explicitly what he or she is trying to say? How do you go from a fictional event or poetic image (an insane man committing murder, two roads that diverge in the woods) or from a dialogue between fictional characters ("Frankly, my dear, I don't give a damn.") to what these events, images, or lines of dialogue mean?

Look for Conflict *in* the Work

There is no simple recipe for figuring out what a literary work means, but one tactic that seems to help our own students is to look for the conflict or debate in the literary work itself and then ask what the text is leading us to think about that conflict. Asking these questions—what is the conflict in the work and which side, if any, should we favor?—will help you think about and formulate a position on what the work means. And since such claims are often ones that literary scholars argue about, thinking about the conflict *in* a literary work will often lead you to discussions and debates *about* the work that you can then respond to in your writing. Because literary authors don't tell us explicitly what the text means, it's always going to be *arguable*—and your task in writing about a literary work is to argue for what *you* think it means. Here are two templates to help get you started responding to other interpretations:

▸ **It might be argued that in the clash between character X and Y in play Z, the author wants us to favor character Y, since she is presented as the play's heroine. I contend, however, that _____ .**

▸ **Several critics seem to assume that poem X endorses the values of discipline and rationality represented by the image of _____ over those of play and emotion represented by the image of _____ . I agree, but with the following caveat: that the poem ultimately sees both values as equally important and even suggests that ideally they should complement one another.**

This tactic of looking for the conflicts in literary works is part of a long tradition of critical thought that sees conflict as central to literature. In ancient Greece, Aristotle argued that conflict between characters or forces underlies the plots of tragic dramas such as *Oedipus*. Indeed, the ancient Greek word *agon*, which means antagonism, conflict, or debate, leaves its traces in the term "protagonist," the hero or leading character of a narrative work who comes into conflict with other characters or with the fates. And Plato noted the pervasiveness of conflict in literature when he banished poets from his ideal community on the grounds that their works depict endless conflict and division.

This emphasis on the centrality of conflict in literature has been echoed by modern theorists like the New Critics of the 1940s and 50s, who focused on such tensions and paradoxes as good and evil or innocence and experience—and more recently by poststructuralists and political theorists who see literature, like society, as saturated by such polarities as male/female, gay/straight, white/black, and so on. Writers today continue to recognize conflict as the engine of good storytelling. As the Hollywood screenwriter Robert McKee puts it, "Nothing moves forward in a story except through conflict."

Building on this idea that conflict is central to literature, we suggest the following four questions to help you understand and formulate your own position on any literary work:

1. What is the central conflict?
2. Which side—if any—does the text seem to favor?
3. What's your evidence? How might others interpret the evidence differently?
4. What's your opinion of the text?

WHAT IS THE CENTRAL CONFLICT?

Conflicts tend to manifest themselves in different ways in different literary genres. In works that take a narrative or story form (novels, short stories, and plays), the central conflict will often be represented in an actual debate between characters. These debates between characters will often reflect larger questions and debates in the society or historical era in which they were written, over such issues as the responsibility of rulers, the consequences of capitalism and consumerism, or the struggle for gender equality. Sometimes these debates will be located within an individual character, appearing as a struggle in someone caught between conflicting or incompatible choices. Whatever form they may take, these debates can provide you with points of entry into the issues raised by the work, its historical context, and its author's vision of the world.

One narrative work that lends itself to such an approach is Flannery O'Connor's 1961 short story "Everything That Rises Must Converge," which is reprinted on pp. 272–91. The story presents a running debate between a mother and her son Julian about the civil rights movement for racial equality that had erupted in the American South at the time the story was written, with Julian defending the outlook of this movement and his mother defending the South's traditional racial hierarchy. The story raises the debatable question of which character we should side with: Julian, his mother, both, or neither?

WHICH SIDE—IF ANY—DOES THE TEXT SEEM TO FAVOR?

When we teach this story, most of our students first assume the story sides with Julian's outlook, which to them as Northern, urban college students in the twenty-first century seems the obviously enlightened position. Who, after all, could fail to see that the mother's views are backward and racist? As our class discussions unfold, however, most students come to reject this view as a misreading, one based more on their own views than on what's in the text. Sooner or later, someone points out that at several points Julian is presented in highly critical ways—and that his apparently progressive sympathy for racial integration rests on arid intellectual abstractions and a hypocritical lack of self-knowledge, in contrast with his mother's heartfelt loyalty to her roots. Eventually another possible interpretation surfaces, that both characters suffer from a common malady, that they're living in a mental bubble that keeps them from being able to see themselves as they really are.

The writing assignment we often give builds on this class discussion by offering students the following template for thinking about which character, if any, the text leads them to favor:

▶ **Some might argue that when it comes to the conflict between Julian and his mother over _____, our sympathies should lie with _____. My own view is that _____.**

WHAT'S YOUR EVIDENCE?

In entering the types of discussions and debates modeled by the above template, how do you determine where your "sympathies should lie"? More generally, how do you arrive at and justify an interpretation of what a literary text says?

The answer lies in the *evidence* provided by the work: its images, dialogue, plot, historical references, tone, stylistic details, and so forth.

It is important to remember, however, that evidence is not set in stone. Students sometimes assume that there exists some fixed code that unlocks the meaning of literary works, symbols, images, and other evidence. A character dies? This must mean that he or she is being condemned. A stairway appears? A symbol for upward mobility. A garden? Must be something sexual.

But evidence itself is open to interpretation and thus to debate. The mother's death in O'Connor's story, for instance, *could* be seen as evidence that we are supposed to disapprove of her as someone whose racial views are regressive and on the way out. On the other hand, her death may instead be evidence that she is to be seen as a heroic martyr too good for this cruel, harsh world. What a character's death means, then, depends—on how he or she is treated in the work, positively or negatively, which in turn may be subject to debate.

As we've repeatedly emphasized in this book, others will often disagree with you and may even use the same evidence you do to support interpretations that are contrary to your own. Like other objects of study, literary works are like the famous ambiguous drawing that can be seen as either a duck or a rabbit, depending how one views it.

Since the same piece of evidence in a literary work will often support differing, even opposing interpretations, you need to argue for what you think the evidence shows—and to acknowledge that others may read that evidence differently.

In writing about literature, then, you need to show that the evidence you are citing supports your interpretation and to anticipate other alternative ones:

▸ **Although some might read the metaphor of _____ in this poem as evidence that, for Author X, modern technology undermines community traditions and values, I see it as _____ .**

To present evidence in such a "they say / I say" way, you need to be alert for how others may read the work differently than you—and even use this very same evidence in support of an opposing interpretation:

▸ **Some might claim that evidence X suggests _____ , but I argue that, on the contrary, it suggests _____ .**

▸ **I agree with my classmate _____ that the image of _____ in novel Y is evidence of childhood innocence that has been lost. Unlike _____ , however, I think this loss of innocence is to be read not as a tragic event but as a necessary, even helpful, stage in human development.**

Are Some Interpretations Simply Wrong?

No matter how flexible and open to debate evidence might be, not all interpretations we arrive at using that evidence are equally valid. And some interpretations are simply unsupported by that evidence. Let us illustrate.

As we noted earlier, some of our students first favored Julian over his mother. One student, let us call her Nancy, cited as evidence a passage early in the story in which Julian is compared to Saint Sebastian, a Christian martyr who is said to have exhibited exceptional faith under extreme suffering and persecution. As the mother stood preparing for Julian to take her to her weekly swimming class, Julian is described as standing "pinned to the door frame, waiting like Saint Sebastian for the arrows to begin piercing him."

Thinking this passage proves that Julian is the more sympathetic character, Nancy pointed to other evidence as well, including the following passage:

> [Julian] was free of prejudice and unafraid to face facts. Most miraculous of all, instead of being blinded by love for [his mother] as she was for him, he had cut himself emotionally free of her and could see her with complete objectivity. He was not dominated by his mother. (412)

Citing passages like this in her essay, Nancy concluded: "Julian represents the future of society, a nonracist and an educated thinker."

After rereading the story, however, and hearing other students' views, Nancy came to realize that the passages she had cited—comparing Julian to a saint, suggesting that he is racially progressive, and that he is "free of" his mother and "objective" about her—were all intended ironically. Julian congratulates *himself* for being saintlike, free of prejudice, and objective, but the story ultimately implies that he deludes himself.

How did the supporters of the ironic reading convince Nancy to revise her initial reading—to see it as wrong, unsupported by the evidence? First, they pointed to the glaring discrepancy between the situations and kinds of suffering endured by Julian and Saint Sebastian. Could anyone be serious, they asked, in comparing something as mundane as being forced to wait a few minutes to go to the YMCA to a martyr dying for his faith? No, they answered, and the jarring incongruity of the events being compared, they argued, suggests that Julian, far from saintlike, is presented in this passage as an impatient, ungrateful, undutiful son. In addition, students pointed out that the gap between Julian's self-image as a progressive man of "complete objectivity" and "facts," "free of [his mother]" and the blubbering young man crying "Mama, Mama!" with "guilt and sorrow" at the end of the story suggests that Julian's righteous, high-minded image of himself is not to be taken at face value.

At this point you may be wondering, how can we say that some interpretations of literature must be ruled out as *wrong*? Isn't the great thing about interpreting literary works—in contrast to scientific and historical texts—that there are no wrong answers? Are we saying that there is one "correct" way to read a literary work—the one way the work itself tells us we "should" read it?

No, we aren't saying that there is only one way to read a literary work. If we believed there were, we would not be offering a method of literary analysis based on multiple interpretations and debate. But yes, acknowledging that literary interpretations are open to debate is not to say that a work can mean anything we want it to mean, as if all interpretations are equally good. In our view, and that of most literature teachers, some interpretations are better than others—more persuasively reasoned and better grounded in the evidence of the text.

If we maintain that all interpretations are equally valid, we risk confusing the perspective of the work's author with our own, as did the students who confused their own views on the civil rights movement of the 1960s with Flannery O'Connor's. Such misreadings are reminiscent of what we call "the closest cliché syndrome," where what's summarized is not the view the author actually expresses but a familiar cliché—or, in O'Connor's case, a certain social belief—that the writer believes and mistakenly assumes the author must too. The view that there are no wrong answers in literary interpretation encourages a kind of solipsism that erases the difference between us and others and transforms everything we encounter into a version of ourselves. See p. 33 for more on the closest cliché syndrome.

As the literary theorist Robert Scholes puts it, reading, conceived "as a submission to the intentions of another is the first step" to understanding what a literary work is saying. For "if we do not postulate the existence of [an author] behind the verbal text," we will "simply project our own subjective modes of thought and desire upon the text." In other words, unless we do the best we can to get at what the author is saying, we will never truly recognize his or her ideas except as some version of our own. Scholes acknowledges that good reading often involves going beyond the author's intention, pointing out contradictions and ideological blind spots, but he argues that we must recognize the author's intention *before* we can try to see beyond it in these ways.

WHAT'S YOUR OPINION OF THE TEXT?

In accord with the principle that we must try to understand the text on its own terms before responding to it, we have thus far in this chapter focused on how to understand and unpack what literary texts say and do. Our approach to get at what they say involves looking for the central conflict in the work and then asking yourself how the author uses various types of evidence (characters, dialogue, imagery, events, plot, etc.) to guide you in thinking about that conflict. Ultimately, your job as a reader of literature is to be open to a work as its author presents it, or else your reading will fail to see what makes that work worth reading and thinking about.

But once you have reached a good understanding of the work, it is time to allow your own opinion to come into play. Offering your own interpretation of a work and opening that interpretation to response are crucial steps in any act of literary analysis, but they are not the end of the process. The final step involves offering your own insight into or critique of the work and its vision, assessing whether, as you see it, it is morally justified or questionable, unified or contradictory, historically regressive or progressive, and so forth. For example:

> Though she is one of the most respected Southern authors of the American literary canon, Flannery O'Connor continually denigrates the one character in her 1961 story who represents the civil rights movement, and in so doing disparages progressive ideas that I believe deserve a far more sympathetic hearing.

Offering a critique, however, doesn't necessarily mean finding fault:

> Some criticize O'Connor's story by suggesting that it has a politically regressive agenda. But I see the story as a laudable critique of politics as such. In my view, O'Connor's story rightly criticizes the polarization of political conflicts—North vs. South, liberal vs. conservative, and the like—and suggests that they need to come together: to "converge," as O'Connor's title implies, through religious love, understanding, and forgiveness.

We realize that the prospect of critiquing a literary work can be daunting. Indeed, simply stating what you think an author is saying can be intimidating, since it means going out on a limb, asserting something about highly respected figures—works that are often complex, contradictory, and connected to larger historical movements. Nevertheless, if you can master these challenges, you may find that figuring out what a literary work is saying, offering an opinion about it, and entering into conversation and debate with others about such questions is what makes literature matter. And if you do it well, what *you* say will invite its own response: your "I say" will become someone else's "they say," and the conversation will go on and on.

SIXTEEN

"THE DATA SUGGEST"

Writing in the Sciences

CHRISTOPHER GILLEN

CHARLES DARWIN DESCRIBED *On the Origin of Species* as "one long argument." In *Dialogue Concerning the Two Chief World Systems*, Galileo Galilei cast his argument for a sun-centered solar system as a series of conversations. As these historical examples show, scientific writing is fundamentally argumentative. Like all academic writers, scientists make and defend claims. They address disagreements and explore unanswered questions. They propose novel mechanisms and new theories. And they advance certain explanations and reject others. Though their vocabulary may be more technical and their emphasis more numerical, science writers use the same

---

CHRISTOPHER GILLEN is a professor of biology at Kenyon College and the faculty director of the Kenyon Institute in Biomedical and Scientific Writing. He teaches courses in animal physiology, biology of exercise, and introductory biology, all stressing the critical reading of primary research articles.

rhetorical moves as other academic writers. Consider the following example from a book about the laws of physics.

> The common refrain that is heard in elementary discussions of quantum mechanics is that a physical object is in some sense both a wave and a particle, with its wave nature apparent when you measure a wave property such as wavelength, and its particle nature apparent when you measure a particle property such as position. But this is, at best, misleading and, at worst, wrong.
>
> V. J. STENGER, *The Comprehensible Cosmos*

The "they say / I say" structure of this passage is unmistakable: They say that objects have properties of both waves and particles; I say they are wrong. This example is not a lonely argumentative passage cherry-picked from an otherwise non-argumentative text. Rather, Stenger's entire book makes the argument that is foreshadowed by its title, *The Comprehensible Cosmos*: that although some might see the universe as hopelessly complex, it is essentially understandable.

Here's another argumentative passage, this one from a research article about the role of lactic acid in muscle fatigue:

> In contrast to the often suggested role for acidosis as a cause of muscle fatigue, it is shown that in muscles where force was depressed by high $[K^+]_o$, acidification by lactic acid produced a pronounced recovery of force.
>
> O. B. NIELSEN, F. DE PAOLI, AND K. OVERGAARD,
> "Protective Effects of Lactic Acid on Force Production in
> Rat Skeletal Muscle," *The Journal of Physiology*

In other words: Many scientists think that lactic acid causes muscle fatigue, but our evidence shows that it actually promotes recovery. Notice that the authors frame their claim with a version of the "they say / I say" formula: Although previous work suggests _____, our data argue _____. This basic move and its many variations are widespread in scientific writing. The essential argumentative moves taught in this book transcend disciplines, and the sciences are no exception. The examples in this chaper were written by professional scientists, but they show moves that are appropriate in any writing that addresses scientific issues.

Despite the importance of argument in scientific writing, newcomers to the genre often see it solely as a means for communicating uncontroversial, objective facts. It's easy to see how this view arises. The objective tone of scientific writing can obscure its argumentative nature, and many textbooks reinforce a nonargumentative vision of science when they focus on accepted conclusions and ignore ongoing controversies. And because science writers base their arguments on empirical data, a good portion of many scientific texts *does* serve the purpose of delivering uncontested facts.

However, scientific writing often does more than just report facts. Data are crucial to scientific argumentation, but they are by no means the end of the story. Given important new data, scientists assess their quality, draw conclusions from them, and ponder their implications. They synthesize the new data with existing information, propose novel theories, and design the next experiments. In short, scientific progress depends on the insight and creativity that scientists bring to their data. The thrill of doing science, and writing about it, comes from the ongoing struggle to use data to better understand our world.

START WITH THE DATA

Data are the fundamental currency of scientific argument. Scientists develop hypotheses from existing data and then test those by comparing their predictions to new experimental data. Summarizing data is therefore a basic move in science writing. Because data can often be interpreted in different ways, describing the data opens the door to critical analysis, creating opportunities to critique previous interpretations and develop new ones.

Describing data requires more than simply reporting numbers and conclusions. Rather than jumping straight to the punch line—to what X concluded—it is important first to describe the hypotheses, methods, and results that led to the conclusion: "To test the hypothesis that _____, X measured _____ and found that _____. Therefore, X concluded _____." In the following sections, we explore the three key rhetorical moves for describing the data that underpin a scientific argument: presenting the prevailing theories, explaining methodologies, and summarizing findings.

See how a physicist begins with data on pp. 252–59.

Present the Prevailing Theories

Readers must understand the prevailing theories that a study responds to before they can fully appreciate the details. So before diving into specifics, place the work in context by describing the prevailing theories and hypotheses. In the following passage from a journal article about insect respiration, the authors discuss an explanation for discontinuous gas exchange (DGC), a phenomenon where insects periodically close valves on their breathing tubes.

Lighton (1996, 1998; see also Lighton and Berrigan, 1995) noted the prevalence of DGC in fossorial insects, which inhabit microclimates where CO_2 levels may be relatively high. Consequently, Lighton proposed the chthonic hypothesis, which suggests that

DGC originated as a mechanism to improve gas exchange while at the same time minimizing respiratory water loss.

A. G. GIBBS AND R. A. JOHNSON, "The Role of Discontinuous Gas Exchange in Insects: The Chthonic Hypothesis Does Not Hold Water," *The Journal of Experimental Biology*

Notice that Gibbs and Johnson not only describe Lighton's hypothesis but also recap the evidence that supports it. By presenting this evidence, Gibbs and Johnson set the stage for engaging with Lighton's ideas. For example, they might question the chthonic hypothesis by pointing out shortcomings of the data or flaws in its interpretation. Or they might suggest new approaches that could verify the hypothesis. The point is that by incorporating a discussion of experimental findings into their summary of Lighton's hypothesis, Gibbs and Johnson open the door to a conversation with Lighton.

Here are some templates for presenting the data that underpin prevailing explanations:

▸ **Experiments showing _____ and _____ have led scientists to propose _____ .**

▸ **Although most scientists attribute _____ to _____ , X's result _____ leads to the possibility that _____ .**

Explain the Methods

Even as we've argued that scientific arguments hinge on data, it's important to note that the quality of data varies depending on how they were collected. Data obtained with sloppy techniques or poorly designed experiments could lead to faulty conclusions. Therefore, it's crucial to explain the methods used to collect data. In order for readers to evaluate a method, you'll need to indicate its purpose, as the following passage from a journal article about the evolution of bird digestive systems demonstrates:

> To test the hypothesis that flowerpiercers have converged with hummingbirds in digestive traits, we compared the activity of intestinal enzymes and the gut nominal area of cinnamon-bellied flowerpiercers (Diglossa baritula) with those of eleven hummingbird species.
>
> J. E. SCHONDUBE AND C. MARTINEZ DEL RIO,
> "Sugar and Protein Digestion in Flowerpiercers and
> Hummingbirds: A Comparative Test of Adaptive Convergence,"
> *Journal of Comparative Physiology*

You need to indicate purpose whether describing your own work or that of others. Here are a couple of templates for doing so:

▸ **Smith and colleagues evaluated _____ to determine whether _____.**

▸ **Because _____ does not account for _____, we instead used _____.**

Summarize the Findings

Scientific data often come in the form of numbers. Your task when presenting numerical data is to provide the context readers need to understand the numbers—by giving supporting information and making comparisons. In the following passage from a book about the interaction between organisms and their environments, Turner uses numerical data to support an argument about the role of the sun's energy on Earth.

> The potential rate of energy transfer from the Sun to Earth is prodigious—about 600 W m^{-2}, averaged throughout the year. Of this, only a relatively small fraction, on the order of 1–2 percent,

is captured by green plants. The rest, if it is not reflected back into space, is available to do other things. The excess can be considerable: although some natural surfaces reflect as much as 95% of the incoming solar beam, many natural surfaces reflect much less (Table 3.2), on average about 15–20 percent. The remaining absorbed energy is then capable of doing work, like heating up surfaces, moving water and air masses around to drive weather and climate, evaporating water, and so forth.

J. S. TURNER, The Extended Organism

Turner supports his point that a huge amount of the sun's energy is directly converted to work on Earth by quoting an actual value (600) with units of measurement (W m^{-2}, watts per square meter). Readers need the units to evaluate the value; 600 watts per square inch is very different from 600 W m^{-2}. Turner then makes comparisons using percent values, saying that only 1 to 2 percent of the total energy that reaches Earth is trapped by plants. Finally, Turner describes the data's variability by reporting comparisons as ranges—1 to 2 percent and 15 to 20 percent—rather than single values.

Supporting information—such as units of measurement, sample size (n), and amount of variability—helps readers assess the data. In general, the reliability of data improves as its sample size increases and its variability decreases. Supporting information can be concisely presented as:

▸ _____ ± _____ (*mean ± variability*) _____ (*units*),
n = _____ (*sample size*).

For example: Before training, resting heart rate of the subjects was 56 ± 7 beats per minute, n = 12. Here's another way to give supporting information:

▸ We measured _____ (*sample size*) subjects, and the average response was _____ (*mean with units*) with a range of _____ (*lower value*) to _____ (*upper value*).

To help readers understand the data, make comparisons with values from the same study or from other similar work.

Here are some templates for making comparisons:

▸ Before training, average running speed was _____ ± _____ kilometers per hour, _____ kilometers per hour slower than running speed after training.

▸ We found athletes' heart rates to be _____ ± _____ % lower than nonathletes'.

▸ The subjects in X's study completed the maze in _____ ± _____ seconds, _____ seconds slower than those in Y's study.

You will sometimes need to present qualitative data, such as that found in some images and photographs, that cannot be reduced to numbers. Qualitative data must be described precisely with words. In the passage below from a review article about connections between cellular protein localization and cell growth, the author describes the exact locations of three proteins: Scrib, Dlg, and Lgl.

> Epithelial cells accumulate different proteins on their apical (top) and basolateral (bottom) surfaces. . . . Scrib and Dlg are localized at the septate junctions along the lateral cell surface, whereas Lgl coats vesicles that are found both in the cytoplasm and "docked" at the lateral surface of the cell.
>
> M. Peifer, "Travel Bulletin—Traffic Jams Cause Tumors," *Science*

EXPLAIN WHAT THE DATA MEAN

Once you summarize experiments and results, you need to say what the data mean. Consider the following passage from a study in which scientists fertilized plots of tropical rainforest with nitrogen (N) and / or phosphorus (P).

> Although our data suggest that the mechanisms driving the observed respiratory responses to increased N and P may be different, the large CO_2 losses stimulated by N and P fertilization suggest that knowledge of such patterns and their effects on soil CO_2 efflux is critical for understanding the role of tropical forests in a rapidly changing global C [carbon] cycle.
>
> C. C. CLEVELAND AND A. R. TOWNSEND, "Nutrient Additions to a Tropical Rain Forest Drive Substantial Soil Carbon Dioxide Losses to the Atmosphere," *Proceedings of the National Academy of Sciences*

Notice that in discussing the implications of their data, Cleveland and Townsend use language—including the verbs "suggest" and "may be"—that denotes their level of confidence in what they say about the data.

Whether you are summarizing what others say about their data or offering your own interpretation, pay attention to the verbs that connect data to interpretations.

To signify a moderate level of confidence:

▸ The data *suggest / hint / imply* _____.

To express a greater degree of certainty:

▸ Our results *show / demonstrate* _____.

Almost never will you use the verb "prove" in reference to a single study, because even very powerful evidence generally falls short of proof unless other studies support the same conclusion.

Scientific consensus arises when multiple studies point toward the same conclusion; conversely, contradictions among studies often signal research questions that need further work. For these reasons, you may need to compare one study's findings to those of another study. Here, too, you'll need to choose your verbs carefully.

▸ Our data *support / confirm / verify* the work of **X** by showing that _____ .

▸ By demonstrating _____ , **X's** work *extends* the findings of **Y**.

▸ The results of **X** *contradict / refute* **Y's** conclusion that _____ .

▸ **X's** findings *call into question* the widely accepted theory that _____ .

▸ Our data *are consistent with* **X's** hypothesis that _____ .

MAKE YOUR OWN ARGUMENTS

Now we turn toward the part of scientific writing where you express your own opinions. One challenge is that the statements of other scientists about their methods and results usually must be accepted. You probably can't argue, for example, that "X and Y claim to have studied 6 elephants, but I think they actually only studied 4." However, it might be fair to say, "X and Y studied only 6 elephants, and this small sample size casts doubts on their conclusions." The second statement doesn't question what the scientists did or found but instead examines how the findings are interpreted.

When developing your own arguments—the "I say"—you will often start by assessing the interpretations of other scientists. Consider the following example from a review article about the beneficial acclimation hypothesis (BAH), the idea that organisms exposed to a particular environment become better suited to that environment than unexposed animals.

> To the surprise of most physiologists, all empirical examinations of the BAH have rejected its generality. However, we suggest that these examinations are neither direct nor complete tests of the functional benefit of acclimation.
>
> R. S. Wilson and C. E. Franklin, "Testing the Beneficial Acclimation Hypothesis," *Trends in Ecology & Evolution*

Wilson and Franklin use a version of the "twist it" move: They acknowledge the data collected by other physiologists but question how those data have been interpreted, creating an opportunity to offer their own interpretation.

For more on the "twist it" move, see p. 60.

You might ask whether we should question how other scientists interpret their own work. Having conducted a study, aren't they in the best position to evaluate it? Perhaps, but as the above example demonstrates, other scientists might see the work from a different perspective or through more objective eyes. And in fact the culture of science depends on vigorous debate in which scientists defend their own findings and challenge those of others—a give and take that helps improve science's reliability. So expressing a critical view about someone else's work is an integral part of the scientific process. Let's examine some of the basic moves for entering scientific conversations: agreeing, with a difference; disagreeing and explaining why; simultaneously agreeing and disagreeing; anticipating objections; and saying why it matters.

Agree, But with a Difference

Scientific research passes through several levels of critical analysis before being published. Scientists get feedback when they discuss work with colleagues, present findings at conferences, and receive reviews of their manuscripts. So the juiciest debates may have been resolved before publication, and you may find little to disagree with in the published literature of a research field. Yet even if you agree with what you've read, there are still ways to join the conversation—and reasons to do so.

One approach is to suggest that further work should be done:

▸ **Now that _____ has been established, scientists will likely turn their attention toward _____ .**

▸ **X's work leads to the question of _____ . Therefore, we investigated _____ .**

▸ **To see whether these findings apply to _____ , we propose to _____ .**

Another way to agree and at the same time jump into the conversation is to concur with a finding and then propose a mechanism that explains it. In the following sentence from a review article about dietary deficiencies, the author agrees with a previous finding and offers a probable explanation.

> Inadequate dietary intakes of vitamins and minerals are widespread, most likely due to excessive consumption of energy-rich, micronutrient-poor, refined food.
>
> B. AMES, "Low Micronutrient Intake May Accelerate the Degenerative Diseases of Aging through Allocation of Scarce Micronutrients by Triage," *Proceedings of the National Academy of Sciences*

Here are some templates for explaining an experimental result.

▸ **One explanation for X's finding of _____ is that _____ .**
  An alternative explanation is _____ .

▸ **The difference between _____ and _____ is probably**
  due to _____ .

Disagree—and Explain Why

Although scientific consensus is common, healthy disagreement is not unusual. While measurements conducted by different teams of scientists under the same conditions should produce the same result, scientists often disagree about which techniques are most appropriate, how well an experimental design tests a hypothesis, and how results should be interpreted. To illustrate such disagreement, let's return to the debate about whether or not lactic acid is beneficial during exercise. In the following passage, Lamb and Stephenson are responding to work by Kristensen and colleagues, which argues that lactic acid might be beneficial to resting muscle but not to active muscle.

The argument put forward by Kristensen and colleagues (12) . . . is not valid because it is based on observations made with isolated whole soleus muscles that were stimulated at such a high rate that >60% of the preparation would have rapidly become completely anoxic (4). . . . Furthermore, there is no reason to expect that adding more H+ to that already being generated by the muscle activity should in any way be advantageous. It is a bit like opening up the carburetor on a car to let in too much air or throwing gasoline over the engine and then concluding that air and gasoline are deleterious to engine performance.

G. D. LAMB AND D. G. STEPHENSON,
"Point: Lactic Acid Accumulation Is an Advantage during Muscle Activity," *Journal of Applied Physiology*

Lamb and Stephenson bring experimental detail to bear on their disagreement with Kristensen and colleagues. First, they criticize methodology, arguing that the high muscle stimulation rate used by Kristensen and colleagues created very low oxygen levels (anoxia). They also criticize the logic of the experimental design, arguing that adding more acid (H+) to a muscle that is already producing it isn't informative. It's also worth noting how they drive home their point, likening Kristensen and colleagues' methodology to flooding an engine with air or gasoline. Even in technical scientific writing, you don't need to set aside your own voice completely.

In considering the work of others, look for instances where the experimental design and methodology fail to adequately test a hypothesis.

▸ **The work of Y and Z appears to show that _____, but their experimental design does not control for _____.**

Also, consider the possibility that results do not lead to the stated conclusions.

▸ **While X and Y claim that _____, their finding of _____ actually shows that _____.**

Okay, But . . .

Science tends to progress incrementally. New work may refine or extend previous work but doesn't often completely overturn it. For this reason, science writers frequently agree up to a point and then express some disagreement. In the following example from a commentary about methods for assessing how proteins interact, the authors acknowledge the value of the two-hybrid studies, but they also point out their shortcomings.

> The two-hybrid studies that produced the protein interaction map for *D. melanogaster* (12) provide a valuable genome-wide view of protein interactions but have a number of shortcomings (13). Even if the protein-protein interactions were determined with high accuracy, the resulting network would still require careful interpretation to extract its underlying biological meaning. Specifically, the map is a representation of all possible interactions, but one would only expect some fraction to be operating at any given time.
>
> J. J. RICE, A. KERSHENBAUM, AND G. STOLOVITZKY,
> "Lasting Impressions: Motifs in Protein-Protein Maps
> May Provide Footprints of Evolutionary Events."
> *Proceedings of the National Academy of Sciences*

Delineating the boundaries or limitations of a study is a good way to agree up to a point. Here are templates for doing so.

▸ While X's work clearly demonstrates _____ , _____ will be required before we can determine whether _____ .

▸ Although Y and Z present firm evidence for _____ , their data can not be used to argue that _____ .

▸ In summary, our studies show that _____ , but the issue of _____ remains unresolved.

Anticipate Objections

Skepticism is a key ingredient in the scientific process. Before an explanation is accepted, scientists demand convincing evidence and assess whether alternative explanations have been thoroughly explored, so it's essential that scientists consider possible objections to their ideas before presenting them. In the following example from a book about the origin of the universe, Tyson and Goldsmith first admit that some might doubt the existence of the poorly understood "dark matter" that physicists have proposed, and then they go on to respond to the skeptics.

> Unrelenting skeptics might compare the dark matter of today with the hypothetical, now defunct "ether," proposed centuries ago as the weightless, transparent medium through which light moved. . . . But dark matter ignorance differs fundamentally from ether ignorance. While ether amounted to a placeholder for our incomplete understanding, the existence of dark matter derives from not from mere presumption but from the observed effects of its gravity on visible matter.
>
> N. D. TYSON AND D. GOLDSMITH,
> *Origins: Fourteen Billion Years of Cosmic Evolution*

Anticipating objections in your own writing will help you clarify and address potential criticisms. Consider objections to your overall approach, as well as to specific aspects of your interpretations. Here are some templates for doing so.

▸ Scientists who take a _____ (*reductionist / integrative / biochemical / computational / statistical*) approach might view our results differently.

217

▸ This interpretation of the data might be criticized by X, who has argued that _____ .

▸ Some may argue that this experimental design fails to account for _____ .

Say Why It Matters

Though individual studies can be narrowly focused, science ultimately seeks to answer big questions and produce useful technologies. So it's essential when you enter a scientific conversation to say why the work—and your arguments about it—matter. The following passage from a commentary on a research article notes two implications of work that evaluated the shape of electron orbitals.

> The classic textbook shape of electron orbitals has now been directly observed. As well as confirming the established theory, this work may be a first step to understanding high-temperature superconductivity.
>
> C. J. HUMPHREYS, "Electrons Seen in Orbit," *Nature*

Humphreys argues that the study confirms an established theory and that it may lead to better understanding in another area. When thinking about the broad significance of a study, consider both the practical applications and the impact on future scientific work.

▸ These results open the door to studies that _____ .

▸ The methodologies developed by X will be useful for _____ .

▸ Our findings are the first step toward _____ .

▶ **Further work in this area may lead to the development of**
_____ .

READING AS A WAY OF ENTERING
SCIENTIFIC CONVERSATIONS

In science, as in other disciplines, you'll often start with work done by others, and therefore you will need to critically evaluate their work. To that end, you'll need to probe how well their data support their interpretations. Doing so will lead you toward your own interpretations—your ticket into an ongoing scientific conversation. Here are some questions that will help you read and respond to scientific research.

How well do the methods test the hypothesis?

- Is the sample size adequate?

- Is the experimental design valid?
  Were the proper controls performed?

- What are the limitations of the methodology?

- Are other techniques available?

How fairly have the results been interpreted?

- How well do the results support the stated conclusion?

- Has the data's variability been adequately considered?

- Do other findings verify (or contradict) the conclusion?

- What other experiments could test the conclusion?

What are the broader implications of the work, and why does it matter?

- Can the results be generalized beyond the system that was studied?

- What are the work's practical implications?

- What questions arise from the work?

- Which experiments should be done next?

The examples in this chapter show that scientists do more than simply collect facts; they also interpret those facts and make arguments about their meaning. On the frontiers of science, where we are probing questions that are just beyond our capacity to answer, the data are inevitably incomplete and controversy is to be expected. Writing about science presents the opportunity to add your own arguments to the ongoing discussion.

SEVENTEEN

"ANALYZE THIS"

Writing in the Social Sciences

ERIN ACKERMAN

SOCIAL SCIENCE is the study of people—how they behave and relate to one another, and the organizations and institutions that facilitate these interactions. People are complicated, so any study of human behavior is at best partial, taking into account some elements of what people do and why, but not always explaining those actions definitively. As a result, it is the subject of constant conversation and argument.

Consider some of the topics studied in the social sciences: minimum wage laws, immigration policy, health care, employment discrimination. Got an opinion on any of these topics? You aren't alone. But in the writing you do as a student of the social sciences, you need to write about more than just your

ERIN ACKERMAN is the Social Sciences Librarian at the College of New Jersey and formerly taught political science at John Jay College, City University of New York. Her research and teaching interests include women and American law, the law and politics of reproductive health, and information literacy in the social sciences.

opinions. Good writing in the social sciences, as in other aca-demic disciplines, requires that you demonstrate that you have thought about what it is you think. The best way to do that is to bring your views into conversation with those expressed by others and to test what you and others think against a review of data. In other words, you'll need to start with what others say and then present what you say as a response.

Consider the following example from a book about contemporary American political culture:

> Claims of deep national division were standard fare after the 2000 elections, and to our knowledge few commentators have publicly challenged them. . . . In sum, contemporary observers of American politics have apparently reached a new consensus around the proposition that old disagreements about economics now pale in comparison to new divisions based on sexuality, morality, and religion, divisions so deep as to justify fears of violence and talk of war in describing them.
>
> This short book advocates a contrary thesis: the sentiments expressed in the previously quoted pronouncements of scholars, journalists, and politicos range from simple exaggeration to sheer nonsense. . . . Many of the activists in the political parties and vari-ous cause groups do, in fact, hate each other and regard themselves as combatants in a war. But their hatreds and battles are not shared by the great mass of the American people. . . .
>
> MORRIS P. FIORINA, *Culture War?*
> *The Myth of a Polarized America*

In other words, "they" (journalists, pundits, other political scientists) say that the American public is deeply divided, whereas Fiorina replies that they have misinterpreted the evidence—specifically, that they have generalized from a few exceptional cases (activists). Even the title of the book calls into question an idea held by others, one Fiorina labels a "myth."

This chapter explores some of the basic moves social science writers make. In addition, writing in the social sciences generally includes several core components: a strong introduction and thesis, a literature review, and the writer's own analysis, including presentation of data and consideration of implications. Much of your own writing will include one or more of these components as well. The introduction sets out the thesis, or point, of the paper, briefly explaining what you will say in your text and how it fits into the preexisting conversation. The literature review summarizes what has already been said on your topic. Your analysis allows you to present data—the information about human behavior you are measuring or testing against what other people have said—and to explain the conclusions you have drawn based on your investigation. Do you agree, disagree, or some combination of both, with what has been said by others? What reasons can you give for why you feel that way? And so what? Who should be interested in what you have to say, and why?

THE INTRODUCTION AND THESIS:
"THIS PAPER CHALLENGES . . ."

Your introduction sets forth what you plan to say in your essay. You might evaluate the work of earlier scholars or certain widely held assumptions and find them incorrect when measured against new data. Alternatively, you might point out that an author's work is largely correct, but that it could use some qualifications or be extended in some way. Or you might identify a gap in our knowledge—we know a great deal about topic X but almost nothing about some other closely related topic. In each of these instances, your introduction needs to cover both "they say" and "I say" perspectives. If you stop after the "they say," your readers won't know what you are bringing to the conversation. Similarly, if you were to jump right to the "I say" portion of your argument, readers might wonder why you need to say anything at all.

Sometimes you join the conversation at a point where the discussion seems settled. One or more views about a topic have become so widely accepted among a group of scholars or society at large that these views are essentially the conventional way of thinking about the topic. You may wish to offer new reasons to support this interpretation, or you may wish to call these standard views into question. To do so, you must first introduce and identify these widely held beliefs and then present your own view. In fact, much of the writing in the social sciences takes the form of calling into question that which we think we already know. Consider the following example from an article in *The Journal of Economic Perspectives*:

> Fifteen years ago, Milton Friedman's 1957 treatise *A Theory of the Consumption Function* seemed badly dated. Dynamic optimization theory had not been employed much in economics when Friedman wrote, and utility theory was still comparatively primitive, so his statement of the "permanent income hypothesis" never actually specified a formal mathematical model of behavior derived explicitly from utility maximization . . . [W]hen other economists subsequently found multiperiod maximizing models that could be solved explicitly, the implications of those models differed sharply from Friedman's intuitive description of his "model." Furthermore, empirical tests in the 1970s and 1980s often rejected these rigorous versions of the permanent income hypothesis in favor of an

alternative hypothesis that many households simply spent all of their current income.

Today, with the benefit of a further round of mathematical (and computational) advances, Friedman's (1957) original analysis looks more prescient than primitive . . .

CHRISTOPHER D. CARROLL, "A Theory of Consumption Function, With and Without Liquidity Constraints," *The Journal of Economic Perspectives*

This introduction makes clear that Carroll will defend Milton Friedman against some major criticisms of his work. Carroll mentions what has been said about Friedman's work and then goes on to say that the critiques turn out to be wrong and to suggest that Friedman's work reemerges as persuasive. A template of Carroll's introduction might look something like this: Economics research in the last fifteen years suggested Friedman's 1957 treatise was _____ because _____. In other words, they say that Friedman's work is not accurate because of _____, _____, and _____. Recent research convinces me, however, that Friedman's work makes sense.

In some cases, however, there may not be a strong consensus among experts on a topic. You might enter the ongoing debate by casting your vote with one side or another or by offering an alternative view. In the following example, Shari Berman identifies two competing accounts of how to explain world events in the twentieth century and then puts forth a third view.

> Conventional wisdom about twentieth-century ideologies rests on two simple narratives. One focuses on the struggle for dominance between democracy and its alternatives. . . . The other narrative focuses on the competition between free-market capitalism and its rivals. . . . Both of these narratives obviously contain some truth. . . . Yet both only tell part of the story, which is why their common

conclusion—neoliberalism as the "end of History"—is unsatisfying and misleading.

What the two conventional narratives fail to mention is that a third struggle was also going on: between those ideologies that believed in the primacy of economics and those that believed in the primacy of politics.

> SHARI BERMAN, "The Primacy of Economics versus the
> Primacy of Politics: Understanding the Ideological Dynamics
> of the Twentieth Century," *Perspectives on Politics*

After identifying the two competing narratives, Berman suggests a third view—and later goes on to argue that this third view explains current debates over globalization. A template for this type of introduction might look something like this: In recent discussions of _____, a controversial aspect has been _____. On the one hand, some argue that _____. On the other hand, others argue that _____. Neither of these arguments, however, considers the alternative view that _____.

Given the complexity of many of the issues studied in the social sciences, however, you may sometimes agree *and* disagree with existing views—pointing out things that you believe are correct or have merit, while disagreeing with or refining other points. In the example below, anthropologist Sally Engle Merry agrees with another scholar about something that is a key trait of modern society but argues that this trait has a different origin than the other author identifies.

For more on different ways of responding, see Chapter 4.

Although I agree with Rose that an increasing emphasis on governing the soul is characteristic of modern society, I see the transformation not as evolutionary but as the product of social mobilization and political struggle.

> SALLY ENGLE MERRY, "Rights, Religion, and Community:
> Approaches to Violence against Women in the
> Context of Globalization," *Law and Society Review*

Here are some templates for agreeing and disagreeing:

▶ **Although I agree with X up to a point, I cannot accept his overall conclusion that _____ .**

▶ **Although I disagree with X on _____ and _____ , I agree with her conclusion that _____ .**

▶ **Political scientists studying _____ have argued that it is caused by _____ . While _____ contributes to the problem, _____ is also an important factor.**

In the process of examining people from different angles, social scientists sometimes identify gaps—areas that have not been explored in previous research. In an article on African American neighborhoods, sociologist Mary Pattillo identifies such a gap.

> The research on African Americans is dominated by inquiries into the lives of the black poor. Contemporary ethnographies and journalistic descriptions have thoroughly described deviance, gangs, drugs, intergender relations and sexuality, stymied aspiration, and family patterns in poor neighborhoods (Dash 1989; Hagedorn 1988; Kotlowitz 1991; Lemann 1991; MacLeod 1995; Sullivan 1989; Williams 1989). Yet, the majority of African Americans are not

poor (Billingsley 1992). A significant part of the black experience, namely that of working and middle-class blacks, remains unexplored. We have little information about what black middle-class neighborhoods look like and how social life is organized within them. . . . this article begins to fill this empirical and theoretical gap using ethnographic data collected in Groveland, a middle-class black neighborhood in Chicago.

MARY E. PATTILLO,
"Sweet Mothers and Gangbangers: Managing Crime
in a Black Middle-Class Neighborhood," *Social Forces*

Pattillo explains that much has been said about poor African American neighborhoods. But, she says, we have little information about the experience of working-class and middle-class black neighborhoods—a gap that her article will address.

Here are some templates for introducing gaps in the existing research:

▸ **Studies of X have indicated _____. It is not clear, however, that this conclusion applies to _____.**

▸ **_____ often take for granted that _____. Few have investigated this assumption, however.**

▸ **X's work tells us a great deal about _____. Can this work be generalized to _____?**

Again, a good introduction indicates what you have to say in the larger context of what others have said. Throughout the rest of your paper, you will move back and forth between the "they say" and the "I say," adding more details.

THE LITERATURE REVIEW:
"PRIOR RESEARCH INDICATES . . ."

In the literature review, you explain what "they say" in more detail, summarizing, paraphrasing, or quoting the viewpoints to which you are responding. But you need to balance what they are saying with your own focus. You need to characterize someone else's work fairly and accurately but set up the points you yourself want to make by selecting the details that are relevant to your own perspective and observations.

It is common in the social sciences to summarize several arguments at once, identifying their major arguments or findings in a single paragraph.

> How do employers in a low-wage labor market respond to an increase in the minimum wage? The prediction from conventional economic theory is unambiguous: a rise in the minimum wage leads perfectly competitive employers to cut employment (George J. Stigler, 1946). Although studies in the 1970's based on aggregate teenage employment rates usually confirmed this prediction, earlier studies based on comparisons of employment at affected and unaffected establishments often did not (e.g., Richard A. Lester, 1960, 1964). Several recent studies that rely on a similar comparative methodology have failed to detect a negative employment effect of higher minimum wages. Analyses of the 1990–1991 increases in the federal minimum wage (Lawrence F. Katz and Krueger, 1992; Card, 1992a) and of an earlier increase in the minimum wage in California (Card, 1992b) find no adverse employment impact.
>
> DAVID CARD AND ALAN KRUEGER,
> "Minimum Wages and Employment: A Case Study of the
> Fast-Food Industry in New Jersey and Pennsylvania,"
> *The American Economic Review*

Card and Krueger cite the key findings and conclusions of works that are relevant to the question they are investigating and the point they plan to address, asking "How do employers in a low-wage labor market respond to an increase in the minimum wage?" They go on, as good writers should, to answer the question they ask. And they do so by reviewing others who have answered that question, noting that this question has been answered in different, sometimes contradictory, ways.

Such summaries are brief, bringing together relevant arguments by several scholars to provide an overview of scholarly work on a particular topic. In writing such a summary, you need to ask yourself how the authors themselves might describe their positions and also consider what in their work is relevant for the point you wish to make. This kind of summary is especially appropriate when you have a large amount of research material on a topic and want to identify the major strands of a debate or to show how the work of one author builds on that of another. Here are some templates for overview summaries:

▶ In addressing the question of _____, political scientists have considered several explanations for _____. X argues that _____. According to Y and Z, another plausible explanation is _____.

▶ What is the effect of _____ on _____? Previous work on _____ by X and by Y and Z supports _____.

Sometimes you may need to say more about the works you cite. On a midterm or final exam, for example, you may need to demonstrate that you have a deep familiarity with a particular work. And in some disciplines of the social sciences, longer, more detailed literature reviews are the standard. Your instructor and the articles he or she has assigned are your best guides for the length and level of detail of your literature review. Other times, the work of certain authors is especially important for your argument, and therefore you need to provide more details to explain what these authors have said. See how Martha Derthick summarizes an argument that is central to her book about the politics of tobacco regulation.

> The idea that governments could sue to reclaim health care costs from cigarette manufacturers might be traced to "Cigarettes and Welfare Reform," an article published in the *Emory Law Journal* in 1977 by Donald Gasner, a law professor at the University of Southern Illinois. Garner suggested that state governments could get a cigarette manufacturer to pay the direct medical costs "of looking after patients with smoking diseases." He drew an analogy to the Coal Mine Health and Safety Act of 1969, under which coal mine operators are required to pay certain disability benefits for coal miners suffering from pneumoconiosis, or black lung disease.
>
> MARTHA DERTHICK, *Up In Smoke:*
> *From Legislation to Litigation in Tobacco Politics*

Note that Derthick identifies the argument she is summarizing, quoting its author directly and then adding details about a precedent for the argument.

You may want to include direct quotations of what others have said, as Derthick does. Using an author's exact words helps you demonstrate that you are representing him or her fairly. But you cannot simply insert a quotation; you need to explain to your readers what it means for your point. Consider the following example drawn from a political science book on the debate over tort reform.

> The essence of *agenda setting* was well enunciated by E. E. Schattschneider: "In politics as in everything else, it makes a great

difference whose game we play" (1960, 47). In short, the ability to define or control the rules, terms, or perceived options in a contest over policy greatly affects the prospects for winning.

WILLIAM HALTOM AND MICHAEL McCANN,
Distorting the Law: Politics, Media, and the Litigation Crisis

Notice how Haltom and McCann first quote Schattschneider and then explain in their own words how political agenda setting can be thought of as a game, with winners and losers.

Remember that whenever you summarize, quote, or paraphrase the work of others, credit must be given in the form of a citation to the original work. The words may be your own, but if the idea comes from someone else you must give credit to the original work. There are several formats for documenting sources. Consult your instructor for help choosing which citation style to use.

THE ANALYSIS

The literature review covers what others have said on your topic. The analysis allows you to present and support your own response. In the introduction you indicate whether you agree, disagree, or some combination of both with what others have said. You will want to expand on how you have formed your opinion and why others should care about your topic.

"The Data Indicate . . ."

The social sciences use data to develop and test explanations. Data can be quantitative or qualitative and can come from a number of sources. You might use statistics related to GDP growth, unemployment, voting rates, or demographics. Or you could use surveys, interviews, or other first-person accounts.

Regardless of the type of data used, it is important to do three things: define your data, indicate where you got the data, and then say what you have done with your data. In a journal article, political scientist Joshua C. Wilson examines a court case about protests at an abortion clinic and asks whether each side of the conflict acts in a way consistent with their general views on freedom of speech.

[T]his paper relies on close readings of in-person, semi-structured interviews with the participants involved in the real controversy that was the *Williams* case.

Thirteen interviews ranging in length from 40 minutes to 1 hour and 50 minutes were conducted for this paper. Of those interviewed, all would be considered "elites" in terms of political psychology / political attitude research—six were active members of Solano Citizens for Life . . . ; two were members of Planned Parenthood Shasta-Diablo management; one was the lawyer who obtained the restraining order, temporary injunction, and permanent injunction for Planned Parenthood; one was the lawyer for the duration of the case for Solano Citizens for Life; two were lawyers for Planned Parenthood on appeal; and one was the Superior Court judge who heard arguments for, and finally crafted, the restraining order and injunctions against Solano Citizens for Life. During the course of the interviews, participants were asked a range of questions about their experiences and thoughts in relation to the Williams case, as well as their beliefs about the interpretation and limits of the First Amendment right to free speech—both in general, and in relation to the Williams case.

JOSHUA C. WILSON. "When Rights Collide:
Anti-Abortion Protests and the Ideological Dilemma
in *Planned Parenthood Shasta-Diablo, Inc. v. Williams*,"
Studies in Law, Politics, and Society

Wilson identifies and describes his qualitative data—interviews conducted with key parties in the conflict—and explains the nature of the questions he asked.

If your data are quantitative, you will need to explain them similarly. See how political scientist Brian Arbour explains the quantitative data he used to study for an article in *The Forum* how a change of rules might have affected the outcome of the 2008 Democratic primary contest between Hillary Clinton and Barack Obama.

> I evaluate these five concerns about the Democratic system of delegate allocation by "rerunning" the Obama-Clinton contest with a different set of allocation rules, those in effect for the 2008 Republican presidential contest. . . . Republicans allow each state to make their own rules, leading to "a plethora of selection plans" (Shapiro & Bello 2008, 5) . . . To "rerun" the Democratic primary under Republican rules, I need data on the results of the Democratic primary for each state and congressional district and on the Republican delegate allocation rules for each state. The Green Papers (www.thegreenpapers.com), a website that serves as an almanac of election procedures, rules, and results, provides each of these data sources. By "rerunning" the Democratic primaries and caucuses, I use the exact results of each contest.
>
> BRIAN ARBOUR, "Even Closer, Even Longer: What If the 2008 Democratic Primary Used Republican Rules?" *The Forum*

Note that Arbour identifies his data as primary voting results and the rules for Republican primaries. In the rest of the paper, Arbour shows how his use of these data suggests that political commentators who thought Republican rules would have clarified the close race between Clinton and Obama were wrong and the race would have been "even closer, even longer."

Here are some templates for discussing data:

▸ In order to test the hypothesis that _____, we assessed _____. Our calculations suggest _____.

▸ I used _____ to investigate _____. The results of this investigation indicate _____.

"But Others May Object . . ."

No matter how strongly your data support your argument, there are almost surely other perspectives (and thus other data) that you need to acknowledge. By considering possible objections to your argument and taking them seriously, you demonstrate that you've done your work and that you're aware of other perspectives—and most important, you present your own argument as part of an ongoing conversation.

See how economist Christopher Carroll acknowledges that there may be objections to his argument about how people allocate their income between consumption and savings.

> I have argued here that the modern version of the dynamically optimizing consumption model is able to match many of the important features of the empirical data on consumption and saving behavior. There are, however, several remaining reasons for discomfort with the model.
>
> CHRISTOPHER D. CARROLL, "A Theory of Consumption
> Function, With and Without Liquidity Constraints,"
> *The Journal of Economic Perspectives*

Carroll then goes on to identify the possible limitations of his mathematical analysis.

Someone may object because there are related phenomena that your analysis does not explain or because you do not have the right data to investigate a particular question. Or perhaps someone may object to assumptions underlying your argument or how you handled your data. Here are some templates for considering naysayers:

▶ _____ might object that _____.

▶ Is my claim realistic? I have argued _____, but readers may question _____.

▶ My explanation accounts for _____ but does not explain _____. This is because _____.

"Why Should We Care?"

Who should care about your research, and why? Since the social sciences attempt to explain human behavior, it is important to consider how your research affects the assumptions we make about human behavior. In addition, you might offer recommendations for how other social scientists might continue to explore an issue, or what actions policymakers should take.

In the following example, sociologist Devah Pager identifies the implications of her study of the way having a criminal record affects a person applying for jobs.

[I]n terms of policy implications, this research has troubling conclusions. In our frenzy of locking people up, our "crime control" policies may in fact exacerbate the very conditions that lead to crime in the first place. Research consistently shows that finding quality steady employment is one of the strongest predictors of desistance from crime (Shover 1996; Sampson and Laub 1993; Uggen 2000). The fact that a criminal record severely limits employment opportunities—particularly among blacks—suggests that these individuals are left with few viable alternatives.

DEVAH PAGER, "The Mark of a Criminal Record,"
The American Journal of Sociology

Pager's conclusion that a criminal record negatively affects employment chances creates a vicious circle, she says: steady employment discourages recidivism, but a criminal record makes it harder to get a job.

In answering the "so what?" question, you need to explain why your readers should care. Although sometimes the implications of your work may be so broad that they would be of interest to almost anyone, it's never a bad idea to identify explicitly any groups of people who will find your work important.

Templates for establishing why your claims matter:

▸ **X is important because _____.**

▸ **Ultimately, what is at stake here is _____.**

▸ **The finding that _____ should be of interest to _____ because _____.**

As noted at the beginning of this chapter, the complexity of people allows us to look at their behavior from many different viewpoints. Much has been, and will be, said about how and why people do the things they do. As a result, we can look at writing in the social sciences as an ongoing conversation.

When you join this conversation, the "they say / I say" framework will help you figure out what has already been said (they say) and what you can add (I say). The components of social science writing presented in this chapter are tools to help you join that conversation.

READINGS

READINGS

Don't Blame the Eater

DAVID ZINCZENKO

—◻—

IF EVER THERE WERE a newspaper headline custom-made for Jay Leno's monologue, this was it. Kids taking on McDonald's this week, suing the company for making them fat. Isn't that like middle-aged men suing Porsche for making them get speeding tickets? Whatever happened to personal responsibility?

I tend to sympathize with these portly fast-food patrons, though. Maybe that's because I used to be one of them.

I grew up as a typical mid-1980s latchkey kid. My parents were split up, my dad off trying to rebuild his life, my mom working long hours to make the monthly bills. Lunch and dinner, for me, was a daily choice between McDonald's, Taco Bell, Kentucky Fried Chicken or Pizza Hut. Then as now, these were the only available options for an American kid to get an affordable meal. By age 15, I had packed 212 pounds of torpid teenage tallow on my once lanky 5-foot-10 frame.

Then I got lucky. I went to college, joined the Navy Reserves and got involved with a health magazine. I learned how to

DAVID ZINCZENKO, who was for many years the editor-in-chief of the fitness magazine *Men's Health*, is president of Galvanized Brands, a global health and wellness media company. This piece was first published on the op-ed page of the *New York Times* on November 23, 2002.

manage my diet. But most of the teenagers who live, as I once did, on a fast-food diet won't turn their lives around: They've crossed under the golden arches to a likely fate of lifetime obesity. And the problem isn't just theirs—it's all of ours.

Before 1994, diabetes in children was generally caused by a genetic disorder—only about 5 percent of childhood cases were obesity-related, or Type 2, diabetes. Today, according to the National Institutes of Health, Type 2 diabetes accounts for at least 30 percent of all new childhood cases of diabetes in this country.

For tips on saying why it matters, see Chapter 7.

Not surprisingly, money spent to treat diabetes has skyrocketed, too. The Centers for Disease Control and Prevention estimate that diabetes accounted for $2.6 billion in health care costs in 1969. Today's number is an unbelievable $100 billion a year.

Shouldn't we know better than to eat two meals a day in fast-food restaurants? That's one argument. But where, exactly, are consumers—particularly teenagers—supposed to find alternatives? Drive down any thoroughfare in America, and I guarantee you'll see one of our country's more than 13,000 McDonald's restaurants. Now, drive back up the block and try to find someplace to buy a grapefruit.

Complicating the lack of alternatives is the lack of information about what, exactly, we're consuming. There are no calorie information charts on fast-food packaging, the way there are on grocery items. Advertisements don't carry warning labels the way tobacco ads do. Prepared foods aren't covered under Food and Drug Administration labeling laws. Some fast-food purveyors will provide calorie information on request, but even that can be hard to understand.

For example, one company's Web site lists its chicken salad as containing 150 calories; the almonds and noodles that come with it (an additional 190 calories) are listed separately. Add a serving of the 280-calorie dressing, and you've got a healthy lunch alternative that comes in at 620 calories. But that's not all. Read the small print on the back of the dressing packet and you'll realize it actually contains 2.5 servings. If you pour what you've been served, you're suddenly up around 1,040 calories, which is half of the government's recommended daily calorie intake. And that doesn't take into account that 450-calorie super-size Coke.

Make fun if you will of these kids launching lawsuits against the fast-food industry, but don't be surprised if you're the next plaintiff. As with the tobacco industry, it may be only a matter of time before state governments begin to see a direct line between the $1 billion that McDonald's and Burger King spend each year on advertising and their own swelling health care costs.

And I'd say the industry is vulnerable. Fast-food companies are marketing to children a product with proven health hazards and no warning labels. They would do well to protect themselves, and their customers, by providing the nutrition information people need to make informed choices about their products. Without such warnings, we'll see more sick, obese children and more angry, litigious parents. I say, let the deep-fried chips fall where they may.

Hidden Intellectualism

GERALD GRAFF

—◻—

EVERYONE KNOWS SOME YOUNG PERSON who is impressively "street smart" but does poorly in school. What a waste, we think, that one who is so intelligent about so many things in life seems unable to apply that intelligence to academic work. What doesn't occur to us, though, is that schools and colleges might be at fault for missing the opportunity to tap into such street smarts and channel them into good academic work.

Nor do we consider one of the major reasons why schools and colleges overlook the intellectual potential of street smarts: the fact that we associate those street smarts with anti-intellectual concerns. We associate the educated life, the life of the mind, too narrowly and exclusively with subjects and texts that we consider inherently weighty and academic. We assume

———

GERALD GRAFF, the co-author of this book, is a professor of English and education at the University of Illinois at Chicago. He is a past president of the Modern Language Association, the world's largest professional association of university scholars and teachers. This essay is adapted from his 2003 book *Clueless in Academe: How Schooling Obscures the Life of the Mind*.

that it's possible to wax intellectual about Plato, Shakespeare, the French Revolution, and nuclear fission, but not about cars, dating, fashion, sports, TV, or video games.

The trouble with this assumption is that no neces- See pp. 58–61 sary connection has ever been established between any for tips on disagreeing, text or subject and the educational depth and weight with reasons. of the discussion it can generate. Real intellectuals turn any subject, however lightweight it may seem, into grist for their mill through the thoughtful questions they bring to it, whereas a dullard will find a way to drain the interest out of the richest subject. That's why a George Orwell writing on the cultural meanings of penny postcards is infinitely more substantial than the cogitations of many professors on Shakespeare or globalization (104–16).

Students do need to read models of intellectually challenging writing—and Orwell is a great one—if they are to become intellectuals themselves. But they would be more prone to take on intellectual identities if we encouraged them to do so at first on subjects that interest them rather than ones that interest us.

I offer my own adolescent experience as a case in point. 5 Until I entered college, I hated books and cared only for sports. The only reading I cared to do or could do was sports magazines, on which I became hooked, becoming a regular reader of *Sport* magazine in the late forties, *Sports Illustrated* when it began publishing in 1954, and the annual magazine guides to professional baseball, football, and basketball. I also loved the sports novels for boys of John R. Tunis and Clair Bee and autobiographies of sports stars like Joe DiMaggio's *Lucky to Be a Yankee* and Bob Feller's *Strikeout Story*. In short, I was your typical teenage anti-intellectual—or so I believed for a long time. I have recently come to think, however, that my preference for sports over schoolwork was not anti-intellectualism so much as intellectualism by other means.

In the Chicago neighborhood I grew up in, which had become a melting pot after World War II, our block was solidly middle class, but just a block away—doubtless concentrated there by the real estate companies—were African Americans, Native Americans, and "hillbilly" whites who had recently fled postwar joblessness in the South and Appalachia. Negotiating this class boundary was a tricky matter. On the one hand, it was necessary to maintain the boundary between "clean-cut" boys like me and working-class "hoods," as we called them, which meant that it was good to be openly smart in a book-ish sort of way. On the other hand, I was desperate for the approval of the hoods, whom I encountered daily on the play-ing field and in the neighborhood, and for this purpose it was not at all good to be book-smart. The hoods would turn on you if they sensed you were putting on airs over them: "Who you lookin' at, smart ass?" as a leather-jacketed youth once said to me as he relieved me of my pocket change along with my self-respect.

I grew up torn, then, between the need to prove I was smart and the fear of a beating if I proved it too well; between the need not to jeopardize my respectable future and the need to impress the hoods. As I lived it, the conflict came down to a choice between being physically tough and being verbal. For a boy in my neighborhood and elementary school, only being "tough" earned you complete legitimacy. I still recall endless, complicated debates in this period with my closest pals over who was "the toughest guy in the school." If you were less than negligible as a fighter, as I was, you settled for the next best thing, which was to be inarticulate, carefully hiding telltale marks of literacy like correct grammar and pronunciation.

In one way, then, it would be hard to imagine an adolescence more thoroughly anti-intellectual than mine. Yet in retrospect, I see that it's more complicated, that I and the 1950s themselves were not simply hostile toward intellectualism, but divided and ambivalent. When Marilyn Monroe married the playwright Arthur Miller in 1956 after divorcing the retired baseball star Joe DiMaggio, the symbolic triumph of geek over jock suggested the way the wind was blowing. Even Elvis, according to his biographer Peter Guralnick, turns out to have supported Adlai over Ike in the presidential election of 1956. "I don't dig the intellectual bit," he told reporters. "But I'm telling you, man, he knows the most" (327).

Though I too thought I did not "dig the intellectual bit," I see now that I was unwittingly in training for it. The germs had actually been planted in the seemingly philistine debates about which boys were the toughest. I see now that in the interminable analysis of sports teams, movies, and toughness that my friends and I engaged in—a type of analysis, needless to say, that the real toughs would never have stooped to—I was already betraying an allegiance to the egghead world. I was practicing being an intellectual before I knew that was what I wanted to be.

It was in these discussions with friends about toughness and sports, I think, and in my reading of sports books and magazines, that I began to learn the rudiments of the intellectual life: how to make an argument, weigh different kinds of evidence, move between particulars and generalizations, summarize the views of others, and enter a conversation about ideas. It was in reading and arguing about sports and toughness that

I experienced what it felt like to propose a generalization, restate and respond to a counterargument, and perform other intellectualizing operations, including composing the kind of sentences I am writing now.

Only much later did it dawn on me that the sports world was more compelling than school because it was *more intellectual than school,* not less. Sports after all was full of challenging arguments, debates, problems for analysis, and intricate statistics that you could care about, as school conspicuously was not. I believe that street smarts beat out book smarts in our culture not because street smarts are nonintellectual, as we generally suppose, but because they satisfy an intellectual thirst more thoroughly than school culture, which seems pale and unreal.

They also satisfy the thirst for community. When you entered sports debates, you became part of a community that was not limited to your family and friends, but was national and public. Whereas schoolwork isolated you from others, the pennant race or Ted Williams's .400 batting average was something you could talk about with people you had never met. Sports introduced you not only to a culture steeped in argument, but to a public argument culture that transcended the personal. I can't blame my schools for failing to make intellectual culture resemble the Super Bowl, but I do fault them for failing to learn anything from the sports and entertainment worlds about how to organize and represent intellectual culture, how to exploit its gamelike element and turn it into arresting public spectacle that might have competed more successfully for my youthful attention.

For here is another thing that never dawned on me and is still kept hidden from students, with tragic results: that the real intellectual world, the one that existed in the big world beyond school, is organized very much like the world of team sports, with rival texts, rival interpretations and evaluations of texts, rival theories of why they should be read and taught, and elaborate team competitions in which "fans" of writers, intellectual systems, methodologies, and -isms contend against each other.

To be sure, school contained plenty of competition, which became more invidious as one moved up the ladder (and has become even more so today with the advent of high-stakes testing). In this competition, points were scored not by making arguments, but by a show of information or vast reading, by grade-grubbing, or other forms of one-upmanship. School competition, in short, reproduced the less attractive features of sports culture without those that create close bonds and community.

And in distancing themselves from anything as enjoyable 15 and absorbing as sports, my schools missed the opportunity to capitalize on an element of drama and conflict that the intellectual world shares with sports. Consequently, I failed to see the parallels between the sports and academic worlds that could have helped me cross more readily from one argument culture to the other.

Sports is only one of the domains whose potential for literacy training (and not only for males) is seriously underestimated by educators, who see sports as competing with academic development rather than a route to it. But if this argument suggests why it is a good idea to assign readings and topics that are close to students' existing interests, it also suggests the limits of this tactic. For students who get excited about the chance to write about their passion for cars will often write as poorly and unreflectively on that topic as on Shakespeare or Plato. Here is the flip side of what I pointed out before: that there's no necessary relation between the degree of interest a student shows in a text or subject and the quality of thought or expression such a student manifests in writing or talking about it. The challenge, as college professor Ned Laff has put it, "is not simply to exploit students' nonacademic interests, but to get them to see those interests through academic eyes."

To say that students need to see their interests "through academic eyes" is to say that street smarts are not enough. Making students' nonacademic interests an object of academic study is useful, then, for getting students' attention and overcoming their boredom and alienation, but this tactic won't in itself necessarily move them closer to an academically rigorous treatment of those interests. On the other hand, inviting students to write about cars, sports, or clothing fashions does not have to be a pedagogical cop-out as long as students are required to see these interests "through academic eyes," that is, to think and write about cars, sports, and fashions in a reflective, analytical way, one that sees them as microcosms of what is going on in the wider culture.

If I am right, then schools and colleges are missing an opportunity when they do not encourage students to take their nonacademic interests as objects of academic study. It is self-defeating to decline to introduce any text or subject that figures to engage students who will otherwise tune out academic work entirely. If a student cannot get interested in Mill's *On Liberty* but will read *Sports Illustrated* or *Vogue* or the hip-hop magazine *Source* with absorption, this is a strong argument for assigning the magazines over the classic. It's a good bet that if students get hooked on reading and writing by doing term papers on *Source*, they will eventually get to *On Liberty*. But even if they don't, the magazine reading will make them more literate and reflective than they would be otherwise. So it makes pedagogical sense to develop classroom units on sports, cars, fashions, rap music, and other such topics. Give me the student anytime who writes a sharply argued, sociologically acute analysis of an issue in *Source* over the student who writes a lifeless explication of *Hamlet* or Socrates' *Apology*.

WORKS CITED

Cramer, Richard Ben. *Joe DiMaggio: The Hero's Life*. New York: Simon, 2000. Print.

DiMaggio, Joe. *Lucky to Be a Yankee*. New York: Bantam, 1949. Print.

Feller, Bob. *Strikeout Story*, New York: Bantam, 1948. Print.

Guralnick, Peter. *Last Train to Memphis: The Rise of Elvis Presley*. Boston: Little, Brown, 1994. Print.

Orwell, George. *A Collection of Essays*. New York: Harcourt, 1953. Print.

Nuclear Waste

RICHARD A. MULLER

—▭—

As PEOPLE RECOGNIZE THE DANGERS of fossil fuel plants—
especially the risk of global warming from carbon dioxide
production—nuclear power begins to look more attractive.
But what about the waste—all that highly radioactive debris
that will endure for thousands of years? Do we have the right
to leave such a legacy to our children?

Nuclear waste is one of the biggest technical issues that any
future president is likely to face. The problem seems totally
intractable. Plutonium—just one of the many highly radioactive waste products—has a half-life of 24,000 years. Even in
that unimaginable amount of time, its intense radioactivity will
decrease by only half. After 48,000 years it will still emit deadly
radiation at a quarter of its original level. Even after 100,000
years the radiation will still be above 10% of the level it had
when it left the reactor. What if it leaks into the ground and

_____

RICHARD A. MULLER is professor of physics at the University of
California at Berkeley. He is a past winner of the MacArthur "genius"
Fellowship. This piece was given originally as a lecture in his physics
course for non-science students and was then published in a collection
of his course lectures, *Physics for Future Presidents* (2008).

reaches human water supplies? How can we possibly certify that this material can be kept safe for 100,000 years?

Still, the US government persists in its pursuit of "safe" nuclear waste disposal. It has created a prototype nuclear waste facility buried deep within Yucca Mountain, Nevada, as shown in the figure below. To keep the waste safe, the storage rooms are 1000 feet below the surface. To store even part of the present nuclear waste requires a vast area, nearly 2 square miles. The cost of the facility is expected to reach $100 billion, with hundreds of billions of dollars more in operating costs.

To make matters worse, the Yucca Mountain region is seismically active. More than 600 earthquakes of magnitude 2.5 and higher have occurred within 50 miles in the last decade

Yucca Mountain, the site of the prototype nuclear waste storage facility.

alone. Moreover, the region was created by volcanic activity. Although that was millions of years ago, how sure can we be that the waste facility won't be torn apart by another eruption?

Many alternatives have been suggested for nuclear waste 5 storage. Why not just send the waste into the sun? Well, maybe that's not such a good idea, since on launch some rockets do crash back down on the Earth. Some scientists have proposed that the waste be put in vessels and sunk under the oceans, in a region where the movement of the Earth's crustal plates will subduct the material, eventually burying it hundreds of miles deep. Yet just the fact that scientists make such suggestions seems to emphasize how severe the problem really is.

Here is the worst part. We have already generated more than enough nuclear waste to fill up Yucca Mountain. That waste won't go away. Yet you, a future president, are considering *more* nuclear power? Are you insane?

My Confession

The furor against nuclear power has been so intense that I felt compelled to reproduce the anti-nuke viewpoint in the opening of this chapter, including at least part of their passion. These are the arguments that you will hear when you are president. Yet it hardly matters whether you are pro-nuke or anti-nuke. The waste is there, and you will have to do something with it. You can't ignore this issue, and to do the right thing (and to convince the public that you're doing the right thing) you must understand the physics.

When I work out the numbers, I find the dangers of storing our waste at Yucca Mountain to be small compared to the dangers of not doing so, and significantly smaller than many other dangers we ignore. Yet the contentious debate continues. More research is demanded, but every bit of additional research seems to raise new questions that exacerbate the public's fear and distrust. I have titled this section "My Confession" because I find it hard to stand aside and present the physics without giving my own personal evaluation. Through most of this book I've tried to present the facts, and just the facts, and let you draw the conclusions. In this section, I confess that I'll depart from that approach. I can't be evenhanded, because the facts seem to point strongly toward a particular conclusion.

I've discussed Yucca Mountain with scientists, politicians, and many concerned citizens. Most of the politicians believe the matter to be a scientific issue, and most of the scientists think it is political. Both are in favor of more research—scientists because that is what they do, and politicians because they think the research will answer the key questions. I don't think it will.

Here are some pertinent facts. The underground tunnels at Yucca Mountain are designed to hold 77,000 tons of high-level nuclear waste. Initially, the most dangerous part of this waste is not plutonium, but fission fragments such as strontium-90, an unstable nucleus created when the uranium nucleus splits. Because these fission fragments have shorter half-lives than uranium, the waste is about 1000 times more radioactive than the original ore. It takes 10,000 years for the waste (not including plutonium, which is also produced in the reactor, and which I'll discuss later) to decay back to the radioactive level of the mined uranium. Largely on the basis of this number, people have searched for a site that will remain secure for 10,000 years. After that, we are better off than if we left the uranium in the ground, so 10,000 years of safety is probably good enough, not the 100,000 years that I mentioned in the chapter introduction.

Ten thousand years still seems impossibly long. What will the world be like 10,000 years from now? Think backward to

10 Chapter 16 has tips on describing the data underpinning a scientific argument.

appreciate the amount of time involved: Ten thousand years ago humans had just discovered agriculture. Writing wouldn't be invented for another 5000 years. Can we really plan 10,000 years into the future? Of course we can't. We have no idea what the world will be like then. There is no way we can claim that we will be able to store nuclear waste for 10,000 years. Any plan to do that is clearly unacceptable.

Of course, calling storage unacceptable is itself an unacceptable answer. We have the waste, and we have to do something with it. But the problem isn't really as hard as I just portrayed it. We don't need absolute security for 10,000 years. A more reasonable goal is to reduce the risk of leakage to 0.1%—that is, to one chance in a thousand. Because the radioactivity is only 1000 times worse than that of the uranium we removed from the ground, the net risk (probability multiplied by danger) is $1000 \times 0.001 = 1$—that is, basically the same as the risk if we hadn't mined the uranium in the first place. (I am assuming the linear hypothesis— that total cancer risk is independent of individual doses or dose rate—but my argument won't depend strongly on its validity.)

Moreover, we don't need this 0.1% level of security for the full 10,000 years. After 300 years, the fission fragment radioactivity will have decreased by a factor of 10; it will be only 100 times as great as the mined uranium. So by then, we no longer need the risk to be at the 0.1% level, but could allow a 1% chance that all of the waste leaks out. That's a lot easier than guaranteeing absolute containment for 10,000 years. Moreover, this calculation assumes that 100% of the waste escapes. For leakage of 1% of the waste, we can accept a 100% probability after 300 years. When you think about it this way, the storage problem begins to seem tractable.

However, the public discussion doesn't take into account these numbers, or the fact that the initial mining actually removed radioactivity from the ground. Instead, the public insists on absolute security. The Department of Energy continues to search Yucca Mountain for unknown earthquake faults, and many people assume that the acceptability of the facility depends on the absence of any such faults. They believe that the discovery of a new fault will rule Yucca Mountain out. The issue, though, should not be whether there will be any earthquakes in the next 10,000 years, but whether after 300 years there will be a 1% chance of a sufficiently large earthquake that 100% of the waste will escape its glass capsules and reach groundwater. Or, we could accept a 100% chance that 1% of the waste will leak, or a 10% chance that 10% will leak. Any of these options leads to a lower risk than if the original uranium had been left in the ground, mixing its natural radioactivity with groundwater. Absolute security is an unnecessarily extreme goal, since even the original uranium in the ground didn't provide it.

The problem is even easier to solve when we ask why we are comparing the danger of waste storage only to the danger of the uranium originally mined. Why not compare it to the larger danger of the natural uranium left in the soil? Colorado, where much of the uranium is obtained, is a geologically active region, full of faults and fissures and mountains rising out of the prairie, and its surface rock contains about a billion tons of uranium. The radioactivity in this uranium is 20 times greater than the legal limit for Yucca Mountain, and it will take more than 13 billion years—not just a few hundred—for the radioactivity to drop by a factor of 10. Yet water that runs through, around, and over this radioactive rock is the source of the Colorado River, which is used for drinking water in much of the West, including Los Angeles and San Diego.

And unlike the glass pellets that store the waste in Yucca Mountain, most of the uranium in the Colorado ground is water-soluble. Here is the absurd-sounding conclusion: if the Yucca Mountain facility were at full capacity and all the waste leaked out of its glass containment immediately and managed to reach groundwater, the danger would still be 20 times less than that currently posed by natural uranium leaching into the Colorado River. The situation brings to mind the resident near Three Mile Island who feared the tiny leakage from the reactor but not the much greater radioactivity of natural radon gas seeping up from the ground.

I don't mean to imply that waste from Yucca Mountain is not dangerous. Nor am I suggesting that we should panic about radioactivity in the Los Angeles water supply. The Colorado River example illustrates only that when we worry about mysterious and unfamiliar dangers, we sometimes lose perspective. Every way I do the calculation, I reach the same conclusion: waste leakage from Yucca Mountain is not a great danger. Put the waste in glass pellets in a reasonably stable geologic formation, and start worrying about real threats—such as the dangers of the continued burning of fossil fuels.

A related issue is the risk of mishaps and attacks during the transportation of nuclear waste to the Yucca Mountain site. The present plans call for the waste to be carried in thick, reinforced concrete cylinders that can survive high-speed crashes without leaking. In fact, it would be very hard for a terrorist to open the containers, or to use the waste in radiological weapons. The smart terrorist is more likely to hijack a tanker truck full of gasoline, chlorine, or another common toxic material and then blow it up in a city. Recall from the chapter on terrorist nukes that al-Qaeda told José Padilla to abandon his effort to make a dirty bomb and instead focus his efforts on natural-gas explosions in apartment buildings.

Why are we worrying about transporting nuclear waste? Ironically, we have gone to such lengths to ensure the safety of the transport that the public thinks the danger is greater than it really is. Images on evening newscasts of concrete containers being dropped from five-story buildings, smashing into the ground and bouncing undamaged, do not reassure the public. This is a consequence of the "where there's smoke there's fire" paradox of public safety. Raise the standards, increase the safety, do more research, study the problem in greater depth, and in the process you will improve safety and frighten the public. After all, would scientists work so hard if the threat weren't real? Scientists who propose rocketing the waste to the sun, or burying it in a subduction zone in the ocean, also seem to be suggesting that the problem is truly intractable, and that premise exacerbates the public fear.

See Chapter 7 for tips on saying why it matters.

The (Futile) Pursuit
of the American Dream

BARBARA EHRENREICH

—▭—

BECAUSE I'VE WRITTEN A LOT ABOUT POVERTY, I'm used to hearing from people in scary circumstances. An eviction notice has arrived. A child has been diagnosed with a serious illness and the health insurance has run out. The car has broken down and there's no way to get to work. These are the routine emergencies that plague the chronically poor. But it struck me, starting in about 2002, that many such tales of hardship were coming from people who were once members in good standing of the middle class—college graduates and former occupants of mid-level white-collar positions. One such writer upbraided me for what she saw as my neglect of hardworking, virtuous people like herself.

———

BARBARA EHRENREICH is an investigative journalist whose articles have appeared in *Harper's*, *The Nation*, the *New York Times*, and many other periodicals. She's the author of a number of books on various topics, including *Bait and Switch: The (Futile) Pursuit of the American Dream* (2005), from which the piece here was taken. Her most recent book is *Bright-Sided: How Positive Thinking Is Undermining America* (2009).

Try investigating people like me who didn't have babies in high school, who made good grades, who work hard and don't kiss a lot of ass and instead of getting promoted or paid fairly must regress to working for $7/hr., having their student loans in perpetual deferment, living at home with their parents, and generally exist in debt which they feel they may never get out of.

Stories of white-collar downward mobility cannot be brushed off as easily as accounts of blue-collar economic woes, which the hard-hearted traditionally blame on "bad choices": failing to get a college degree, for example, failing to postpone child-bearing until acquiring a nest egg, or failing to choose affluent parents in the first place. But distressed white-collar people cannot be accused of fecklessness of any kind; they are the ones who "did everything right." They earned higher degrees, often setting aside their youthful passion for philosophy or music to suffer through dull practical majors like management or finance. In some cases, they were high achievers who ran into trouble precisely because they had risen far enough in the company for their salaries to look like a tempting cost cut. They were the losers, in other words, in a classic game of bait and switch. And while blue-collar poverty has become numbingly routine, white-collar unemployment—and the poverty that often results—remains a rude finger in the face of the American dream.

I realized that I knew very little about the mid- to upper levels of the corporate world, having so far encountered this world almost entirely through its low-wage, entry-level representatives. I was one of them—a server in a national chain restaurant, a cleaning person, and a Wal-Mart "associate"—in the course of researching an earlier book, *Nickel and Dimed: On (Not) Getting By in America*. Like everyone else, I've also encountered the corporate world as a consumer, dealing with people quite far down in the occupational hierarchy—retail clerks, customer service representatives, telemarketers. Of the levels where decisions are made—where the vice presidents, account executives, and regional managers dwell—my experience has been limited to seeing these sorts of people on airplanes, where they study books on "leadership," fiddle with spreadsheets on their laptops, or fall asleep over biographies of the founding fathers.[1] I'm better acquainted with the corporate functionaries of the future, many of whom I've met on my visits to college campuses, where "business" remains the most popular major, if only because it is believed to be the safest and most lucrative (National Center for Education Statistics).

But there have been growing signs of trouble—if not outright misery—within the white-collar corporate workforce. First, starting with the economic downturn of 2001, there has been a rise in unemployment among highly credentialed and experienced people. In late 2003, when I started this project, unemployment was running at about 5.9 percent, but in contrast to earlier economic downturns, a sizable portion—almost 20 percent, or about 1.6 million—of the unemployed were white-collar professionals.[2] Previous downturns had disproportionately hit blue-collar people; this time it was the relative elite of professional, technical, and managerial employees who were being singled out for media sympathy. In April 2003, for example, the *New York Times Magazine* offered a much-discussed cover story about a former $300,000-a-year computer industry executive reduced, after two years of unemployment, to working as a sales associate at the Gap (Mahler). Throughout the first four years of the 2000s, there were similar stories of the mighty or the mere midlevel brought low, ejected from their office suites and forced to serve behind the counter at Starbucks.

Today, white-collar job insecurity is no longer a function of [5] the business cycle—rising as the stock market falls and declining again when the numbers improve.³ Nor is it confined to a few volatile sectors like telecommunications or technology, or a few regions of the country like the rust belt or Silicon Valley. The economy may be looking up, the company may be raking in cash, and still the layoffs continue, like a perverse form of natural selection, weeding out the talented and successful as well as the mediocre. Since the midnineties, this perpetual winnowing process has been institutionalized under various euphemisms such as "downsizing," "right-sizing," "smart-sizing," "restructuring," and "de-layering"—to which we can now add the outsourcing of white-collar functions to cheaper labor markets overseas.

In the metaphor of the best-selling business book of the first few years of the twenty-first century, the "cheese"—meaning a stable, rewarding, job—has indeed been moved. A 2004 survey of executives found 95 percent expecting to move on, voluntarily or otherwise, from their current jobs, and 68 percent concerned about unexpected firings and layoffs (Mackay 94). You don't, in other words, have to lose a job to feel the anxiety and despair of the unemployed.

A second sign of trouble could be called "overemployment." I knew, from my reading, that mid- and high-level corporate executives and professionals today often face the same punishing demands on their time as low-paid wage earners who must work two jobs in order to make ends meet. Economist Juliet Schor, who wrote *The Overworked American*, and business journalist Jill Andresky Fraser, author of *White Collar Sweatshop*, describe stressed-out white-collar employees who put in ten- to twelve-hour-long days at the office, continue to work on their laptops in the evening at home, and remain tethered to the office by cell phone even on vacations and holidays. "On Wall Street, for example," Fraser reports, "it is common for a supervisor to instruct new hires to keep a spare set of clothes and toothbrush in the office for all those late night episodes when it just won't make sense to head home for a quick snooze" (Fraser 23). She quotes an Intel employee:

> If you make the choice to have a home life, you will be ranked and rated at the bottom. I was willing to work the endless hours, come in on weekends, travel to the ends of the earth. I had no hobbies, no outside interests. If I wasn't involved with the company, I wasn't anything (qtd. in Fraser 158).

Something, evidently, is going seriously wrong within a socioeconomic group I had indeed neglected as too comfortable and too powerful to merit my concern. Where I had imagined comfort, there is now growing distress, and I determined to investigate. I chose the same strategy I had employed in *Nickel and Dimed*: to enter this new world myself, as an undercover reporter, and see what I could learn about the problems first-hand. Were people being driven out of their corporate jobs? What did it take to find a new one? And, if things were as bad as some reports suggested, why was there so little protest?

The plan was straightforward enough: to find a job, a "good" job, which I defined minimally as a white-collar position that would provide health insurance and an income of about $50,000 a year, enough to land me solidly in the middle class. The job itself would give me a rare firsthand glimpse into the midlevel corporate world, and the effort to find it would of course place me among the most hard-pressed white-collar corporate workers—the ones who don't have jobs.

Since I wanted to do this as anonymously as possible, certain 10 areas of endeavor had to be excluded, such as higher education, publishing (magazines, newspapers, and books), and nonprofit liberal organizations. In any of these, I would have run the risk of being recognized and perhaps treated differently—more favorably, one hopes—than the average job seeker. But these restrictions did not significantly narrow the field, since of course most white-collar professionals work in other sectors of the for-profit, corporate world—from banking to business services, pharmaceuticals to finance.

The decision to enter corporate life—and an unfamiliar sector of it, at that—required that I abandon, or at least set aside, deeply embedded attitudes and views, including my longstanding critique of American corporations and the people who lead them. I had cut my teeth, as a fledgling investigative journalist in the seventies, on the corporations that were coming to dominate the health-care system: pharmaceutical companies, hospital chains, insurance companies. Then, sometime in the eighties, I shifted my attention to the treatment of blue- and pink-collar employees, blaming America's intractable level of poverty—12.5 percent by the federal government's official count, 25 percent by more up-to-date measures—on the chronically low wages offered to nonprofessional workers. In the last few years, I seized on the wave of financial scandals— from Enron through, at the time of this writing, HealthSouth and Hollingers International—as evidence of growing corruption within the corporate world, a pattern of internal looting without regard for employees, consumers, or even, in some cases, stockholders.

But for the purposes of this project, these criticisms and reservations had to be set aside or shoved as far back in my mind as possible. Like it or not, the corporation is the dominant unit of the global economy and the form of enterprise that our lives depend on in a day-to-day sense. I write this on an IBM laptop while sipping Lipton tea and wearing clothes from the Gap—all major firms or elements thereof. It's corporations that make the planes run (though not necessarily on time), bring us (and increasingly grow) our food, and generally "make it happen." I'd been on the outside of the corporate world, often complaining bitterly, and now I wanted in.

This would not, I knew, be an altogether fair test of the job market, if only because I had some built-in disadvantages as a job seeker. For one thing, I am well into middle age, and since age discrimination is a recognized problem in the corporate world even at the tender age of forty, I was certainly vulnerable to it myself. This defect, however, is by no means unique to me. Many people—from displaced homemakers to downsized executives—now find themselves searching for jobs at an age that was once associated with a restful retirement.

Furthermore, I had the disadvantage of never having held a white-collar job with a corporation. My one professional-level office job, which lasted for about seven months, was in the public sector, at the New York City Bureau of the Budget. It had involved such typical white-collar activities as attending meetings, digesting reports, and writing memos; but that was a long time ago, before cell phones, PowerPoint, and e-mail. In the corporate world I now sought to enter, everything would be new to me: the standards of performance, the methods of evaluation, the lines and even the modes of communication. But I'm a quick study, as you have to be in journalism, and counted on this to get me by.

See Chapter 8 for tips on connecting the parts.

The first step was to acquire a new identity and personal history to go with it, meaning, in this case, a résumé. It is easier to change your identity than you might think. Go to Alavarado and Seventh Street in Los Angeles, for example, and you will be approached by men whispering, "ID, ID." I, however, took the legal route, because I wanted my documents to be entirely in order when the job offers started coming in. My fear, perhaps exaggerated, was that my current name might be recognized, or would at least turn up an embarrassing abundance of Google entries. So in November 2003 I legally changed back to my maiden name, Barbara Alexander, and acquired a Social Security card to go with it.

As for the résumé: although it had to be faked, I wanted it as much as possible to represent my actual skills, which, I firmly believed, would enrich whatever company I went to work for. I am a writer—author of thousands of published articles and about twelve nonfiction books, counting the coauthored ones—and I know that "writing" translates, in the corporate world, into public relations or "communications" generally. Many journalism schools teach PR too, which may be fitting, since PR is really journalism's evil twin. Whereas a journalist seeks the truth, a PR person may be called upon to disguise it or even to advance an untruth. If your employer, a pharmaceutical company, claims its new drug cures both cancer and erectile dysfunction, your job is to promote it, not to investigate the grounds for these claims.

I could do this, on a temporary basis anyway, and have even done many of the things PR people routinely do: I've written press releases, pitched stories to editors and reporters, prepared press packets, and helped arrange press conferences. As an author, I have also worked closely with my publisher's PR people and have always found them to be intelligent and in every way congenial.

I have also been an activist in a variety of causes over the years, and this experience too must translate into something valuable to any firm willing to hire me. I have planned meetings and chaired them; I have worked in dozens of diverse groups and often played a leadership role in them; I am at ease as a public speaker, whether giving a lengthy speech or a brief presentation on a panel—all of which amounts to the "leadership" skills that should be an asset to any company. At the very least, I could claim to be an "event planner," capable of dividing gatherings into plenaries and break-out sessions, arranging the press coverage, and planning the follow-up events.

Even as a rough draft, the résumé took days of preparation. I had to line up people willing to lie for me, should they be called by a potential employer, and attest to the fine work I had done for them. Fortunately, I have friends who were willing to do this, some of them located at recognizable companies. Although I did not dare claim actual employment at these firms, since a call to their Human Resources departments would immediately expose the lie, I felt I could safely pretend to have "consulted" to them over the years. Suffice it to say that I gave Barbara Alexander an exemplary history in public relations, sometimes with a little event planning thrown in, and that the dissimulation involved in crafting my new résumé was further preparation for any morally challenging projects I should be called upon to undertake as a PR person.

I did not, however, embellish my new identity with an affect 20 or mannerisms different from my own. I am not an actor and would not have been able to do this even if I had wanted to. "Barbara Alexander" was only a cover for Barbara Ehrenreich; her behavior would, for better or worse, always be my own. In fact, in a practical sense I was simply changing my occupational status from "self-employed/writer" to "unemployed"—a distinction that might be imperceptible to the casual observer. I would still stay home most days at my computer, only now, instead of researching and writing articles, I would be researching and contacting companies that might employ me. The new name and fake résumé were only my ticket into the ranks of the unemployed white-collar Americans who spend their days searching for a decent-paying job.

The project required some minimal structure; since I was stepping into the unknown, I needed to devise some guidelines for myself. My first rule was that I would do everything possible to land a job, which meant being open to every form of help that presented itself: utilizing whatever books, web sites, and businesses, for example, that I could find offering guidance to job seekers. I would endeavor to behave as I was expected to, insofar as I could decipher the expectations. I did not know exactly what forms of effort would be required of successful job seekers, only that I would, as humbly and diligently as possible, give it my best try.

Second, I would be prepared to go anywhere for a job or even an interview, and would advertise this geographic flexibility in my contacts with potential employers. I was based in Charlottesville, Virginia, throughout this project, but I was prepared to travel anywhere in the United States to get a job and then live there for several months if I found one. Nor would I shun any industry—other than those where I might be recognized—as unglamorous or morally repugnant. My third rule was that I would have to take the first job I was offered that met my requirements as to income and benefits.

I knew that the project would take a considerable investment of time and money, so I set aside ten months[4] and the sum of $5,000 for travel and other expenses that might arise in the course of job searching. My expectation was that I would make the money back once I got a job and probably come out far ahead. As for the time, I budgeted roughly four to six months for the search—five months being the average for unemployed people in 2004—and another three to four months of employment (Leland). I would have plenty of time both to sample the life of the white-collar unemployed and to explore the corporate world they sought to reenter.

From the outset, I pictured this abstraction, *the corporate world*, as a castle on a hill—well fortified, surrounded by difficult checkpoints, with its glass walls gleaming invitingly from on high. I knew that it would be a long hard climb just to get to the door. But I've made my way into remote and lofty places before—college and graduate school, for example. I'm patient and crafty; I have stamina and resolve; and I believed that I could do this too.

In fact, the project, as I planned it, seemed less challenging 25 than I might have liked. As an undercover reporter, I would of course be insulated from the real terrors of the white-collar work world, if only because I was independent of it for my income and self-esteem. Most of my fellow job seekers would probably have come to their status involuntarily, through layoffs or individual firings. For them, to lose a job is to enter a world of pain. Their income collapses to the size of an unemployment insurance check; their self-confidence plummets. Much has been written about the psychological damage incurred by the unemployed— their sudden susceptibility to depression, divorce, substance abuse, and even suicide.[5] No such calamities could occur in my life as an undercover job seeker and, later, jobholder. There would be no sudden descent into poverty, nor any real sting of rejection.

I also started with the expectation that this project would be far less demanding than the work I had undertaken for *Nickel and Dimed*. Physically, it would be a piece of cake—no scrubbing, no heavy lifting, no walking or running for hours on end. As for behavior, I imagined that I would be immune from the constant subservience and obedience demanded of low-wage blue-collar workers, that I would be far freer to be, and express, myself. As it turns out, I was wrong on all counts.

NOTES

[1]Even fiction—my favorite source of insight into culture and times remote from my own—was no help. While the fifties and sixties had produced absorbing novels about white-collar corporate life, including Richard Yates's *Revolutionary Road* and Sloan Wilson's *The Man in the Gray Flannel Suit*, more recent novels and films tend to ignore the white-collar corporate work world except as a backdrop to sexual intrigue.

[2]According to the Bureau of Labor Statistics, women are only slightly more likely than men to be unemployed—6.1 percent compared to 5.7 percent—and white women, like myself, are about half as likely as black women to be unemployed (www.bls.gov).

[3]I was particularly enlightened by Jill Andresky Fraser's *White Collar Sweatshop: The Deterioration of Work and Its Rewards in Corporate America* (New York: Norton, 2001) and Richard Sennett's *The Corrosion of Character: The Personal Consequences of Work in the New Capitalism* (New York: Norton, 1998).

[4]From December 2003 to October 2004, with the exception of most of July, when I had a brief real-life job writing biweekly columns for the *New York Times*.

[5]See, for example, Katherine S. Newman's *Falling from Grace: Downward Mobility in the Age of Affluence* (Berkeley: University of California Press, 1999) or, for a highly readable first-person account, G.J. Meyer's *Executive Blues* (New York: Franklin Square Press, 1995).

WORKS CITED

Fraser, Jill Andresky. *White Collar Sweatshop: The Deterioration of Work and Its Rewards in Corporate America.* New York: Norton, 2001. Print.

Leland, John. "For Unemployed, Wait for New Work Grows Longer." *New York Times* 9 Jan. 2005. Print.

Mackay, Harvey. *We Got Fired! And It's the Best Thing That Ever Happened to Us.* New York: Ballantine, 2004. Print.

Mahler, Jonathan. "Commute to Nowhere." *New York Times Magazine* 13 Apr. 2003. Print.

National Center for Education Statistics. *Undergraduate Enrollments in Academic, Career, and Vocational Education.* Maryland: Issue Brief, 2004. PDF file.

Everything That Rises Must Converge

FLANNERY O'CONNOR

HER DOCTOR HAD TOLD JULIAN'S MOTHER that she must lose twenty pounds on account of her blood pressure, so on Wednesday nights Julian had to take her downtown on the bus for a reducing class at the Y. The reducing class was designed for working girls over fifty, who weighed from 165 to 200 pounds. His mother was one of the slimmer ones, but she said ladies did not tell their age or weight. She would not ride the buses by herself at night since they had been integrated, and because the reducing class was one of her few pleasures, necessary for her health, and *free*, she said Julian could at least put himself out to take her, considering all she did for him. Julian did not

FLANNERY O'CONNOR (1925–1964) was an American writer and essayist. Born in Savannah, Georgia, she authored two novels and over thirty short stories. "Everything That Rises Must Converge" comes from her second short story collection, published posthumously in 1965. Her style is frequently associated with the Southern Gothic, a genre of stories set in the American South in which characters often find themselves in ominous situations.

like to consider all she did for him, but every Wednesday night he braced himself and took her.

She was almost ready to go, standing before the hall mirror, putting on her hat, while he, his hands behind him, appeared pinned to the door frame, waiting like Saint Sebastian for the arrows to begin piercing him. The hat was new and had cost her seven dollars and a half. She kept saying, "Maybe I shouldn't have paid that for it. No, I shouldn't have. I'll take it off and return it tomorrow. I shouldn't have bought it."

Julian raised his eyes to heaven. "Yes, you should have bought it," he said. "Put it on and let's go." It was a hideous hat. A purple velvet flap came down on one side of it and stood up on the other; the rest of it was green and looked like a cushion with the stuffing out. He decided it was less comical than jaunty and pathetic. Everything that gave her pleasure was small and depressed him.

She lifted the hat one more time and set it down slowly on top of her head. Two wings of gray hair protruded on either side of her florid face, but her eyes, sky-blue, were as innocent and untouched by experience as they must have been when she was ten. Were it not that she was a widow who had struggled fiercely to feed and clothe and put him through school and who was supporting him still, "until he got on his feet," she might have been a little girl that he had to take to town.

"It's all right, it's all right," he said. "Let's go." He opened the door himself and started down the walk to get her going. The sky was a dying violet and the houses stood out darkly against it, bulbous liver-colored monstrosities of a uniform ugliness though no two were alike. Since this had been a fashionable neighborhood forty years ago, his mother persisted in thinking they did well to have an apartment in it. Each house had a narrow collar of dirt around it in which sat, usually, a grubby child.

Julian walked with his hands in his pockets, his head down and thrust forward and his eyes glazed with the determination to make himself completely numb during the time he would be sacrificed to her pleasure.

The door closed and he turned to find the dumpy figure, surmounted by the atrocious hat, coming toward him. "Well," she said, "you only live once and paying a little more for it, I at least won't meet myself coming and going."

"Some day I'll start making money," Julian said gloomily—he knew he never would—"and you can have one of those jokes whenever you take the fit." But first they would move. He visualized a place where the nearest neighbors would be three miles away on either side.

"I think you're doing fine," she said, drawing on her gloves. "You've only been out of school a year. Rome wasn't built in a day."

She was one of the few members of the Y reducing class who arrived in hat and gloves and who had a son who had been to college. "It takes time," she said, "and the world is in such a mess. This hat looked better on me than any of the others, though when she brought it out I said, 'Take that thing back. I wouldn't have it on my head,' and she said, 'Now wait till you see it on,' and when she put it on me, I said, 'We-ull,' and she said, 'If you ask me, that hat does something for you and you do something for the hat, and besides,' she said, 'with that hat, you won't meet yourself coming and going.'"

Julian thought he could have stood his lot better if she had been selfish, if she had been an old hag who drank and screamed at him. He walked along, saturated in depression, as if in the midst of his martyrdom he had lost his faith. Catching sight of his long, hopeless, irritated face, she stopped suddenly with a grief-stricken look, and pulled back on his arm. "Wait on me," she said. "I'm going back to the house and take this thing off and tomorrow I'm going to return it. I was out of my head. I can pay the gas bill with that seven-fifty."

He caught her arm in a vicious grip. "You are not going to take it back," he said. "I like it."

"Well," she said, "I don't think I ought . . ."

"Shut up and enjoy it," he muttered, more depressed than ever.

"With the world in the mess it's in," she said, "it's a wonder we can enjoy anything. I tell you, the bottom rail is on the top."

Julian sighed.

"Of course," she said, "if you know who you are, you can go anywhere." She said this every time he took her to the reducing class. "Most of them in it are not our kind of people," she said, "but I can be gracious to anybody. I know who I am."

"They don't give a damn for your graciousness," Julian said savagely. "Knowing who you are is good for one generation only. You haven't the foggiest idea where you stand now or who you are."

She stopped and allowed her eyes to flash at him. "I most certainly do know who I am," she said, "and if you don't know who you are, I'm ashamed of you."

"Oh hell," Julian said.

"Your great-grandfather was a former governor of this state," she said. "Your grandfather was a prosperous landowner. Your grandmother was a Godhigh."

"Will you look around you," he said tensely, "and see where you are now?" and he swept his arm jerkily out to indicate the neighborhood, which the growing darkness at least made less dingy.

"You remain what you are," she said. "Your great-grandfather had a plantation and two hundred slaves."

"There are no more slaves," he said irritably.

"They were better off when they were," she said. He groaned to see that she was off on that topic. She rolled onto it every few days like a train on an open track. He knew every stop, every junction, every swamp along the way, and knew the exact point at which her conclusion would roll majestically into the station: "It's ridiculous. It's simply not realistic. They should rise, yes, but on their own side of the fence."

"Let's skip it," Julian said.

"The ones I feel sorry for," she said, "are the ones that are half white. They're tragic."

"Will you skip it?"

"Suppose we were half white. We would certainly have mixed feelings."

"I have mixed feelings now," he groaned.

"Well let's talk about something pleasant," she said. "I remember going to Grandpa's when I was a little girl. Then the house had double stairways that went up to what was really the second floor—all the cooking was done on the first. I used to like to stay down in the kitchen on account of the way the walls smelled. I would sit with my nose pressed against the plaster and take deep breaths. Actually the place belonged to the Godhighs but your grandfather Chestny paid the mortgage and saved it for them. They were in reduced circumstances," she said, "but reduced or not, they never forgot who they were."

"Doubtless that decayed mansion reminded them," Julian muttered. He never spoke of it without contempt or thought of it without longing. He had seen it once when he was a child before it had been sold. The double stairways had rotted and been torn down. Negroes were living in it. But it remained in his mind as his mother had known it. It appeared in his dreams regularly. He would stand on the wide porch, listening to the rustle of oak leaves, then wander through the high-ceilinged hall into the parlor that opened onto it and gaze at the worn rugs and faded draperies. It occurred to him that it was he, not she, who could have appreciated it. He preferred its threadbare elegance to anything he could name and it was because of it that all the neighborhoods they had lived in had been a torment to him—whereas she had hardly known the difference. She called her insensitivity "being adjustable."

"And I remember the old darky who was my nurse, Caroline. There was no better person in the world. I've always had a great respect for my colored friends," she said. "I'd do anything in the world for them and they'd . . ."

"Will you for God's sake get off that subject?" Julian said. When he got on a bus by himself, he made it a point to sit down beside a Negro, in reparation as it were for his mother's sins.

"You're mighty touchy tonight," she said. "Do you feel all right?"

"Yes I feel all right," he said. "Now lay off."

She pursed her lips. "Well, you certainly are in a vile humor," she observed. "I just won't speak to you at all."

They had reached the bus stop. There was no bus in sight and Julian, his hands still jammed in his pockets and his head thrust forward, scowled down the empty street. The frustration of having to wait on the bus as well as ride on it began to creep up his neck like a hot hand. The presence of his mother was borne in upon him as she gave a pained sigh. He looked at her bleakly. She was holding herself very erect under the preposterous hat, wearing it like a banner of her imaginary dignity. There was in him an evil urge to break her spirit. He suddenly unloosened his tie and pulled it off and put it in his pocket.

She stiffened. "Why must you look like *that* when you take me to town?" she said. "Why must you deliberately embarrass me?"

"If you'll never learn where you are," he said, "you can at least learn where I am."

"You look like a—thug," she said.

"Then I must be one," he murmured.

"I'll just go home," she said. "I will not bother you. If you can't do a little thing like that for me . . ."

Rolling his eyes upward, he put his tie back on. "Restored to my class," he muttered. He thrust his face toward her and hissed, "True culture is in the mind, the *mind*," he said, and tapped his head, "the mind."

"It's in the heart," she said, "and in how you do things and how you do things is because of who you *are*."

"Nobody in the damn bus cares who you are."

"I care who I am," she said icily.

The lighted bus appeared on top of the next hill and as it approached, they moved out into the street to meet it. He put his hand under her elbow and hoisted her up on the creaking step. She entered with a little smile, as if she were going into a drawing room where everyone had been waiting for her. While he put in the tokens, she sat down on one of the broad front seats for three which faced the aisle. A thin woman with protruding teeth and long yellow hair was sitting on the end of it. His mother moved up beside her and left room for Julian beside herself. He sat down and looked at the floor across the aisle where a pair of thin feet in red and white canvas sandals were planted.

His mother immediately began a general conversation meant to attract anyone who felt like talking. "Can it get any hotter?" she said and removed from her purse a folding fan, black with a Japanese scene on it, which she began to flutter before her.

"I reckon it might could," the woman with the protruding teeth said, "but I know for a fact my apartment couldn't get no hotter."

"It must get the afternoon sun," his mother said. She sat forward and looked up and down the bus. It was half filled. Everybody was white. "I see we have the bus to ourselves," she said. Julian cringed.

"For a change," said the woman across the aisle, the owner of the red and white canvas sandals. "I come on one the other day and they were thick as fleas—up front and all through."

"The world is in a mess everywhere," his mother said. "I don't know how we've let it get in this fix."

"What gets my goat is all those boys from good families stealing automobile tires," the woman with the protruding teeth said. "I told my boy, I said you may not be rich but you been raised right and if I ever catch you in any such mess, they can send you on to the reformatory. Be exactly where you belong."

"Training tells," his mother said. "Is your boy in high school?"

"Ninth grade," the woman said.

"My son just finished college last year. He wants to write but he's selling typewriters until he gets started," his mother said.

The woman leaned forward and peered at Julian. He threw her such a malevolent look that she subsided against the seat. On the floor across the aisle there was an abandoned newspaper. He got up and got it and opened it out in front of him. His mother discreetly continued the conversation in a lower tone but the woman across the aisle said in a loud voice, "Well that's nice. Selling typewriters is close to writing. He can go right from one to the other."

"I tell him," his mother said, "that Rome wasn't built in a day."

Behind the newspaper Julian was withdrawing into the inner compartment of his mind where he spent most of his time. This was a kind of mental bubble in which he established himself when he could not bear to be a part of what was going on around him. From it he could see out and judge but in it he was safe from any kind of penetration from without. It was the only place where he felt free of the general idiocy of his fellows. His mother had never entered it but from it he could see her with absolute clarity.

The old lady was clever enough and he thought that if she had started from any of the right premises, more might have been expected of her. She lived according to the laws of her own fantasy world outside of which he had never seen her set foot. The law of it was to sacrifice herself for him after she had first created the necessity to do so by making a mess of things. If he had permitted her sacrifices, it was only because her lack of foresight had made them necessary. All of her life had been a struggle to act like a Chestny without the Chestny goods, and to give him everything she thought a Chestny ought to have; but since, said she, it was fun to struggle, why complain? And when you had won, as she had won, what fun to look back on the hard times! He could not forgive her that she had enjoyed the struggle and that she thought *she* had won.

What she meant when she said she had won was that she had brought him up successfully and had sent him to college and that he had turned out so well—good looking (her teeth had gone unfilled so that his could be straightened), intelligent (he realized he was too intelligent to be a success), and with a future ahead of him (there was of course no future ahead of him). She excused his gloominess on the grounds that he was still growing up and his radical ideas on his lack of practical experience. She said he didn't yet know a thing about "life," that he hadn't even entered the real world—when already he was as disenchanted with it as a man of fifty.

The further irony of all this was that in spite of her, he had turned out so well. In spite of going to only a third-rate college, he had, on his own initiative, come out with a first-rate education; in spite of growing up dominated by a small mind, he had ended up with a large one; in spite of all her foolish views, he was free of prejudice and unafraid to face facts. Most miraculous of all, instead of being blinded by love for her as she was for him, he had cut himself emotionally free of her and could see her with complete objectivity. He was not dominated by his mother.

The bus stopped with a sudden jerk and shook him from his meditation. A woman from the back lurched forward with little steps and barely escaped falling in his newspaper as she righted herself. She got off and a large Negro got on. Julian kept his paper lowered to watch. It gave him a certain satisfaction to see injustice in daily operation. It confirmed his view that with a few exceptions there was no one worth knowing within a radius of three hundred miles. The Negro was well dressed and carried a briefcase. He looked around and then sat down on the other end of the seat where the woman with the red and white canvas sandals was sitting. He immediately unfolded a newspaper and obscured himself behind it. Julian's mother's elbow at once prodded insistently into his ribs. "Now you see why I won't ride on these buses by myself," she whispered.

The woman with the red and white canvas sandals had risen at the same time the Negro sat down and had gone further back in the bus and taken the seat of the woman who had got off. His mother leaned forward and cast her an approving look.

Julian rose, crossed the aisle, and sat down in the place of the woman with the canvas sandals. From this position, he looked serenely across at his mother. Her face had turned an angry red. He stared at her, making his eyes the eyes of a stranger. He felt his tension suddenly lift as if he had openly declared war on her.

He would have liked to get in conversation with the Negro and to talk with him about art or politics or any subject that would be above the comprehension of those around them, but the man remained entrenched behind his paper. He was either ignoring the change of seating or had never noticed it. There was no way for Julian to convey his sympathy.

His mother kept her eyes fixed reproachfully on his face. The woman with the protruding teeth was looking at him avidly as if he were a type of monster new to her.

"Do you have a light?" he asked the Negro.

Without looking away from his paper, the man reached in his pocket and handed him a packet of matches.

"Thanks," Julian said. For a moment he held the matches foolishly. A NO SMOKING sign looked down upon him from over the door. This alone would not have deterred him; he had no cigarettes. He had quit smoking some months before because he could not afford it. "Sorry," he muttered and handed back the matches. The Negro lowered the paper and gave him an annoyed look. He took the matches and raised the paper again.

His mother continued to gaze at him but she did not take advantage of his momentary discomfort. Her eyes retained their battered look. Her face seemed to be unnaturally red, as if her blood pressure had risen. Julian allowed no glimmer of sympathy to show on his face. Having got the advantage, he wanted desperately to keep it and carry it through. He would have liked to teach her a lesson that would last her a while, but there seemed no way to continue the point. The Negro refused to come out from behind his paper.

Julian folded his arms and looked stolidly before him, facing her but as if he did not see her, as if he had ceased to recognize her existence. He visualized a scene in which, the bus having reached their stop, he would remain in his seat and when she said, "Aren't you going to get off?" he would look at her as at a stranger who had rashly addressed him. The corner they got off on was usually deserted, but it was well lighted and it would not hurt her to walk by herself the four blocks to the Y. He decided to wait until the time came and then decide whether or not he would let her get off by herself. He would have to be at the Y at ten to bring her back, but he could leave her wondering if he was going to show up. There was no reason for her to think she could always depend on him.

He retired again into the high-ceilinged room sparsely settled with large pieces of antique furniture. His soul expanded momentarily but then he became aware of his mother across from him and the vision shriveled. He studied her coldly. Her feet in little pumps dangled like a child's and did not quite reach the floor. She was training on him an exaggerated look of reproach. He felt completely detached from her. At that moment he could with pleasure have slapped her as he would have slapped a particularly obnoxious child in his charge.

He began to imagine various unlikely ways by which he could teach her a lesson. He might make friends with some distinguished Negro professor or lawyer and bring him home to spend the evening. He would be entirely justified but her blood pressure would rise to 300. He could not push her to the extent of making her have a stroke, and moreover, he had never been successful at making any Negro friends. He had tried to strike up an acquaintance on the bus with some of the better types, with ones that looked like professors or ministers or lawyers. One morning he had sat down next to a distinguished-looking dark brown man who had answered his questions with a sonorous solemnity but who had turned out to be an undertaker. Another day he had sat down beside a cigar-smoking Negro with a diamond ring on his finger, but after a few stilted pleasantries, the Negro had rung the buzzer and risen, slipping two lottery tickets into Julian's hand as he climbed over him to leave.

He imagined his mother lying desperately ill and his being able to secure only a Negro doctor for her. He toyed with that idea for a few minutes and then dropped it for a momentary vision of himself participating as a sympathizer in a sit-in demonstration. This was possible but he did not linger with it. Instead, he approached the ultimate horror. He brought home a beautiful suspiciously Negroid woman. Prepare yourself, he said. There is nothing you can do about it. This is the woman I've chosen. She's intelligent, dignified, even good, and she's suffered and she hasn't thought it *fun*. Now persecute us, go ahead and persecute us. Drive her out of here, but remember, you're driving me too. His eyes were narrowed and through the indignation he had generated, he saw his mother across the aisle, purple-faced, shrunken to the dwarf-like proportions of her moral nature, sitting like a mummy beneath the ridiculous banner of her hat.

He was tilted out of his fantasy again as the bus stopped. The door opened with a sucking hiss and out of the dark a large, gaily dressed, sullen-looking colored woman got on with a little boy. The child, who might have been four, had on a short plaid suit and a Tyrolean hat with a blue feather in it. Julian hoped that he would sit down beside him and that the woman would push in beside his mother. He could think of no better arrangement.

As she waited for her tokens, the woman was surveying the seating possibilities—he hoped with the idea of sitting where she was least wanted. There was something familiar-looking about her but Julian could not place what it was. She was a giant of a woman. Her face was set not only to meet opposition but to seek it out. The downward tilt of her large lower lip was like a warning sign: DON'T TAMPER WITH ME. Her bulging figure was encased in a green crepe dress and her feet overflowed in red shoes. She had on a hideous hat. A purple velvet flap came down on one side of it and stood up on the other; the rest of it was green and looked like a cushion with the stuffing out. She carried a mammoth red pocketbook that bulged throughout as if it were stuffed with rocks.

To Julian's disappointment, the little boy climbed up on the empty seat beside his mother. His mother lumped all children, black and white, into the common category, "cute," and she thought little Negroes were on the whole cuter than little white children. She smiled at the little boy as he climbed on the seat.

Meanwhile the woman was bearing down upon the empty seat beside Julian. To his annoyance, she squeezed herself into it. He saw his mother's face change as the woman settled herself next to him and he realized with satisfaction that this was more objectionable to her than it was to him. Her face seemed almost gray and there was a look of dull recognition in her eyes, as if suddenly she had sickened at some awful confrontation. Julian saw that it was because she and the woman had, in a sense, swapped sons. Though his mother would not realize the symbolic significance of this, she would feel it. His amusement showed plainly on his face.

The woman next to him muttered something unintelligible to herself. He was conscious of a kind of bristling next to him, muted growling like that of an angry cat. He could not see anything but the red pocketbook upright on the bulging green thighs. He visualized the woman as she had stood waiting for her tokens—the ponderous figure, rising from the red shoes upward over the solid hips, the mammoth bosom, the haughty face, to the green and purple hat.

His eyes widened.

The vision of the two hats, identical, broke upon him with the radiance of a brilliant sunrise. His face was suddenly lit with joy. He could not believe that Fate had thrust upon his mother such a lesson. He gave a loud chuckle so that she would look at him and see that he saw. She turned her eyes on him slowly. The blue in them seemed to have turned a bruised purple. For a moment he had an uncomfortable sense of her innocence, but it lasted only a second before principle rescued him. Justice entitled him to laugh. His grin hardened until it said to her as plainly as if he were saying aloud: Your punishment exactly fits your pettiness. This should teach you a permanent lesson.

Her eyes shifted to the woman. She seemed unable to bear looking at him and to find the woman preferable. He became conscious again of the bristling presence at his side. The woman was rumbling like a volcano about to become active. His mother's mouth began to twitch slightly at one corner. With a sinking heart, he saw incipient signs of recovery on her face and realized that this was going to strike her suddenly as funny and was going to be no lesson at all. She kept her eyes on the woman and an amused smile came over her face as if the woman were a monkey that had stolen her hat. The little Negro was looking up at her with large fascinated eyes. He had been trying to attract her attention for some time.

"Carver!" the woman said suddenly. "Come heah!"

When he saw that the spotlight was on him at last, Carver drew his feet up and turned himself toward Julian's mother and giggled.

"Carver!" the woman said. "You heah me? Come heah!"

Carver slid down from the seat but remained squatting with his back against the base of it, his head turned slyly around toward Julian's mother, who was smiling at him. The woman reached a hand across the aisle and snatched him to her. He righted himself and hung backwards on her knees, grinning at Julian's mother. "Isn't he cute?" Julian's mother said to the woman with the protruding teeth.

"I reckon he is," the woman said without conviction.

The Negress yanked him upright but he eased out of her grip and shot across the aisle and scrambled, giggling wildly, onto the seat beside his love.

"I think he likes me," Julian's mother said, and smiled at the woman. It was the smile she used when she was being particularly gracious to an inferior. Julian saw everything lost. The lesson had rolled off her like rain on a roof.

The woman stood up and yanked the little boy off the seat as if she were snatching him from contagion. Julian could feel the rage in her at having no weapon like his mother's smile. She gave the child a sharp slap across his leg. He howled once and then thrust his head into her stomach and kicked his fret against her shins. "Behave," she said vehemently.

The bus stopped and the Negro who had been reading the newspaper got off. The woman moved over and set the little boy down with a thump between herself and Julian. She held him firmly by the knee. In a moment he put his hands in front of his face and peeped at Julian's mother through his fingers.

"I see yoooooooo!" she said and put her hand in front of her face and peeped at him.

The woman slapped his hand down. "Quit yo' foolishness," she said, "before I knock the living Jesus out of you!"

Julian was thankful that the next stop was theirs. He reached up and pulled the cord. The woman reached up and pulled it at the same time. Oh my God, he thought. He had the terrible intuition that when they got off the bus together, his mother would open her purse and give the little boy a nickel. The gesture would be as natural to her as breathing. The bus stopped and the woman got up and lunged to the front, dragging the child, who wished to stay on, after her. Julian and his mother got up and followed. As they neared the door, Julian tried to relieve her of her pocketbook.

"No," she murmured, "I want to give the little boy a nickel."

"No!" Julian hissed. "No!"

She smiled down at the child and opened her bag. The bus door opened and the woman picked him up by the arm and descended with him, hanging at her hip. Once in the street she set him down and shook him.

Julian's mother had to close her purse while she got down the bus step but as soon as her feet were on the ground, she opened it again and began to rummage inside. "I can't find but a penny," she whispered, "but it looks like a new one."

"Don't do it!" Julian said fiercely between his teeth. There was a streetlight on the corner and she hurried to get under it so that she could better see into her pocketbook. The woman was heading off rapidly down the street with the child still hanging backward on her hand.

"Oh little boy!" Julian's mother called and took a few quick steps and caught up with them just beyond the lamppost. "Here's a bright new penny for you," and she held out the coin, which shone bronze in the dim light.

The huge woman turned and for a moment stood, her shoulders lifted and her face frozen with frustrated rage, and stared at Julian's mother. Then all at once she seemed to explode like a piece of machinery that had been given one ounce of pressure too much. Julian saw the black fist swing out with the red pocketbook. He shut his eyes and cringed as he heard the woman shout, "He don't take nobody's pennies!" When he opened his eyes, the woman was disappearing down the street with the little boy staring wide-eyed over her shoulder. Julian's mother was sitting on the sidewalk.

"I told you not to do that," Julian said angrily. "I told you not to do that!"

He stood over her for a minute, gritting his teeth. Her legs were stretched out in front of her and her hat was on her lap. He squatted down and looked her in the face. It was totally expressionless. "You got exactly what you deserved," he said. "Now get up."

He picked up her pocketbook and put what had fallen out back in it. He picked the hat up off her lap. The penny caught his eye on the sidewalk and he picked that up and let it drop before her eyes into the purse. Then he stood up and leaned over and held his hands out to pull her up. She remained immobile. He sighed. Rising above them on either side were black apartment buildings, marked with irregular rectangles of light. At the end of the block a man came out of a door and walked off in the opposite direction. "All right," he said, "suppose somebody happens by and wants to know why you're sitting on the sidewalk?"

She took the hand and, breathing hard, pulled heavily up on it and then stood for a moment, swaying slightly as if the spots of light in the darkness were circling around her. Her eyes, shadowed and confused, finally settled on his face. He did not try to conceal his irritation. "I hope this teaches you a lesson," he said. She leaned forward and her eyes raked his face. She seemed trying to determine his identity. Then, as if she found nothing familiar about him, she started off with a headlong movement in the wrong direction.

"Aren't you going on to the Y?" he asked.

"Home," she muttered.

"Well, are we walking?"

For answer she kept going. Julian followed along, his hands behind him. He saw no reason to let the lesson she had had go without backing it up with an explanation of its meaning. She might as well be made to understand what had happened to her. "Don't think that was just an uppity Negro woman," he said. "That was the whole colored race which will no longer take your condescending pennies. That was your black double. She can wear the same hat as you, and to be sure," he added gratuitously (because he thought it was funny), "it looked better on her than it did on you. What all this means," he said, "is that the old world is gone. The old manners are obsolete and your graciousness is not worth a damn." He thought bitterly of the house that had been lost for him. "You aren't who you think you are," he said.

She continued to plow ahead, paying no attention to him. Her hair had come undone on one side. She dropped her pocketbook and took no notice. He stooped and picked it up and handed it to her but she did not take it.

"You needn't act as if the world had come to an end," he said, "because it hasn't. From now on you've got to live in a new world and face a few realities for a change. Buck up," he said, "it won't kill you."

She was breathing fast.

"Let's wait on the bus," he said.

"Home," she said thickly.

"I hate to see you behave like this," he said. "Just like a child. I should be able to expect more of you." He decided to stop where he was and make her stop and wait for a bus. "I'm not going any farther," he said, stopping. "We're going on the bus."

She continued to go on as if she had not heard him. He took a few steps and caught her arm and stopped her. He looked into her face and caught his breath. He was looking into a face he had never seen before. "Tell Grandpa to come get me," she said.

He stared, stricken.

"Tell Caroline to come get me," she said.

Stunned, he let her go and she lurched forward again, walking as if one leg were shorter than the other. A tide of darkness seemed to be sweeping her from him. "Mother!" he cried. "Darling, sweetheart, wait!" Crumpling, she fell to the pavement. He dashed forward and fell at her side, crying, "Mamma, Mamma!" He turned her over. Her face was fiercely distorted. One eye, large and staring, moved slightly to the left as if it had become unmoored. The other remained fixed on him, raked his face again, found nothing and closed.

"Wait here, wait here!" he cried and jumped up and began to run for help toward a cluster of lights he saw in the distance ahead of him. "Help, help!" he shouted, but his voice was thin, scarcely a thread of sound. The lights drifted farther away the faster he ran and his feet moved numbly as if they carried him nowhere. The tide of darkness seemed to sweep him back to her, postponing from moment to moment his entry into the world of guilt and sorrow.

INDEX OF TEMPLATES

INTRODUCING WHAT "THEY SAY"
(p. 23)

- ▶ A number of _____ have recently suggested that _____ .

- ▶ It has become common today to dismiss _____ .

- ▶ In their recent work, Y and Z have offered harsh critiques of _____ for _____ .

INTRODUCING "STANDARD VIEWS"
(pp. 23–24)

- ▶ Americans today tend to believe that _____ .

- ▶ Conventional wisdom has it that _____ .

- ▶ Common sense seems to dictate that _____ .

- ▶ The standard way of thinking about topic X has it that _____ .

- ▶ It is often said that _____ .

- ▶ My whole life I have heard it said that _____ .

- ▶ You would think that _____ .

- ▶ Many people assume that _____ .

INDEX OF TEMPLATES

MAKING WHAT "THEY SAY" SOMETHING *YOU* SAY
(pp. 24–25)

▶ I've always believed that _____.

▶ When I was a child, I used to think that _____.

▶ Although I should know better by now, I cannot help thinking that _____.

▶ At the same time that I believe _____, I also believe _____.

INTRODUCING SOMETHING IMPLIED OR ASSUMED
(p. 25)

▶ Although none of them have ever said so directly, my teachers have often given me the impression that _____.

▶ One implication of X's treatment of _____ is that _____.

▶ Although X does not say so directly, she apparently assumes that _____.

▶ While they rarely admit as much, _____ often take for granted that _____.

INTRODUCING AN ONGOING DEBATE
(pp. 25–28)

▶ In discussions of X, one controversial issue has been _____. On the one hand, _____ argues _____. On the other hand, _____ contends _____. Others even maintain _____. My own view is _____.

▶ When it comes to the topic of _____, most of us will readily agree that _____. Where this agreement usually ends, however, is on the question of _____. Whereas some are convinced that _____, others maintain that _____.

▶ In conclusion, then, as I suggested earlier, defenders of _____ can't have it both ways. Their assertion that _____ is contradicted by their claim that _____.

CAPTURING AUTHORIAL ACTION
(pp. 38–40)

▶ X acknowledges that _____.

▶ X agrees that _____.

▶ X argues that _____.

▶ X believes that _____.

▶ X denies/does not deny that _____.

▶ X claims that _____.

▶ X complains that _____.

▶ X concedes that _____.

▶ X demonstrates that _____.

▶ X deplores the tendency to _____.

▶ X celebrates the fact that _____.

▶ X emphasizes that _____.

INDEX OF TEMPLATES

▸ X insists that _____.

▸ X observes that _____.

▸ X questions whether _____.

▸ X refutes the claim that _____.

▸ X reminds us that _____.

▸ X reports that _____.

▸ X suggests that _____.

▸ X urges us to _____.

INTRODUCING QUOTATIONS
(p. 46)

▸ X states, "_____."

▸ As the prominent philosopher X puts it, "_____."

▸ According to X, "_____."

▸ X himself writes, "_____."

▸ In her book, _____, X maintains that "_____"

▸ Writing in the journal _____, X complains that "_____."

▸ In X's view, "_____."

▸ X agrees when she writes, "_____."

▸ X disagrees when he writes, "_____."

▸ X complicates matters further when he writes, "_____."

Index of Templates

EXPLAINING QUOTATIONS
(pp. 46–47)

▶ Basically, X is saying _____.

▶ In other words, X believes _____.

▶ In making this comment, X urges us to _____.

▶ X is corroborating the age-old adage that _____.

▶ X's point is that _____.

▶ The essence of X's argument is that _____.

DISAGREEING, WITH REASONS
(p. 60)

▶ I think X is mistaken because she overlooks _____.

▶ X's claim that _____ rests upon the questionable assumption that _____.

▶ I disagree with X's view that _____ because, as recent research has shown, _____.

▶ X contradicts herself / can't have it both ways. On the one hand, she argues _____. On the other hand, she also says _____.

▶ By focusing on _____, X overlooks the deeper problem of _____.

AGREEING—WITH A DIFFERENCE
(pp. 61–64)

▸ I agree that _____ because my experience _____ confirms it.

▸ X surely is right about _____ because, as she may not be aware, recent studies have shown that _____.

▸ X's theory of _____ is extremely useful because it sheds insight on the difficult problem of _____.

▸ Those unfamiliar with this school of thought may be interested to know that it basically boils down to _____.

▸ I agree that _____, a point that needs emphasizing since so many people believe _____.

▸ If group X is right that _____, as I think they are, then we need to reassess the popular assumption that _____.

AGREEING AND DISAGREEING SIMULTANEOUSLY
(pp. 64–66)

▸ Although I agree with X up to a point, I cannot accept his overall conclusion that _____.

▸ Although I disagree with much that X says, I fully endorse his final conclusion that _____.

▸ Though I concede that _____, I still insist that _____.

▸ Whereas X provides ample evidence that _____, Y and Z's research on _____ and _____ convinces me that _____ instead.

Index of Templates

- X is right that _____, but she seems on more dubious ground when she claims that _____.

- While X is probably wrong when she claims that _____, she is right that _____.

- I'm of two minds about X's claim that _____. On the one hand, I agree that _____. On the other hand, I'm not sure if _____.

- My feelings on the issue are mixed. I do support X's position that _____, but I find Y's argument about _____ and Z's research on _____ to be equally persuasive.

SIGNALING WHO IS SAYING WHAT
(pp. 71–73)

- X argues _____.

- According to both X and Y, _____.

- Politicians _____, X argues, should _____.

- Most athletes will tell you that _____.

- My own view, however, is that _____.

- I agree, as X may not realize, that _____.

- But _____ are real and, arguably, the most significant factor in _____.

- But X is wrong that _____.

- However, it is simply not true that _____.

- Indeed, it is highly likely that _____.

- X's assertion that _____ does not fit the facts.

▶ X is right that _____.

▶ X is wrong that _____.

▶ X is both right and wrong that _____.

▶ Yet a sober analysis of the matter reveals _____.

▶ Nevertheless, new research shows _____.

▶ Anyone familiar with _____ should agree that _____.

EMBEDDING VOICE MARKERS
(pp. 74–75)

▶ X overlooks what I consider an important point about _____.

▶ My own view is that what X insists is a _____ is in fact a _____.

▶ I wholeheartedly endorse what X calls _____.

▶ These conclusions, which X discusses in _____, add weight to the argument that _____.

ENTERTAINING OBJECTIONS
(p. 82)

▶ At this point I would like to raise some objections that have been inspired by the skeptic in me. She feels that I have been ignoring _____. "_____," she says to me, "_____."

▶ Yet some readers may challenge the view that _____.

▶ Of course, many will probably disagree with this assertion that _____.

Index of Templates

NAMING YOUR NAYSAYERS
(pp. 83–84)

▶ Here many _____ would probably object that _____.

▶ But _____ would certainly take issue with the argument that _____.

▶ _____, of course, may want to question whether _____.

▶ Nevertheless, both followers and critics of _____ will probably argue that _____.

▶ Although not all _____ think alike, some of them will probably dispute my claim that _____.

▶ _____ are so diverse in their views that it's hard to generalize about them, but some are likely to object on the grounds that _____.

INTRODUCING OBJECTIONS INFORMALLY
(pp. 84–85)

▶ But is my proposal realistic? What are the chances of its actually being adopted?

▶ Yet is it always true that _____? Is it always the case, as I have been suggesting, that _____?

▶ However, does the evidence I've cited prove conclusively that _____?

▶ "Impossible," some will say. "You must be reading the research selectively."

MAKING CONCESSIONS WHILE STILL
STANDING YOUR GROUND (p. 89)

▸ Although I grant that _____, I still maintain that _____.

▸ Proponents of X are right to argue that _____. But they exaggerate when they claim that _____.

▸ While it is true that _____, it does not necessarily follow that _____.

▸ On the one hand, I agree with X that _____. But on the other hand, I still insist that _____.

INDICATING WHO CARES
(pp. 95–96)

▸ _____ used to think _____. But recently [or within the past few decades] _____ suggests that _____.

▸ These findings challenge the work of earlier researchers, who tended to assume that _____.

▸ Recent studies like these shed new light on _____, which previous studies had not addressed.

▸ Researchers have long assumed that _____. For instance, one eminent scholar of cell biology, _____, assumed in _____, her seminal work on cell structures and functions, that fat cells _____. As _____ herself put it, "_____" (2012). Another leading scientist, _____, argued that fat cells "_____" (2011). Ultimately, when it came to the nature of fat, the basic assumption was that _____.

But a new body of research shows that fat cells are far more complex and that _____.

▶ If sports enthusiasts stopped to think about it, many of them might simply assume that the most successful athletes _____. However, new research shows _____.

▶ These findings challenge neoliberals' common assumptions that _____.

▶ At first glance, teenagers appear to _____. But on closer inspection _____.

ESTABLISHING WHY YOUR CLAIMS MATTER
(pp. 98–99)

▶ X matters / is important because _____.

▶ Although X may seem trivial, it is in fact crucial in terms of today's concern over _____.

▶ Ultimately, what is at stake here is _____.

▶ These findings have important consequences for the broader domain of _____.

▶ My discussion of X is in fact addressing the larger matter of _____.

▶ These conclusions / This discovery will have significant applications in _____ as well as in _____.

▶ Although X may seem of concern to only a small group of _____, it should in fact concern anyone who cares about _____.

COMMONLY USED TRANSITIONS
(pp. 108–10)

ADDITION

also	in fact
and	indeed
besides	moreover
furthermore	so too
in addition	

ELABORATION

actually	to put it another way
by extension	to put it bluntly
in short	to put it succinctly
that is	ultimately
in other words	

EXAMPLE

after all	for instance
as an illustration	specifically
consider	to take a case in point
for example	

CAUSE AND EFFECT

accordingly	since
as a result	so
consequently	then
hence	therefore
it follows, then	thus

Index of Templates

COMPARISON

along the same lines	likewise
in the same way	similarly

CONTRAST

although	nevertheless
but	nonetheless
by contrast	on the contrary
conversely	on the other hand
despite	regardless
even though	whereas
however	while
in contrast	yet

CONCESSION

admittedly	of course
although it is true that	naturally
granted	to be sure
I concede that	

CONCLUSION

as a result	so
consequently	the upshot of all this is that
hence	therefore
in conclusion, then	thus
in short	to sum up
in sum, then	to summarize
it follows, then	

ADDING METACOMMENTARY
(pp. 131–37)

- In other words, _____.

- What _____ really means by this is _____.

- Ultimately, my goal is to demonstrate that _____.

- My point is not _____, but _____.

- To put it another way, _____.

- In sum, then, _____.

- My conclusion, then, is that, _____.

- In short, _____.

- What is more important, _____.

- Incidentally, _____.

- By the way, _____.

- Chapter 2 explores _____, while Chapter 3 examines _____.

- Having just argued that _____, let us now turn our attention to _____.

- Although some readers may object that _____, I would answer that _____.

Index of Templates

STARTING WITH WHAT OTHERS SAY
ABOUT A LITERARY WORK
(pp. 185–88)

▶ Critic X complains that Author Y's story is compromised by his
_____. While there's some truth to this critique, I argue
that Critic X overlooks _____.

▶ According to Critic A, novel X suggests _____. I agree, but
would add that _____.

▶ Several members of our class have suggested that the final message of play X is _____. I agree up to a point, but I still
think that _____.

▶ On first reading play Z, I thought it was an uncritical celebration of _____. After rereading the play and discussing it in
class, however, I see that it is more critical of _____ than
I originally thought.

▶ It might be said that poem Y is chiefly about _____. But
the problem with this reading, in my view, is _____.

▶ Though religious readers might be tempted to analyze poem X
as a parable about _____, a closer examination suggests
that the poem is in fact about _____.

RESPONDING TO OTHER INTERPRETATIONS
OF A LITERARY WORK
(p. 191)

▶ It might be argued that in the clash between character X and
Y in play Z, the author wants us to favor character Y, since she

is presented as the play's heroine. I contend, however, that
_____.

▸ Several critics seem to assume that poem X endorses the values of _____ represented by the image of _____ over those of _____ represented by the image of _____. I agree, but with the following caveat: _____.

SHOWING EVIDENCE WHEN WRITING ABOUT A LITERARY WORK
(pp. 194–96)

▸ Although some might read the metaphor of _____ in this poem as evidence, that for Author X, _____, I see it as _____.

▸ Some might claim that evidence X suggests _____, but I argue that, on the contrary, it suggests _____.

▸ I agree with my classmate _____ that the image of _____ in novel Y is evidence of _____. Unlike _____, however, I think _____.

EXPLAIN WHAT THE DATA MEAN
(p. 211)

▸ Our data *support / confirm / verify* the work of X by showing that _____.

▸ By demonstrating _____, X's work *extends* the findings of Y.

▸ The results of X *contradict/refute* Y's conclusion that _____.

Index of Templates

- X's findings *call into question* the widely accepted theory that _____ .

- Our data *are consistent with* X's hypothesis that _____ .

EXPLAINING AN EXPERIMENTAL RESULT
(p. 214)

- One explanation for X's finding of _____ is that _____ . An alternative explanation is _____ .

- The difference between _____ and _____ is probably due to _____ .

INTRODUCING GAPS IN THE EXISTING RESEARCH
(p. 228)

- Studies of X have indicated _____ . It is not clear, however, that this conclusion applies to _____ .

- _____ often take for granted that _____ . Few have investigated this assumption, however.

- X's work tells us a great deal about _____ . Can this work be generalized to _____ ?

CREDITS

—◫—

TEXT

Barbara Ehrenreich: From *Bait and Switch: The (Futile) Pursuit of the American Dream.* Copyright © 2005. Reprinted by permission of Metropolitan Books of Henry Holt and Company, LLC and International Creative Management.

Gerald Graff: "Hidden Intellectualism," adapted from *Clueless in Academe: How Schooling Obscures the Life of the Mind.* Copyright © 2003 Yale University. Reprinted by permission of Yale University Press.

Richard A. Muller: From *Physics for Future Presidents: The Science Behind the Headlines* by Richard A. Muller. Copyright © 2008 by Richard A. Muller. Used by permission of W.W. Norton & Company, Inc.

Flannery O'Connor: "Everything That Rises Must Converge," from *The Complete Stories.* Copyright © 1946. Reprinted by permission of Farrar, Straus and Giroux and Harold Matson Company, Inc.

Eric Schlosser: "A People's Democratic Platform," *The Nation*, August 2, 2004. Reprinted by permission.

David Zinczenko: "Don't Blame the Eater," *The New York Times*, November 23, 2002, p. A31. © 2002, The New York Times. Reprinted by permission.

PHOTOGRAPHS

Chapter 11: p. 146: *Family Guy* Peter and Stewie: ©20th Century Fox/ Courtesy Everett Collection; p. 154: *Family Guy* family watching TV: ©20th Century Fox/Courtesy Everett Collection. **Chapter 15:** p. 195: Duck or Rabbit: Wikimedia. **Readings:** p. 253: Yucca Mountain, Nevada: Wikimedia.

ACKNOWLEDGMENTS

Like the previous two editions, this one would never have seen print if it weren't for Marilyn Moller, our superb editor at Norton, and the extraordinary job she has done of inspiring, commenting on, rewriting (and then rewriting and rewriting again) our many drafts. Our friendship with Marilyn is one of the most cherished things to have developed from this project.

Our thanks go as well to Tenyia Lee, Julia Reidhead, Marian Johnson, Peter Simon, and Spencer Richardson-Jones for their incisive comments and suggestions on the new chapter on writing about literature; to Ariella Foss, Rebecca Homiski, Andy Ensor, and Ashley Horna for managing the editing and production of this edition; and to Cliff Landesman and Michal Brody for curating and producing the fabulous blog that accompanies this book, **theysayiblog.**

We thank John Darger, our Norton representative, who offered early encouragement to write this book—and give special thanks to Lib Triplett and all the Norton travelers for the superb work they've done on behalf of our book.

We owe a special debt of gratitude to Christopher Gillen and Erin Ackerman for their chapters on writing in the hard and social sciences, respectively. Working with Chris and Erin proved to be an exhilarating experience; we learned a great deal by seeing how they applied our ideas to their disciplines.

ACKNOWLEDGMENTS

We owe special thanks to our colleagues in the English department at the University of Illinois at Chicago: Mark Canuel, our former department head, for supporting our earlier efforts overseeing the university's Writing in the Disciplines requirement; Walter Benn Michaels, our current department head; and Ann Feldman, former Director of University Writing Programs, for encouraging us to teach first-year composition courses at UIC in which we could try out ideas and drafts of our manuscript; Tom Moss, Diane Chin, Vainis Aleksa, and Matt Pavesich, who have also been very supportive of our efforts; and Matt Oakes, our former research assistant. We are also grateful to Ann, Diane, and Mark Bennett for bringing us into their graduate course on the teaching of writing, and to Lisa Freeman, John Huntington, Walter Benn Michaels, and Ralph Cintron, for inviting us to present our ideas in the keynote lecture at UIC's 2013 "Composition Matters" conference.

We are also especially grateful to Steve Benton and Nadya Pittendrigh, who taught a section of composition with us using an early draft of this book. Steve made many helpful suggestions, particularly regarding the exercises. We are grateful to Andy Young, a lecturer at UIC who has tested our book in his courses and who gave us extremely helpful feedback. And we thank Vershawn A. Young, whose work on code-meshing influenced our argument in Chapter 9, and Hillel Crandus, whose classroom handout inspired the chapter on "Entering Classroom Discussions."

We are grateful to the many colleagues and friends who've let us talk our ideas out with them and given extremely helpful responses. UIC's former dean, Stanley Fish, has been central in this respect, both in personal conversations and in his incisive articles calling for greater focus on form in the teaching of writing. Our conversations with Jane Tompkins have also

been integral to this book, as was the composition course that
Jane co-taught with Gerald entitled "Can We Talk?" Lenny
Davis, too, offered both intellectual insight and emotional
support, as did Heather Arnet, Jennifer Ashton, Janet Atwill,
Kyra Auslander, Noel Barker, Jim Benton, Jack Brereton,
Tim Cantrick, Marsha Cassidy, David Chinitz, Lisa Chinitz,
Pat Chu, Duane Davis, Bridget O'Rourke Flisk, Steve Flisk,
Judy Gardiner, Howard Gardner, Rich Gelb, Gwynne Gertz,
Jeff Gore, Bill Haddad, Ben Hale, Scott Hammerl, Patricia
Harkin, Andy Hoberek, John Huntington, Joe Janangelo, Paul
Jay, David Jolliffe, Nancy Kohn, Don Lazere, Jo Liebermann,
Steven Mailloux, Deirdre McCloskey, Maurice J. Meilleur,
Alan Meyers, Greg Meyerson, Anna Minkov, Chris Newfield,
Jim Phelan, Paul Psilos, Bruce Robbins, Charles Ross, Eileen
Seifert, Evan Seymour, David Shumway, Herb Simons, Jim
Sosnoski, David Steiner, Harold Veeser, Chuck Venegoni,
Marla Weeg, Jerry Wexler, Joyce Wexler, Virginia Wexman,
Jeffrey Williams, Lynn Woodbury, and the late Wayne Booth,
whose friendship we dearly miss.

We are grateful for having had the opportunity to present
our ideas to a number of schools: University of Arkansas at
Little Rock, Augustana College, Brandeis University, Brigham
Young University, Bryn Mawr College, Case Western University, Columbia University, Community College of Philadelphia, California State University at Bakersfield, California
State University at Northridge, University of California at
Riverside, University of Delaware, DePauw University, Drew
University, Duke University, Duquesne University, Elmhurst
College, Emory University, Fontbonne University, Furman
University, Gettysburg College, Harper College, Harvard
University, Haverford College, Hawaii Office of Secondary
School Curriculum Instruction, Hunter College, University of

ACKNOWLEDGMENTS

Illinois College of Medicine, Illinois State University, John Carroll University, Kansas State University, Lawrence University, the Lawrenceville School, University of Louisiana at Lafayette, MacEwan University, University of Maryland at College Park, Massachusetts Institute of Technology, University of Memphis, Miami University, University of Missouri at Columbia, New Trier High School, State University of New York at Geneseo, State University of New York at Stony Brook, North Carolina A&T University, University of North Florida, Northern Michigan University, Norwalk Community College, Northwestern University Division of Continuing Studies, University of Notre Dame, Ohio Wesleyan University, Oregon State University, University of Portland, University of Rochester, St. Ambrose University, St. Andrew's School, St. Charles High School, Seattle University, Southern Connecticut State University, South Elgin High School, University of South Florida, University of Southern Mississippi, Swarthmore College, Teachers College, University of Tennessee at Knoxville, University of Texas at Arlington, Tulane University, Union College, Ursinus College, Wabash College, Washington College, University of Washington, Western Michigan University, Westinghouse/Kenwood High Schools, University of West Virginia at Morgantown, Wheaton Warrenville English Chairs, and the University of Wisconsin at Whitewater.

We particularly thank those who helped arrange these visits and discussed writing issues with us: Jeff Abernathy, Herman Asarnow, John Austin, Greg Barnheisel, John Bean, Crystal Benedicks, Joe Bizup, Sheridan Blau, Dagne Bloland, Chris Breu, Mark Brouwer, Joan Johnson Bube, John Caldwell, Gregory Clark, Irene Clark, Dean Philip Cohen, Cathy D'Agostino, Tom Deans, Gaurav Desai, Lisa Dresdner, Kathleen Dudden-Rowlands, Lisa Ede, Alexia Ellett, Emory Elliott,

Acknowledgments

Anthony Ellis, Kim Flachmann, Ronald Fortune, Rosanna Fukuda, George Haggerty, Donald Hall, Joe Harris, Gary Hatch, Elizabeth Hatmaker, Harry Hellenbrand, Nicole Henderson, Donna Heiland, Doug Hesse, Van Hillard, Andrew Hoberek, Michael Hustedde, Sara Jameson, T. R. Johnson, David Jones, Ann Kaplan, Don Kartiganer, Linda Kinnahan, Dean Georg Kleine, Albert Labriola, Craig Lawrence, Lori Lopez, Tom Liam Lynch, Hiram Maxim, Michael Mays, Thomas McFadden, Sean Meehan, Connie Mick, Joseph Musser, Margaret Oakes, John O'Connor, Gary Olson, Tom Pace, Les Perelman, Emily Poe, Dominick Randolph, Clancy Ratliff, Monica Rico, Kelly Ritter, Jack Robinson, Warren Rosenberg, Laura Rosenthal, Dean Howard Ross, Deborah Rossen-Knill, Paul Schacht, Petra Schatz, Evan Seymour, Rose Shapiro, Mike Shea, Cecilia M. Shore, Erec Smith, Nancy Sommers, Stephen Spector, Timothy Spurgin, Ron Strickland, Trig Thoreson, Josh Toth, Judy Trost, Aiman Tulamait, Charles Tung, John Webster, Robert Weisbuch, Sandi Weisenberg, Karin Westman, Martha Woodmansee, and Lynn Worsham.

We also wish to extend particular thanks to two Chicago area educators who have worked closely with us: Les Lynn of the Chicago Debate League and Eileen Murphy of CERCA. Lastly, we wish to thank two high school teachers for their excellent and inventive adaptations of our work: Mark Gozonsky in his YouTube video clip, "Building Blocks," and Dave Stuart, Jr., in his blog, "Teaching the Core."

For inviting us to present our ideas at their conferences we are grateful to John Brereton and Richard Wendorf at the Boston Athenaeum; Wendy Katkin of the Reinvention Center of State University of New York at Stony Brook; Luchen Li of the Michigan English Association; Lisa Lee and Barbara Ransby of the Public Square in Chicago; Don Lazere of the

ACKNOWLEDGMENTS

University of Tennessee at Knoxville; Dennis Baron of the
University of Illinois at Urbana-Champaign; Alfie Guy of Yale
University; Irene Clark of the California State University of
Northridge; George Crandell and Steve Hubbard, co-directors
of the ACETA conference at Auburn University; Mary Beth
Rose of the Humanities Institute at the University of Illinois
at Chicago; Diana Smith of St. Anne's Belfield School and
the University of Virginia; Jim Maddox and Victor Luftig of
the Bread Loaf School of English; Jan Fitzsimmons and Jerry
Berberet of the Associated Colleges of Illinois; and Rosemary
Feal, Executive Director of the Modern Language Association.

A very special thanks goes to those who reviewed materials
for the third edition: Carrie Bailey (Clark College); Heather
Barrett (Boston University); Amy Bennett-Zendzian (Boston
University); Seth Blumenthal (Boston University); Ron Brooks
(Oklahoma State University); Jonathan Cook (Durham Tech-
nical Community College); Tessa Croker (Boston University);
Perry Cumbie (Durham Technical Community College); Rob-
ert Danberg (Binghamton University); Elias Dominguez Barajas
(University of Arkansas); Nancy Enright (Seton Hall Uni-
versity); Jason Evans (Prairie State College); Ted Fitts (Bos-
ton University); Karen Gaffney (Raritan Valley Community
College); Karen Gardiner (University of Alabama); Stephen
Hodin (Boston University); Michael Horwitz (University of
Hartford); John Hyman (American University); Claire Kervin
(Boston University); Melinda Kreth (Central Michigan Uni-
versity); Heather Marcovitch (Red Deer College); Chris-
tina Michaud (Boston University); Marisa Milanese (Boston
University); Theresa Mooney (Austin Community College);
Roxanne Munch (Joliet Junior College); Sarah Quirk (Wau-
bonsee Community College); Lauri Ramey (California State
University, Los Angeles); David Shawn (Boston University);

Jennifer Sia (Boston University); Laura Sonderman (Marshall University); Katherine Stebbins McCaffrey (Boston University); K. Sullivan (Lane Community College); Anne-Marie Thomas (Austin Community College at Riverside); Eliot Treichel (Lane Community College); Rosanna Walker (Lane Community College); Mary Erica Zimmer (Boston University).

We also thank those who reviewed the literature chapter: Julie Bowman (Carnegie Mellon University); Jim Burke (Burlingame High School); Ana Cooke (Carnegie Mellon University); Lisa Ede (Oregon State University); Thomas Cooley (The Ohio State University); Priscilla Glanville (State College of Florida); Melissa Goldthwaite (Saint Joseph's University); Rafey Habib (Rutgers University at Camden); Michael Hennessy (Texas State University); Alexis Teagarden (Carnegie Mellon University).

Thanks to those who reviewed the materials for the second edition: Erin Ackerman (City University of New York–John Jay College); Mary Angeline (University of Northern Colorado); Ned Bachus (Community College of Philadelphia); Michelle Ballif (University of Georgia); Jonathan Barz (University of Dubuque); Mary Bauer Morley (University of North Dakota); Benjamin Bennett-Carpenter (Oakland University); Michelle Boswell (University of Maryland); Laura Bowles (University of Central Arkansas); E. Brand (Broome Community College); Beth Buyserie (Washington State University); Dana Cairns Watson (University of California, Los Angeles); Genevieve Carminati (Montgomery College); Brent Chesley (Aquinas College); Joseph Colavito (Butler University); Tara DaPra (University of Minnesota); Emily Detmer-Goebel (Northern Kentucky University); J. Michael Duvall (College of Charleston); Adriana Estill (Carleton College); Ralph Faris (Community College of Philadelphia); Chris Gillen (Kenyon

ACKNOWLEDGMENTS

College); Patricia Gillikin (University of New Mexico Valencia
Campus); Kenneth Grant (University of Wisconsin–Baraboo/
Sauk County); Kevin Griffith (Capital University); Annemarie
Hamlin (Central Oregon Community College); Rick Hansen
(California State University, Fresno); John Hare (Montgomery
College); Wendy Hayden (Hunter College of the City Uni-
versity of New York); Karen Head (Georgia Institute of Tech-
nology); Chene Heady (Longwood University); Nels Highberg
(University of Hartford); Victoria Holladay (California State
University, Los Angeles); D. Kern Holoman (University
of California, Davis); Elizabeth Huergo (Montgomery Col-
lege); Sara Jameson (Oregon State University); Joseph Jones
(University of Memphis); Andrew Keitt (University of Ala-
bama at Birmingham); Kurt Koenigsberger (Case Western
Reserve University); Gary Leising (Utica College); Gary
Lewandowski (Monmouth University); Michelle Maher
(La Roche College); Lisa Martin (University of Wisconsin–
Baraboo/Sauk County); Miles McCrimmon (J. Sargeant
Reynolds Community College); Jacqueline Megow (Oklahoma
State University); Bruce Michelson (University of Illinois at
Urbana-Champaign); Megan Morton (Purdue University);
Steven Muhlberger (Nipissing University); Lori Muntz (Iowa
Wesleyan College); Ann Murphy (Assumption College); Sarah
Perrault (University of Nevada, Reno); Christine Pipitone-
Herron (Raritan Valley Community College); David Samper
(University of Oklahoma); Rose Shapiro (Fontbonne Univer-
sity); Jennifer Stewart (Indiana University–Purdue University
Fort Wayne); Sandra Stollman (Broward College); Linda Sturtz
(Beloit College); Mark Sutton (Kean University); Tobin von
der Nuell (University of Colorado at Boulder); Brody Waybrant
(Bay Mills Community College); Gina Weaver (Southern

320

Nazarene University); Amy Whitson (Missouri State University); Susan Wright (Montclair State University).

Thanks also to those who reviewed the manuscript for the original version of "*They Say*"; their suggestions contributed enormously to this book: Alan Ainsworth (Houston Community College); Rise Axelrod (University of California, Riverside); Bob Baron (Mesa Community College); David Bartholomae (University of Pittsburgh); Diane Belcher (Georgia State University); Michel De Benedictis (Miami Dade College); Joseph Bizup (Boston University); Patricia Bizzell (College of the Holy Cross); John Brereton (Harvard University); Richard Bullock (Wright State University); Charles Cooper (University of California, San Diego); Christine Cozzens (Agnes Scott College); Sarah Duerden (Arizona State University); Russel Durst (University of Cincinnati); Joseph Harris (Duke University); Paul Heilker (Virginia Polytechnic Institute); Michael Hennessy (Texas State University); Karen Lunsford (University of California, Santa Barbara); Libby Miles (University of Rhode Island); Mike Rose (University of California, Los Angeles); William H. Smith (Weatherford College); Scott Stevens (Western Washington University); Patricia Sullivan (University of Colorado); Pamela Wright (University of California, San Diego); Daniel Zimmerman (Middlesex Community College).

Finally, a special thank you to David Bartholomae for suggesting the phrase that became the subtitle of this book.

GERALD GRAFF, a professor of English and Education at the University of Illinois at Chicago and the 2008 President of the Modern Language Association of America, has had a major impact on teachers through such books as *Professing Literature: An Institutional History*, *Beyond the Culture Wars: How Teaching the Conflicts Can Revitalize American Education*, and, most recently, *Clueless in Academe: How Schooling Obscures the Life of the Mind*. The new Common Core State Standards for K–12 cite his work on the importance of argument literacy for college and career readiness. **CATHY BIRKENSTEIN**, a lecturer at the University of Illinois at Chicago, has published essays on writing, most recently in *College English*, and, with Gerald, in *The Chronicle of Higher Education*, *Academe*, and *College Composition and Communication*. She and Gerald have given over a hundred lectures and workshops at colleges, conferences, and high schools—and are at present working on a book contending that our currently confusing school and college curriculum needs to be clarified by making the practice of argument the common thread across all disciplines.